FREEDOM OF CONSCIENCE AND RELIGION

SECOND EDITION

Other Books in the *Essentials of Canadian Law* Series

International Trade Law

Family Law

Copyright Law

The Law of Sentencing

Administrative Law

Computer Law 2/e

International Human Rights Law

Franchise Law

Legal Ethics and Professional
Responsibility 2/e

Public International Law 2/e

Individual Employment Law 2/e

Civil Litigation

Canadian Telecommunications Law

Intellectual Property Law 2/e

Animals and the Law

Income Tax Law 2/e

Youth Criminal Justice Law 3/e

Bank and Customer Law in Canada 2/e

The Law of Equitable Remedies 2/e

Remedies: The Law of Damages 3/e

The Law of Trusts 3/e

Ethics and Criminal Law 2/e

Insurance Law 2/e

Immigration Law 2/e

Bankruptcy and Insolvency Law 2/e

Legal Research and Writing 4/e

Canadian Maritime Law 2/e

Public Lands and Resources
in Canada

Conflict of Laws 2/e

Statutory Interpretation 3/e

Constitutional Law 5/e

Land-Use Planning

Refugee Law 2/e

Religious Institutions and the Law 4/e

The Law of Partnerships and
Corporations 4/e

Environmental Law 5/e

Fundamental Justice 2/e

International and Transnational
Criminal Law 3/e

The Law of Torts 6/e

Mergers, Acquisitions, and Other
Changes of Corporate Control 3/e

Criminal Procedure 4/e

Information and Privacy Law
in Canada

The Law of Evidence 8/e

The Law of Contracts 3/e

National Security Law 2/e

Canadian Competition Law
and Policy

The Law of Property

Pension Law 3/e

The Charter of Rights and
Freedoms 7/e

Personal Property Security Law 3/e

Criminal Law 8/e

Securities Law 3/e

Search and Seizure

Detention and Arrest 3/e

FREEDOM OF CONSCIENCE AND RELIGION

SECOND EDITION

RICHARD MOON

Faculty of Law, University of Windsor

UNIVERSITY OF TORONTO PRESS
Toronto Buffalo London

© University of Toronto Press 2024
Irwin Law
An imprint of University of Toronto Press
Toronto Buffalo London
utorontopress.com
Printed in the USA

ISBN 978-1-5522-1736-8 (paper)   ISBN 978-1-5522-1737-5 (PDF)

Cataloguing in Publication available from Library and Archives Canada

We wish to acknowledge the land on which the University of Toronto Press operates. This land is the traditional territory of the Wendat, the Anishnaabeg, the Haudenosaunee, the Métis, and the Mississaugas of the Credit First Nation.

University of Toronto Press acknowledges the financial support of the Government of Canada and the Ontario Arts Council, an agency of the Government of Ontario, for its publishing activities.

To Adina

SUMMARY TABLE OF CONTENTS

DETAILED
TABLE OF CONTENTS

CHAPTER 3:
THE RESTRICTION AND ACCOMMODATION OF RELIGIOUS PRACTICES   59

CHAPTER 4:
CONSCIENTIOUS OBJECTIONS   106

PREFACE

When the *Canadian Charter of Rights and Freedoms*[1] was enacted in 1982, the first of its fundamental freedoms, freedom of conscience and religion (section 2(a)), seemed less significant and less interesting than many of its other rights. Religion in Canada was generally regarded as a private matter, with little visible presence in the country's political life. There were, of course, individuals and groups who were motivated by a religious commitment to take political action, but their objectives were almost always civic — to eradicate child poverty, ban landmines, or prohibit abortion — and not to advance the particular practices of their faith. Indeed, political actors seldom spoke publicly about their faith and did not justify their public actions explicitly on religious grounds. Some of the early support for a charter of rights in Canada had been a reaction to acts of state suppression of religious and cultural practices, such as the "war without mercy" against the proselytizing activities of the Jehovah's Witness community in 1950s Quebec.[2] But by 1982, the state seemed no longer to be engaged in the direct suppression of religious practice.

Yet in 1982 there were also several reasons to think that issues of religious freedom might again become significant. Those who had predicted the ineluctable decline of religious belief had begun to rethink

---

1   *Canadian Charter of Rights and Freedoms,* Part 1 of the *Constitution Act, 1982,* being Schedule B to the *Canada Act 1982* (UK), 1982, c 11 [*Charter*].

2   Maurice Duplessis quoted in William Kaplan, *State and Salvation: The Jehovah's Witnesses and Their Fight for Civil Rights* (Toronto: University of Toronto Press, 1989) at 230.

this assumption. Religious commitment seemed not only to be stubbornly persistent, but indeed to be experiencing a revival in evangelical, fundamentalist, and spiritualist forms. Even if most religious adherents accepted that religion and politics should remain separate, they did not always agree about where the line between private spirituality and public secularism should be drawn. As well, immigration in the latter part of the twentieth century had significantly added to the religious diversity of the country. The number of adherents to non-Christian belief systems, including Sikhism, Islam, and Hinduism, grew significantly in this period. This growth in diversity raised questions about the historic ordering of public life on the basis of Christian practice. Even if the majority in the country saw the imprint of Christian practice on public life as "just the way things are," or as cultural rather than religious in character, other religious groups viewed the public traces of Christian practice differently.

In the freedom of religion cases that arose in the first decades of the *Charter*, the courts and other state actors were asked to remove the vestiges of Christian practice from the public sphere (for example, Sunday closing laws or the recitation of the Lord's Prayer in public schools and town council meetings) or to exempt religious minority group members from legal standards that privileged mainstream Christian practice and failed to take account of minority practices (such as the RCMP uniform requirement or statutory holidays). These issues, though, seemed manageable, requiring only minor adjustments to existing practices. They could be, and often were, worked out in particular settings by the affected parties.[3]

However, the Salman Rushdie affair, the 9/11 attacks, and later the publication of the "Danish Cartoons" helped to move religion or religious difference to the forefront of public consciousness. These events confirmed to some in the community that religion represented a threat to the values of liberal-democratic society and that different religious worldviews were so fundamentally at odds that social coexistence, if possible, was bound to be difficult. Religious freedom issues that may have been minor and easily resolved "on the ground" were increasingly seen through this lens of intractable conflict. In Canada, anxiety about religion has been far less acute than in Europe, where it is perceived as an internal threat to liberal-democratic values, or in the United States, where the threat was once viewed as external and is now often seen as

---

3   The RCMP voluntarily made changes to its dress code to permit turbans and other religious headgear. A constitutional challenge to the decision of the RCMP to accommodate religious dress was rejected by the Federal Court of Appeal in *Grant et al v Canada*, [1995] 1 FC 158, 1994 CanLII 3507.

internal. Nevertheless, in Canada concern about the character of religion or certain religions has shaped the public reaction to religious diversity and freedom. This has been most powerfully so in Quebec where, as in Europe, concerns about national identity remain strong, and the political role of the Catholic church in the recent past has caused many to be wary of the visibility of religion in the public sphere.

While the first wave of freedom of religion cases was concerned with state support for Christian rituals and the presence of religious symbols in public spaces, more recent cases have been concerned with indirect restrictions on minority religious practices (and the reasonable accommodation of these practices), the autonomy of religious associations (their right to operate according to their own norms and practices), and conscientious objection claims (the right of religious believers to be exempted from a law that requires them to perform an act they consider to be immoral or that implicates them in what they see as the immoral actions of others).

The introductory chapter of this book sets out the basic history of religious freedom in Canada, including the early justifications for religious freedom or tolerance. A central theme of this book, which is introduced in Chapter 1, is the shift in the courts' conception of religious freedom from a liberty-based to an equality-based right. In their early *Charter* judgments, the courts described religious freedom as a liberty that has two dimensions—the freedom to engage in religious practice without state restriction (unless necessary to advance the public interest) and the freedom from state compulsion to perform a religious practice.

However, in later cases the courts have said that the freedom does not simply prohibit state coercion in matters of religion or conscience but requires also that the state treat religious belief systems or communities in an equal or even-handed manner—that it remain neutral in religious matters. Freedom of religion, on this account, is a form of equality right—a right to equal treatment or equal respect by the state without discrimination on the grounds of religious belief or association. The state must not support or prefer the practices of one religious group over those of another, or religious belief over atheism and vice versa (religion, or at least religious contest, should be excluded from politics), and it must not restrict the practices of a religious group, unless this is necessary to protect an important public interest (religion should be insulated from politics). Religion is bracketed off—separated—from politics.

This separation of religion and politics rests on a recognition of the deep and rooted nature of religious commitment. Religious commitment is treated as an identity and not simply as a choice or judgment. When the state supports or prefers a particular religious tradition or belief system, it sends a message that some in the community should be included and others not. Or when the state takes action that has the effect of restricting the practices of a particular religious group, it excludes the members of that group from full participation in community life. Accommodation should be made for the beliefs or practices of different religious groups, because the group and its practices are a source of identity and meaning for the group's members. More practically, accommodations should sometimes be made to avoid the marginalization of religious groups within the larger political community. If the law prevents the members of some religious groups from fully participating in society, their identification or connection with the society may be negatively affected, which in turn may lead to social conflict. The ties between religious group members, which may be intergenerational and comprehensive, mean these groups are often the object of suspicion, discrimination, and marginalization.

This shift in the courts' understanding of the freedom's justification from a liberty to an equality right has been accompanied by a narrowing of the freedom's scope. Despite the apparent breadth of section 2(a) and the courts' formal acknowledgment that freedom of conscience and religion protects both religious and nonreligious (fundamental) beliefs, the former have been at the centre of the freedom of religion/conscience jurisprudence. The protection of nonreligious beliefs and practices (the freedom of conscience component of section 2(a)) appears to be limited to practices that resemble in content and structure familiar religious practices.

Chapter 2 considers the issue of state support for religion, including the place of religious practices and symbols in state-run institutions, such as public schools, and the role of religious values in public decision making. While the courts have said that the state should remain neutral in matters of religion and should not support or favour the practices of a particular religion, they have not interpreted section 2(a) as excluding religion entirely from the political sphere. First, the courts have held that the state may support religious practices and organizations provided it does so in an even-handed way, and (in the case of schools and other services) ensures the availability of a secular option. Second, the courts have recognized that religious practices have shaped the traditions or customs of the community and cannot simply be erased from the public sphere. The Supreme Court of Canada has said that "the state's duty of neutrality does not require it to abstain from celebrating and preserving its religious heritage."[4] Third, the courts have recognized that as long

---

4   *Mouvement laïque québécois v Saguenay (City)*, 2015 SCC 16 at para 116.

as religion remains part of private life, it is bound to affect the shape of public action. If a large part of the population is Christian, the state may take the practices of this group into account when, for example, selecting statutory holidays or establishing a "pause day" from work. Finally, the courts have said that political actors may draw on religious values when making public decisions—that they should not be expected to leave their values behind when they enter the legislative chamber. When a religious belief addresses a civic matter, it will be treated by the courts as a political or moral judgment that may play a role in public decision making, rather than as a religious practice towards which the state should remain neutral. Where the courts draw the line between the "civic" and "spiritual" elements of a religious belief system (between religious values and religious practices) will depend on their views about the ordinary forms of religious worship, the nature of human welfare, and the proper scope of political action.

Behind the courts' limited application of the religious neutrality requirement lies a complex conception of religious commitment in which religion is viewed as both a cultural identity and a personal commitment to a set of beliefs about truth and right. The challenge for the courts is to find a way to fit this complex conception of religious commitment into a constitutional framework that relies on a distinction between individual choices or commitments that should be protected as a matter of liberty, and individual attributes that should be respected as a matter of equality. The constitutional framework (and perhaps, more deeply, our conception of rights) imposes this distinction between judgment and identity on the rich and complex experience of religious commitment.

Chapter 3 addresses the other dimension of religious freedom: the right to hold and manifest religious beliefs without interference from the state. Section 2(a) protects any belief or practice that the individual regards as spiritually significant — something that for the individual has a "nexus" with the divine — regardless of whether the belief/practice is part of an established belief system or is shared with others. The issue for the court at this stage is whether the individual has a sincere belief in the spiritual significance of the practice. According to the courts, the state breaches section 2(a) any time it restricts a religious practice in a nontrivial way. Even when a law advances a legitimate public purpose, such as the prevention of drug use or cruelty to animals, the state must justify, under section 1 of the *Charter* (the limitations provision), the law's nontrivial interference with a religious practice.

The courts' focus on *individual* belief raises questions not simply about the scope of section 2(a) protection but also about the substance of that protection. Why should the state be required to compromise its policies to make space for the beliefs/practices of a particular individual?

Despite the courts' formal declaration that the state must justify any nontrivial restriction of a religious practice (or reasonably accommodate the practice), they have given this requirement little substance. The courts appear willing to uphold a legal restriction if it has a legitimate objective (that is, an objective other than the suppression of an erroneous religious practice) that would be noticeably compromised if an exception to the law were made for a religious practice. In other words, even though the courts have structured their approach to section 2(a) so that it has the form of an equality right, they have adopted in practice a very weak standard of justification under section 1, so that the right protects only a limited form of liberty.

While the courts purport to resolve these issues through the balancing of civic and religious interests, they have, in almost all cases, attached little value or weight to the religious belief/practice and given priority to the state's policies. From a secular or public perspective, a religious belief/practice has no necessary value; indeed, it is said that a court should take no position concerning its value — that the court should remain neutral on the question of religious truth. To the believer, the state is wrong to restrict their religious practices, because these practices express or reflect a deeper truth. Secular institutions such as the courts do not — in fact, cannot — value the practice for the reason the believer values it (that is, because it is true). The belief/practice is significant from a civic-secular perspective only because it matters deeply to the group and its members, because it is part of their cultural identity, and because its restriction may lead to the marginalization or alienation of the group. But there is no way to balance the subjective value of the practice to the believer and the secular concern about group identity with the value of the restrictive law. The courts' task then is not to trade off or balance competing public and religious values/interests but is instead to mark out a protected (private) space for religious communities or ways of life — to define the scope of personal or communal religious practice that can be practically insulated (and excluded) from legal regulation. The protection of religious freedom requires the courts to draw a line between the spheres of spiritual and civic life, even if that line often appears to be porous and moveable, as the courts try to protect "private" space for religious belief and practice.

Chapter 4 will examine conscientious objection claims. In most religious accommodation cases, an individual (or group) seeks to be exempted from a law that prevents them from engaging in a religious practice — for example, from wearing religious dress or keeping religious holidays. In conscientious objection cases, however, the individual asks to be exempted from a law that requires them to perform an act that is inconsistent with their religious commitments. In many of these cases the claimant asks to be excused from performing an act that is not itself immoral but that supports or facilitates (what they see as) the immoral action of others and thus makes them complicit in this immorality.

The issue in conscientious objection cases is not, as the courts present it, the reasonable balance between the individual's religious interests or commitments and the interests or rights of others in the community, but is instead whether the individual's religiously based objection should be viewed as an expression of personal religious conscience that should be accommodated, provided this can be done without noticeable harm to others, or as a (religiously grounded) civic position that falls outside the scope of religious freedom protection and may be the subject of legal regulation. An individual's spiritual practices are both excluded and insulated from political decision making. However, their beliefs concerning civic issues, such as the rights and interests of others in the community, even if grounded in a religious system, must be subject to the give-and-take of ordinary politics.

In determining whether a particular (conscientious) objection should be viewed as a personal/spiritual matter or a civic/political position, two factors may be relevant. The first is whether the individual is being required to perform the particular act (to which they object) because they hold a special position not held by others, notably some form of public appointment. The other factor is the relative remoteness/ proximity of the act that the objector is required to perform to the act that they consider to be inherently immoral. When the required action is remote from the "sinful" act, the objection can be seen as a position about how others should behave or about the correctness of the law, rather than as an expression of personal conscience.

Chapter 5 discusses the extent to which religious organizations may be insulated from state regulation. When an individual believer seeks an exemption from the law for their religious practice, the key issue for the court is whether the exemption (the accommodation) will negatively affect the public interest or the rights of others. In some cases, though, the accommodation claim is made not by an individual who is seeking exemption for a specific practice, but by a religious organization or institution that is seeking a degree of autonomy in the governance of its affairs—that is, in the operation of its internal decision-making processes. In these institutional autonomy cases, the court must determine not only whether the exemption from state law will impact the rights and interests of others (whether the group's application of its own rules will negatively affect outsiders to the group), but also whether vulnerable members of the group should be protected by state law from oppressive internal rules and practices. The deep communal connections that are part of the value of religious life may also be the source of what the courts regard as harm—the lack of meaningful choice or opportunity open to the members of such communities. The state then may sometimes decide to intervene in the affairs of a religious community that is hierarchical or insular when the community's practices are thought to be harmful to some of its members, even though the members have, in a formal sense, chosen to participate in those practices.

While the courts will not ordinarily intervene in the internal affairs of a religious organization, they may do so when property or other legal rights are at issue. The courts, though, are understandably cautious when interpreting or enforcing agreements made between religious group members that give legal form to the norms or practices of the group for the same reasons they have sometimes declined to enforce "family bargains"—because these agreements are embedded in larger relationships and are inseparable from deeper obligations. The parties may not have intended to form a legal relationship and may consider themselves bound not by secular law but by the spiritual norms of their community (by a higher law) and by their commitment to each other as members of a spiritual community. The particular norm or practice that is the subject of the agreement may be embedded within (and only understandable in relation to) a larger system of religious norms and practices.

Chapter 6 looks at freedom of religion in two related contexts, the family and education. It is not surprising that some of the most contentious freedom of religion cases involve the claim of parents to make religiously based decisions concerning their children, including decisions about education and medical care. In these cases, the parents' claim to oversee the spiritual welfare of their children, and to transmit their faith to their children, is often pitted against their children's interest in developing as independent agents who are capable of making their own judgments, including spiritual judgments, or the interest of the larger community in ensuring the development of children as citizens who are tolerant and able to contribute to society. In this way, the debate about religious freedom in the family context exposes most starkly the central tension in the courts' understanding of religion as both a personal commitment and a cultural identity, and of religious freedom as both the right of the individual to make spiritual choices and the right of religious believers or communities to be treated with equal respect.

The courts have held that section 2(a) precludes the state from supporting the practices or institutions of a particular religion but does not prevent the state from providing general support for religious practices or institutions. A province then may fund religious schools as long as it does so in an even-handed way. There is, however, a constitutional exception to the requirement of equal treatment. Section 93 of the *Constitution Act, 1867*[5] protects the rights of "Separate" or "Dissentient" schools (principally Roman Catholic schools) that were legally established in a province at the time of Confederation or its later entry into the union. (The constitutional terms under which each of the provinces entered the union included a recognition of the rights of denominational schools). However, the courts found that in many provinces the provision had no application since, at the time of their entry, these provinces had no legally established denominational schools. The Constitution protects separate school rights in Ontario, Saskatchewan, and Alberta. While the provinces of Quebec and Newfoundland and Labrador were originally bound under the Constitution to provide support for denominational schools, these obligations were ended (in the case of Quebec) or substantially removed (in the case of Newfoundland and Labrador) by constitutional amendment.

Section 93 was included in the Constitution at a time when the dominant public or common school system in Ontario (and most other provinces) had a clear Protestant ethos. The section 93 protection of separate school rights ensured that members of the minority Roman Catholic community would not be financially pressured to send their children to the Protestant common schools. However, the character of the public school system in Ontario, Saskatchewan, and Alberta has changed dramatically since 1867, with all vestiges of religion now removed from the curriculum, a change that was accelerated by the *Charter*. At the same time, Canada has become far more religiously diverse. The funding of separate schools then is no longer about the protection of a religious minority but involves instead the privileging of one religious group. In the absence of section 93, this privileging would unquestionably breach both section 2(a) and section 15 of the *Charter*.

Many of the recent section 93 cases have been concerned with the right of separate schools to maintain their religious (denominational) character, even when this involves adherence to values or practices that are at odds with public values, such as 2SLGBTQ+ equality. At the same time, separate schools, because of their special status in Ontario, Saskatchewan, and Alberta as the only fully funded religious schools, are considered by the courts to be government actors that are subject to

---

5   *Constitution Act, 1867,* (UK), 30 & 31 Vict, c 3, reprinted in RSC 1985, Appendix II, No 5.

the *Charter*. There is something odd, even paradoxical, about treating religious institutions as government actors that must respect the rights of citizens, including the right to be free from discrimination, but are permitted to hire only Catholic teachers and to teach Catholic doctrine, including the belief that homosexuality is sinful.

Finally, Chapter 7 looks at the freedom of conscience component of section 2(a). The term "freedom of conscience" was once used interchangeably with "freedom of religion" to refer to the individual's freedom to hold beliefs that are spiritual or moral in character. At this earlier time, the moral beliefs of most individuals were rooted in a religious system. Freedom of conscience, though, is now viewed as an alternative to, or an extension of, religious freedom. While freedom of religion protects fundamental religious beliefs and practices, freedom of conscience extends protection to fundamental beliefs and practices that are not part of a religious system—to deeply held secular or humanist beliefs/practices. Together, then, freedom of conscience and freedom of religion protect the individual's most fundamental moral beliefs or commitments.

Yet despite the courts' formal definition of the scope of freedom of conscience and religion as encompassing both religious and nonreligious beliefs, very few freedom of conscience claims have come before the courts. If section 2(a) requires not just that the state refrain from compelling or restricting religious practices (individual liberty in religious matters), but also that the state remain neutral in religious matters, then it is less obvious that equivalent protection should be extended to an individual's nonreligious practices. If the duty to accommodate religious practices rests on a recognition of the deep connection between the individual and their religious/cultural group and on a concern about the standing of such groups in the larger society (and is a matter of social equality rather than individual liberty), then it may not extend to practices that are idiosyncratic and have no link to a religious or cultural group/tradition.

Political decision making involves the adoption of some moral/political views and the rejection of others. The protection of freedom of conscience under section 2(a) then must be confined to beliefs that appear to fall outside the scope of ordinary political debate not just because they are fundamental to the individual but because they are part of a distinctive worldview or moral framework. Freedom of conscience will not extend, for example, to beliefs about matters of fact (such as the safety or effectiveness of vaccines or seatbelts) or beliefs about civic or collective action that affects others. A conscientiously held belief may fall within the protection of section 2(a) when it resembles a paradigmatic religious belief or practice (a faith-based commitment) that is fundamental in significance, specific in content, peremptory in force, perceived by nonbelievers as inaccessible or unconventional, and minor in its impact on others. A belief of this kind, though, is less likely to be sustained outside a religious or cultural community. It is not an accident that many nonreligious "conscientious" practices are historically linked to religious practices. It might then be said that when "religion" looks like civic morality, it will be subject to the give-and-take of ordinary politics (as discussed in Chapter 3), and when "conscience" (secular morality) looks like religion and can be treated as a private matter, it will fall within the protection of section 2(a).

ACKNOWLEDGMENTS

The material in this book draws from my previous writing, including the following:

- "Liberty, Neutrality and Inclusion: Freedom of Religion under the *Canadian Charter of Rights*" (2003) 41 *Brandeis LJ* 563
- "From Liberty to Equal Respect: Religious Freedom under the *Canadian Charter of Rights and Freedoms*" in M Habibi et al, eds, *Theoretical Foundations of Human Rights* (Qom, Iran: Mofid University Publications, 2007)
- "Religious Commitment and Identity: *Syndicat Northcrest v. Amselem*" (2005) 29 *Sup Ct L Rev* (2d) 201
- "Government Support for Religious Practice" and "Introduction" in R Moon, ed, *Law and Religious Pluralism in Canada* (Vancouver: UBC Press, 2008)
- "Divorce and the Marriage of Law and Religion: Comment on *Bruker v. Marcovitz*" (2008) 42 *Sup Ct L Rev* (2d) 37
- "Accommodation without Compromise: Comment on *Alberta v. Hutterian Brethren of Wilson Colony*" (2010) 51 *Sup Ct L Rev* (2d) 95
- "The Supreme Court of Canada's Attempt to Reconcile Freedom of Religion and Sexual Orientation Equality in the Public Schools" in D Rayside & C Wilcox, eds, *Faith, Politics and Sexual Diversity* (Vancouver: UBC Press, 2011)
- "Christianity, Multiculturalism, and National Identity: A Canadian Comment on *Lautsi and Others v. Italy*" in Jeroen Temperman, ed, *The*

Lautsi Papers: Multidisciplinary Reflections on Religious Symbols in the Public School Classroom (Leiden: Martinus Nijhoff, 2012)
- "Freedom of Religion under the *Charter of Rights*: The Limits of State Neutrality" (2012) 45 *UBC L Rev* 497
- "Freedom of Conscience and Religion" in S Beaulac & E Mendes, eds, *Canadian Charter of Rights and Freedoms* (5th ed) (Markham, ON: LexisNexis, 2013)
- "Religious Accommodation and Its Limits: The York University Case" (2014) 23 *Constitutional Forum* 1
- "Neutrality and Prayers: *Mouvement laique v. Saguenay*" (2015) 4 *Oxford J of Law and Religion* 512
- "Conscientious Objections by Civil Servants: The Case of Marriage Commissioners and Same-Sex Civil Marriages" in B Berger & R Moon, eds, *Religion and the Exercise of Public Authority* (Oxford: Hart/Bloomsbury, 2016)
- "Conscientious Objections in Canada: Pragmatic Accommodation and Principled Adjudication" (2018) 7 *Oxford J of Law and Religion* 279
- "Conscience in the Image of Religion" in John Adenitire, ed, *Religious Beliefs and Conscientious Exemptions in a Liberal State* (Oxford: Hart/Bloomsbury, 2019)
- "*LSBC v. TWU*: Complicated Answers to a Simple Question" (2019) 94 *Sup Ct L Rev* (2d) 335
- "Conscientious Objection and the Politics of Cake-Baking" (2020) 9 *Oxford J of Law and Religion* 329
- "The Conscientious Objection of Medical Practitioners to the CPSO's Effective Referral Requirement" 29(1) *Constitutional Forum* (2020)
- "*Ktunaxa v. BC* and the Shape of Religious Freedom" in J Hewitt & R Moon, eds, *Indigenous Spirituality and Religious Freedom* (Toronto: University of Toronto Press, 2024)

I am grateful to Lesley Steeve and Irwin Law for their support. As always, though, my greatest debt is to my partner Audrey Macklin and to my children, Sibyl, Ellie, Hope, and Adina.

CHAPTER 1

INTRODUCTION

A. RELIGIOUS TOLERANCE IN CANADA

Canada's early history as a colony and a nation was marked by periods of harsh religious suppression and moments of pragmatic religious tolerance. The early efforts of European colonizers, first the French and later the British, to convert Indigenous Peoples to a version of Christianity sometimes involved the active suppression of spiritual practices. Cultural suppression became standard practice with the growth of European settlement and the extension of political control by colonial and Canadian authorities over lands occupied by Indigenous Peoples. Because the spiritual practices of Indigenous communities were often tied to the land, the removal of these communities from their traditional territories significantly undermined their spiritual and economic life. In the late 1800s, spiritual practices, such as spirit dancing in the Prairies and the potlatch on the West Coast, were banned by the federal government. Perhaps the most significant program of cultural suppression was the residential school system, which involved the forcible removal of Indigenous children from their families and communities and their placement in state-sanctioned Christian schools, where they were prevented from speaking their language and engaging in the practices of their culture. The residential school program began in the late 1800s and continued until the mid 1990s.

Yet the country's early history was also marked by significant acts of religious tolerance. With the conquest of New France by the British in the middle of the eighteenth century, a Protestant monarch came to rule over the colony's French Catholic population.[1] The practice, common at the time, in which the conquering power imposed its faith on its new subjects gave way to the practical necessities of government in colonial Canada. Under the *Treaty of Paris, 1763*,[2] which formally ended the Seven Years' War between Britain and France, the British government agreed that the French Catholic inhabitants of Canada would retain the right to practise their religion. Specifically, the treaty stated that

> His Britannick Majesty, on his side, agrees to grant the liberty of the Catholick religion to the inhabitants of Canada: he will, in consequence, give the most precise and most effectual orders, that his new Roman Catholic subjects may profess the worship of their religion according to the rites of the Romish church, as far as the laws of Great Britain permit.[3]

As MH Ogilvie notes, this concession was not free of ambiguity, since at the time Roman Catholics in England were subject to a number of significant criminal restrictions.[4] However, the *Quebec Act, 1774* of the British Parliament formally extended to the colony's inhabitants the right to maintain the French language, the civil law system, and the Roman Catholic faith.[5] The British government's motives, though, were entirely

---

1   The earliest settlers in New France included both Roman Catholics and Huguenots (French Protestants), although Huguenot immigration was subsequently halted and the Huguenot settlers already residing in the colony came under significant restriction.

2   *Treaty of Paris, 1763*, France, Britain, and Spain, 10 February 1763.

3   *Ibid*, art IV. Acadia had been ceded to the British in 1713 by the *Treaty of Utrecht*, Britain and France, 11 April 1713. While this treaty included language similar to that in the *Treaty of Paris, 1763*, a very different strategy was employed following the British acquisition of Acadia. To ensure political stability, the British government in 1755 expelled a significant portion of the French-speaking population. The expelled Acadians either returned to France or resettled in Louisiana or the American colonies.

4   MH Ogilvie, *Religious Institutions and the Law in Canada*, 3rd ed (Toronto: Irwin Law, 2010) at 34.

5   The *Quebec Act, 1774* (UK), 14 Geo III, c 83 [*Quebec Act*] provides the following:

> V. And, for the more perfect Security and Ease of the Minds of the Inhabitants of the said Province, it is hereby declared, That his Majesty's Subjects, professing the Religion of the Church of Rome of and in the said Province of Quebec, may have, hold, and enjoy, the free Exercise of the Religion of the Church of Rome, subject to the King's Supremacy, declared and established by an Act, made in the first Year of the Reign of Queen Elizabeth, over all the Dominions and Countries which then did, or thereafter should belong, to the Imperial Crown of this Realm; and that the Clergy of the said Church may hold, receive,

pragmatic: to ensure the stability of the Quebec colony and the loyalty of its inhabitants at a time when the American colonies were becoming disenchanted with British rule.

The growth of English-speaking, Protestant settlement in Lower and Upper Canada (later Canada East and Canada West, and then Quebec and Ontario) in the late 1700s and early 1800s (with Protestants soon forming the majority in Upper Canada) led to increasing conflict between Catholics and Protestants. During this period, the assumption of many English-speaking settlers, which was given expression in the *Durham Report* of 1839, was that continued immigration from Britain and the political unification of Canada East and Canada West would eventually result in the assimilation of the "French race."[6] Nevertheless, the colonial government maintained its formal commitment to religious freedom. In 1851 the legislature for Canada East and West recognized the "legal equality among all religious denominations ... [as a] principle of Colonial legislation" and "the free exercise and enjoyment of Religious Profession and Worship, without discrimination or preference ... allowed to all Her Majesty's subjects."[7] In this period the most significant religious accommodation was the extension of support to minority Roman Catholic schools in Canada West, where the dominant school system was non-denominational Protestant, and to Protestant schools in Canada East, alongside the larger Roman Catholic system.[8]

The *Quebec Act* permitted the Roman Catholic church in Lower Canada (Canada East) to continue collecting tithes from parishioners, as provided for in the *Civil Code*.[9] During the early period of British rule in Upper Canada, the Anglican church was also granted certain privileges, reflecting its status as the established church in England. Most significantly, the *Constitutional Act, 1791* required that a certain proportion of lands, designated as clergy reserves, be set aside for "the Maintenance and Support of a Protestant Clergy," which in practice meant the Anglican

---

and enjoy, their accustomed Dues and Rights, with respect to such Persons only as shall profess the said Religion.

6   John George Lambton, Earl of Durham, *Report on the Affairs of British North America* (London: Robert Stanton, 1839) [*Durham Report*]. This report, which followed the rebellions in Lower and Upper Canada, also recommended the establishment of a system of responsible government and the creation of a single legislature for Canada East and West (Lower and Upper Canada).

7   *An Act to Repeal so much of the Imperial Act 31, Geo III, c 31, as relates to Rectories, and the presentation of Incumbents to the same*, S Prov C 1851 (3 & 4 Vict), c 55.

8   *An Act to repeal certain Acts therein mentioned, and to make further provision for the establishment and maintenance of Common Schools throughout the Province*, S Prov C (4 & 5 Vict), c 18.

9   Above note 5 at V.

clergy.[10] While the political elite in Upper Canada in the early 1800s was composed principally of Anglicans, the largest part of the population, particularly in rural areas, was composed of Methodists, Baptists, Congregationalists, and Presbyterians, and pressure from these groups eventually led to the ending of the clergy-reserve system in the mid-1800s, and with it of any semblance of religious establishment. While the Anglican church had been formally established by the colonial legislatures in Nova Scotia (1758), New Brunswick (1784), and Prince Edward Island (1802), the privileged status of the church in each of these colonies came to an end in the mid-1800s.[11] Nevertheless, in each of the colonies the ties between church(es) and state remained significant, particularly in the delivery of social services. What has been described as a "shadow establishment" of the Roman Catholic church in Quebec and of non-denominational Protestantism in the other provinces continued well into the twentieth century, manifested in the choice of civic holidays and the inclusion of religious lessons and rituals in public schools.[12]

Confederation in 1867 was an act of union, bringing together several of the British North American colonies (Canada East and West, New Brunswick, and Nova Scotia), but also an act of separation. Canada East

---

10   *Constitutional Act, 1791* (UK), 31 Geo III, c 31, s XXXV. The law also provided in section XXXV for the setting aside of special rectory land "according to the Establishment of the Church of England." See Alan Wilson, *The Clergy Reserves of Upper Canada*, Booklet #23 (Ottawa: Canadian Historical Association, 1969). The other established church in Great Britain, the Church of Scotland (the Presbyterian church), laid claim to a percentage of the reserves.

11   But as Ogilvie notes, above note 4 at 37–38:

> Since there would appear to be no legislation in these provinces disestablishing the Church of England, in legal theory at least, it is still the established church! However, legislation in each province dating from the late eighteenth century in relation to a variety of matters, from rights to conduct marriage, to vote, to hold property, and to hold military and civil office, among others, have resulted in complete equality before the law for all religious groups.

12   David Martin, "Canada in Comparative Perspective" in David Lyon & Marguerite Van Die, eds, *Rethinking Church, State, and Modernity: Canada between Europe and America* (Toronto: University of Toronto Press, 2000) 23 at 23. See also George Egerton, "Trudeau, God, and the Canadian Constitution: Religion, Human Rights, and Government Authority in the Making of the 1982 Constitution" in Lyon & Van Die, *ibid*, 90 at 92:

> Although the Canadian church-state relationship was distinct from the separationist model of America, the establishmentarianism of England, and the secularism of republican France, what the retreat from state confessionalism amounted to was a quasi-establishment of the major denominations, or "national churches", which, in the Canadian experience, included Roman Catholicism.

and West, governed since 1842 by a single legislature, was split into two provinces, Quebec and Ontario, each with its own legislature. The *BNA Act, 1867* (*Constitution Act, 1867*) gave provincial governments the power to regulate cultural matters, family relationships, and civil obligations, and the federal government the power to establish and maintain a national economic infrastructure and to protect public order and security.[13] In this way, the federal system ensured the continuation and protection of a level of religious and cultural diversity in the country, at least at a regional level. The *BNA Act*, though, also provided some protection for religious diversity within the provinces by establishing certain rights for minority religious schools. While section 93 of the *BNA Act* gave the provinces jurisdiction in relation to education, it also protected the rights of dissentient schools in Ontario (principally, Roman Catholic schools) and Protestant and Roman Catholic schools in Quebec that were legally established at the time of Confederation. The Supreme Court of Canada later described the constitutional protection of minority religious schools as a "bargain" that made Confederation possible.[14] The recognition of Roman Catholic school rights was also one of the terms of entry into the union of Manitoba in 1870 and Saskatchewan and Alberta in 1905.[15] However, anti-Catholic sentiment, which was prevalent in "Orange Ontario," not only contributed to significant local conflict in Ontario and the Western provinces but also surfaced at the national level in the Manitoba Schools Crisis of the 1890s, which led to the denial of Roman Catholic education rights in that province.[16]

The political accommodation between Roman Catholic and Protestant communities, while always imperfect and often precarious, shaped the new country's response to the growth of religious plurality in the late nineteenth and early twentieth centuries.[17] This response involved the

---

13 *Constitution Act, 1867* (UK), 30 & 31 Vict, c 3, ss 91 & 92, reprinted in RSC 1985, App II, No 5 [*BNA Act*].

14 *Reference re Bill 30, An Act to amend the Education Act (Ontario)*, [1987] 1 SCR 1148 at para 27, Wilson J [*Reference re Bill 30*]. The constitutional rights of dissentient schools are discussed more fully in Chapter 6.

15 Each of the provinces was formally subject to such a provision; however, the courts found that the provision had no application in many of the provinces because they did not have a legally established separate school system at the time they entered Confederation. For a more detailed account, see Chapter 6.

16 A political compromise brokered at the federal level permitted Roman Catholic instruction after regular school hours. See Ogilvie, above note 4 at 49.

17 See Mark Noll, "Constitutional Divides: North American Civil War and Religion in at Least Three Stories" in Marguerite Van Die, ed, *Religion and Public Life in Canada: Historical and Comparative Perspectives* (Toronto: University of Toronto Press, 2001) 153 at 157: "Canada ... developed under the necessity of accommodating in one nation Quebec, a traditional Old World society with church and

general protection of individual liberty in religious practice but also the pragmatic accommodation of certain minority group practices within the context of a public privileging of Christian or non-denominational Protestant practices. In the late 1800s and early 1900s, the Government of Canada, seeking to attract settlers to the western part of the country, agreed to exempt certain religious groups from public obligations that were inconsistent with the group's practices. For example, Anabaptist groups, such as the Mennonites and the Hutterites, were assured at the time of their arrival in Canada that they would be exempted from compulsory military service and standard schooling requirements.[18]

Yet, despite the country's general commitment to religious liberty, the first half of the twentieth century was marred by a number of significant and traumatic acts of religious oppression by the state, including the banning of the Jehovah's Witness community during World War II[19] and the removal of children in the Doukhobor community from parents who refused to send them to public schools.[20] Perhaps the most significant instance of religious oppression, at least in terms of its role in shaping the contemporary Canadian conception of religious freedom, was the suppression by the province of Quebec of the proselytizing activities of the Jehovah's Witness community in the 1950s.[21] Maurice Duplessis, the

---

state linked together organically, and English-language societies in Upper Canada and the Atlantic provinces shaped by both British Protestant paternalism and the American separation of church and state."

18   In 1873 the federal government assured the Mennonites settling in Manitoba that they could operate their own schools. The government stated that "[t]he fullest privilege of exercising their religious principles is by law afforded the Mennonites without any kind of molestation or restriction whatever" (quoted in Frank H Epp, *Mennonites in Canada, 1786–1920: The History of a Separate People* (Toronto: Macmillan, 1974) at 338). The commitment regarding schools, though, was not binding on the provinces. Earlier in Upper Canada, the Quakers and Mennonites, who arrived as United Empire Loyalists, were exempted from military service under the *Militia Act, 1793* (UK), 33 Geo III, c 1. See William Janzen, *Limits on Liberty: The Experience of Mennonite, Hutterite, and Doukhobor Communities in Canada* (Toronto: University of Toronto Press, 1990) at 163.

19   For an account, see William Kaplan, *State and Salvation: The Jehovah's Witnesses and Their Fight for Civil Rights* (Toronto: University of Toronto Press, 1989) ch 4. The ban was lifted in 1943.

20   For an account of the seizure of Doukhobor children under child protection laws in British Columbia, see John McLaren, "The State, Child Snatching, and the Law: The Seizure and Indoctrination of Sons of Freedom Children in British Columbia, 1950–60" in Dorothy E Chunn, John McLaren & Robert Menzies, eds, *Regulating Lives: Historical Essays on the State, Society, the Individual, and the Law* (Vancouver: UBC Press, 2002) 259.

21   For an examination of the attempt to suppress Jehovah's Witness proselytization in Quebec during the 1950s, see Kaplan, above note 19, ch 8.

premier (who also served as the attorney general of Quebec), conducted what he described as a "war without mercy" on the province's Jehovah's Witness community.[22]

B. A PRINCIPLED ACCOUNT OF RELIGIOUS FREEDOM

While much of Canada's early commitment to religious freedom was simply a pragmatic compromise to ensure social peace and political stability, in several judgments in the 1950s the Supreme Court of Canada sought to articulate a principled account of religious freedom. In *Saumur v City of Quebec*, the Supreme Court struck down a bylaw that forbade the distribution of literature in the streets of Quebec City without the prior consent of the chief of police—a bylaw that was intended to limit the proselytizing activities of the Jehovah's Witness community.[23] After setting out some of the history of religious tolerance in Canada, Rand J in the *Saumur* decision observed that

> [f]rom 1760, therefore, to the present moment religious freedom has, in our legal system, been recognized as a principle of fundamental character; and although we have nothing in the nature of an established church, that the untrammelled affirmations of religious belief and its propagation, personal or institutional, remain as of the greatest constitutional significance throughout the Dominion is unquestionable.[24]

Justice Rand went on to hold that the provinces lacked the authority, under the constitutional division of powers, to restrict religious freedom and other fundamental rights — that "legislation 'in relation' to religion and its profession is not a local or private matter . . . ; the dimensions of this interest are nationwide; . . . it appertains to a boundless field of ideas, beliefs and faiths with the deepest roots and loyalties; a religious incident reverberates from one end of this country to the other. "[25] He described religious freedom as one of the "original freedoms which are at once the necessary attributes and modes of self-expression of human beings and the primary conditions of their community life within a legal order."[26]

In *Chaput v Romain*, the Quebec provincial police "broke up," without a warrant, an orderly religious meeting of Jehovah's Witnesses in a

---

22   Quoted in Kaplan, *ibid* at 230.
23   [1953] 2 SCR 299 [*Saumur*].
24   *Ibid* at 327.
25   *Ibid* at 329.
26   *Ibid*.

private home, seizing bibles and other religious literature.[27] The Supreme Court found that the police action breached the *Criminal Code*[28] prohibition against obstructing a minister who is conducting a religious meeting. In reaching this conclusion, Taschereau J declared that in Canada there is no state religion and that all denominations enjoy the same freedom of speech and thought.[29]

The concern for the protection of rights that emerged in Europe and elsewhere following the atrocities of World War II found expression in international human rights treaties such as the *Universal Declaration of Human Rights*[30] and the *International Covenant on Civil and Political Rights*,[31] both of which gave protection to freedom of conscience and religion. In Canada, as in other countries, this concern led to the enactment of human rights code restrictions on private sector discrimination, including discrimination based on religion or creed, beginning in the late 1940s,[32] to the passage of the *Canadian Bill of Rights* in 1960,[33] and eventually to the constitutional entrenchment of the *Canadian Charter of Rights and Freedoms* in 1982.[34]

Section 2(a) of the *Charter*, which protects the fundamental right of "freedom of conscience and religion," is framed in terms similar to

---

27   [1955] SCR 834.

28   RSC 1985, c C-46.

29   *Ibid* at 840:

> Dans notre pays, il n'existe pas de religion d'Etat. Personne n'est tenu d'adhérer à une croyance quelconque. Toutes les religions sont sur un pied d'égalité, et tous les catholiques comme d'ailleurs tous les protestants, les juifs, ou les autres adhérents des diverses dénominations religieuses, ont la plus entière liberté de penser comme ils le désirent. La conscience de chacun est une affaire personnelle, et l'affaire de nul autre. Il serait désolant de penser qu'une majorité puisse imposer ses vues religieuses à une minorité. Ce serait une erreur fâcheuse de croire qu'on sert son pays ou sa religion, en refusant dans une province, à une minorité, les mêmes droits que l'on revendique soi-même avec raison, dans une autre province.

30   GA Res 217(III), UNGAOR, 3d Sess, Supp No 13, UN Doc A/810, (1948) [*UDHR*], online (pdf): www.ohchr.org/EN/UDHR/Documents/UDHR_Translations/eng.pdf.

31   GA Res 2200A(XXI), 21 UNGAOR Supp (No 16) at 52, UN Doc A/6316 (1966) (entered into force 23 March 1976) [*ICCPR*], online: www.ohchr.org/en/professionalinterest/pages/ccpr.aspx.

32   See *The Saskatchewan Bill of Rights Act, 1947*, SS 1947, c 35.

33   SC 1960, c 44, s 1, reprinted in RSC 1985, App III: "It is hereby recognized and declared that in Canada there have existed and shall continue to exist without discrimination by reason of race, national origin, colour, religion or sex, the following human rights and fundamental freedoms, namely, . . . (c) freedom of religion . . ."

34   Part 1 of the *Constitution Act, 1982*, being Schedule B to the *Canada Act 1982* (UK), 1982, c 11 [*Charter*].

article 18 of the *UDHR*[35] (as well as other provisions derived from article 18 such as article 18 of the *ICCPR*[36] and article 9 of the *European Convention on Human Rights*[37]). Because section 2(a) uses language similar to that used in these other charters, was enacted in the same historical context, and was inspired by the same concerns and events, it is not surprising that the Canadian courts' interpretation of section 2(a) is in many respects similar to the interpretation given to these other provisions. At the same time, though, the Canadian courts' understanding of the scope and limits of the section 2(a) right has been shaped by the particular history and circumstances of Canada — a country in which there has been no formal religious establishment similar to that in the United Kingdom and other European countries nor a historical resistance to state support for religion, as in the United States.[38]

---

35   Above note 30: "Everyone has the right to freedom of thought, conscience and religion; this right includes freedom to change his religion or belief, and freedom, either alone or in community with others and in public or private, to manifest his religion or belief in teaching, practice, worship and observance."

36   Above note 31:

1.   Everyone shall have the right to freedom of thought, conscience and religion. This right shall include freedom to have or to adopt a religion or belief of his choice, and freedom, either individually or in community with others and in public or private, to manifest his religion or belief in worship, observance, practice and teaching.
2.   No one shall be subject to coercion which would impair his freedom to have or to adopt a religion or belief of his choice.
3.   Freedom to manifest one's religion or beliefs may be subject only to such limitations as are prescribed by law and are necessary to protect public safety, order, health, or morals or the fundamental rights and freedoms of others.
4.   The States Parties to the present Covenant undertake to have respect for the liberty of parents and, when applicable, legal guardians to ensure the religious and moral education of their children in conformity with their own convictions.

37   *Convention for the Protection of Human Rights and Fundamental Freedoms*, Rome, 4 November 1950, online (pdf): www.echr.coe.int/Documents/Convention_ENG.pdf:

1.   Everyone has the right to freedom of thought, conscience and religion; this right includes freedom to change his religion or belief and freedom, either alone or in community with others and in public or private, to manifest his religion or belief, in worship, teaching, practice and observance.
2.   Freedom to manifest one's religion or beliefs shall be subject only to such limitations as are prescribed by law and are necessary in a democratic society in the interests of public safety, for the protection of public order, health or morals, or for the protection of the rights and freedoms of others.

38   The role of the courts under the *Charter* is not to make strategic judgments about the most effective way to ensure social peace but is instead to define and defend

C. A JUSTIFICATION FOR RELIGIOUS FREEDOM

The story of religious freedom in the West begins with the religious wars that disrupted Europe in the sixteenth and early seventeenth centuries.[39] It was in this context that writers such as John Locke sought to develop a principled argument for religious tolerance.[40] They argued not just that religious tolerance (rather than state-enforced religious conformity) was the better route to social peace but that it was morally required. At the centre of their principled defence of religious tolerance was the claim that spiritual matters lay within the sphere of individual conscience — the individual's divinely endowed capacity to recognize spiritual truth.

John Locke's *Letter Concerning Toleration* is regarded as the seminal defence of religious tolerance and freedom in the West.[41] Indeed, his central arguments are referred to, and partly relied on, by the Supreme Court of Canada in *R v Big M Drug Mart*, the Court's first religious freedom decision under the *Charter*.[42] Locke argues that it is essential "to distinguish exactly the business of civil government from that of religion and to settle the just bounds that lie between the one and the other."[43]

---

the basic rights of individuals or minority groups in the larger community. However, as I have noted elsewhere, few rights can be interpreted in a way that does not entangle the courts in complex sociopolitical issues. This claim is made about s 2(b), freedom of expression, in Richard Moon, *The Constitutional Protection of Freedom of Expression* (Toronto: University of Toronto Press, 2000).

39 See Perez Zagorin, *How the Idea of Religious Toleration Came to the West* (Princeton, NJ: Princeton University Press, 2003) at xii:

> The rationale of religious toleration and the theological, moral, and philosophical justification of religious freedom had their real beginning in the sixteenth century; they were forged in the bitter denominational conflicts, the continued struggle against persecution, and the fierce intellectual controversies arising out of the religious divisions created in Europe by the Protestant Reformation.

40 See Zagorin, *ibid*, for an examination of the various advocates of religious tolerance in this period.

41 John Locke, "Letter Concerning Toleration" in John Locke, *Treatise of Civil Government and a Letter Concerning Toleration* (1689; repr, New York: Irvington Publishers, 1979). This, of course, is not the only starting point for the Western story of religious freedom — just the standard one. As well, there are other stories of religious freedom or tolerance, including stories from the Islamic world and from the Indian subcontinent where Hinduism and Islam met. For a discussion of the former and its contemporary relevance, see Anver M Emon, *Religious Pluralism and Islamic Law: Dhimmis and Others in the Empire of Law* (Oxford: Oxford University Press, 2012).

42 [1985] 1 SCR 295 [*Big M Drug Mart*].

43 Above note 41 at 171.

The state, he says, should concern itself only with "civil interests" such as life, liberty, health, and property: "The commonwealth seems to me to be a society of men constituted only for the procuring, preserving, and advancing their own civil interests."[44] The authority of the state, argues Locke, does not extend to spiritual matters — "the salvation of the soul" — which lies within the exclusive domain of the individual. The individual is responsible for their own spiritual welfare and cannot delegate this responsibility to anyone else because religious belief depends on "inner persuasion":

> [N]o man can so far abandon the care of his own salvation as blindly to leave to the choice of any other, whether prince or subject, to prescribe to him what faith or worship he shall embrace. For no man can, if he would, conform his faith to the dictates of another. All the life and power of true religion consist in the inward and full persuasion of the mind; and faith is not faith without believing. Whatever profession we make, to whatever outward worship we conform, if we are not fully satisfied in our own mind that the one is true and the other well pleasing unto God, such profession and such practice, far from being any furtherance, are indeed great obstacles to our salvation.[45]

Locke observes that the power of government is exercised through coercion. But coercive power, he points out, is ineffective in spiritual matters. A government can require its citizens to conform to certain standards in their outward behaviour, but it cannot compel them to embrace spiritual truth — to sincerely believe. According to Locke, "It is only light and evidence that can work a change in men's opinions":[46]

> For laws are of no force at all without penalties, and penalties in this case are absolutely impertinent, because they are not proper to convince the mind. Neither the profession of any articles of faith, nor the conformity to any outward form of worship ... can be available to the salvation of souls, unless the truth of the one and the acceptableness of the other unto God be thoroughly believed by those that so profess and practise. But penalties are no way capable to produce such belief.[47]

---

44   *Ibid* at 172.

45   *Ibid* at 173. Locke continues: "For in this manner, instead of expiating other sins by the exercise of religion, I say, in offering thus unto God Almighty such a worship as we esteem to be displeasing unto Him, we add unto the number of our other sins those also of hypocrisy and contempt of His Divine Majesty."

46   *Ibid* at 174.

47   *Ibid.* See also *ibid* at 173:

> In the second place, the care of souls cannot belong to the civil magistrate, because his power consists only in outward force; but true and saving religion

It may even be an offence to God when an individual worships in the correct form without "inward sincerity."

Locke supplements this argument about the nature of religious commitment with a number of practical considerations. He notes that even if the government could change "men's minds" through coercion, there would be no reason to think that the faith it imposed was the true one. While "princes" may have particular skill or knowledge in civil matters, their spiritual judgment is not superior to that of other persons. After all, there are many different "princes" (or governments) in Europe, and each seems to hold a different view about the true faith. They cannot all be right. Moreover, says Locke, while governments may often be able to correct their mistakes in civil matters, they have no power to correct their spiritual mistakes. If the government forces the wrong religion onto its citizens, the otherworldly consequences of its error will be borne by its citizens, and the government will be able to do nothing to mitigate their spiritual loss or injury.

Locke's defence of religious tolerance raised a variety of issues, several of which persist in the contemporary debates about the justification and scope of religious freedom. The first concerns his conception of religious commitment. Locke's claim that state coercion will be at best ineffective and at worst blasphemous follows from his belief that religious commitment must be based on individual judgment. He thought that the individual would come to know religious truth through the reasoned assessment of evidence rather than blind obedience to authority and indeed that an individual's religious commitment would only be acceptable to God if it was the outcome of "inner persuasion."[48] Yet

---

consists in the inward persuasion of the mind, without which nothing can be acceptable to God. And such is the nature of the understanding, that it cannot be compelled to the belief of anything by outward force. Confiscation of estate, imprisonment, torments, nothing of that nature can have any such efficacy as to make men change the inward judgement that they have framed of things.

And see also *ibid* at 192: "It is in vain for an unbeliever to take up the outward show of another man's profession. Faith only and inward sincerity are the things that procure acceptance with God."

48   Some have disputed this, arguing that state coercion might well be effective in bringing the individual to "the truth" over time or across generations. Locke also assumes that the state should be prohibited not only from compelling religious practice but also from restricting practices it regards as erroneous (*ibid* at 197–98):

As the magistrate has no power to impose by his laws the use of any rites and ceremonies in any Church, so neither has he any power to forbid the use of such rites and ceremonies as are already received, approved, and practised by any Church; because, if he did so, he would destroy the Church itself: the end of whose institution is only to worship God with freedom after its own manner.

religious commitment is often viewed as faith-based or as a matter of cultural identity rather than individual judgment.[49] If religion is viewed in this way, then its protection may not rest simply on respect for individual autonomy or liberty in spiritual matters.

The second issue concerns Locke's exclusive focus on state coercion. Even if we agree with him that attempts by the state to compel its citizens to embrace the true faith will be ineffective, the state may advance "the truth" in other ways. The state, at least in the contemporary context, does not act exclusively through coercion. It supports a variety of values and goals using noncoercive means, such as subsidy and advocacy. Locke's argument, then, may not preclude the state from intervening in religious matters, provided it employs noncoercive measures.[50]

The third issue is Locke's narrow, otherworldly understanding of religion. In his view, spiritual salvation is distinct from the civil interests addressed by the state and falls exclusively within the individual's personal domain. Religions, though, often have something to say about how we should treat others and the kind of society we should work to create. Indeed, Locke took for granted that public morality was grounded in religion and dependent on a belief in God. It is worth recalling that Locke thought atheists ought not to be tolerated because without a belief

---

But this may not follow from his argument about the ineffectiveness of compulsion. It might reasonably be claimed that the spiritual welfare of citizens is advanced when the state inhibits the practice and promotion of a "false" religion. Locke's rejection of state restriction of religious practice appears to be based either on a skepticism about the state's ability to determine spiritual truth or on a belief that spiritual matters are the exclusive concern of the individual — a matter of individual liberty.

49   See, for example, Timothy Macklem, "Faith as a Secular Value" (2000) 45 *McGill LJ* 1.

50   Locke seems to be aware that his argument does not preclude the state from supporting particular religious practices (above note 41 at 173):

> It may indeed be alleged that the magistrate may make use of arguments, and thereby draw the heterodox into the way of truth, and procure their salvation. I grant it; but this is common to him with other men. In teaching, instructing, and redressing the erroneous by reason, he may certainly do what becomes any good man to do. Magistracy does not oblige him to cut off either humanity or Christianity.

For a discussion of this claim, see Rex Adhar & Ian Leigh, "Is Establishment Consistent with Religious Freedom?" (2004) 49 *McGill LJ* 635. Locke's statement can be reconciled with his claim that the spiritual and civil spheres are distinct only if he is referring to the magistrate in their personal capacity rather than as a lawmaker or state authority — a distinction that may depend on Locke's assumption that the state acts exclusively by coercive means.

in God and the afterlife, there was nothing to bind their consciences in civil society. As Perez Zagorin observes:

> [The early defenders of religious tolerance] certainly did not intend to banish religion from the polity or common life. Such a thought could hardly have occurred to them, nor could they ever have imagined as a proper setting for religious freedom a completely secular society in which the Christian religion had ceased to be a dominant public presence and a pervasive force in morals and conduct and was largely relegated to the realm of personal and private belief.[51]

D. RELIGIOUS FREEDOM UNDER THE *CHARTER*

In *Big M Drug Mart*, the first section 2(a) case decided by the Supreme Court of Canada, Dickson CJ held that section 2(a) protects the individual's freedom "to hold and to manifest whatever beliefs and opinions his or her conscience dictates, provided inter alia only that such manifestations do not injure his or her neighbours."[52] The freedom, he said, precludes the state from compelling an individual to engage in a religious practice and from restricting their ability to practise their religion unless it has a legitimate public reason. According to Dickson CJ, the protection of freedom of religion rests on "the centrality of individual conscience and the inappropriateness of governmental intervention to compel or to constrain its manifestation."[53] The chief justice traced this understanding of religious freedom back to Locke and other post-Reformation writers who based their opposition to state coercion in religious matters on a recognition that "belief . . . was not amenable to compulsion" and that

---

51   Above note 39 at 289–90.

52   Above note 42 at para 123. He continued, at para 94:

> Religious belief and practice are historically prototypical and, in many ways, paradigmatic of conscientiously-held beliefs and manifestations and are therefore protected by the Charter. Equally protected, and for the same reasons, are expressions and manifestations of religious non-belief and refusals to participate in religious practice." He also noted, "[t]he essence of the concept of freedom of religion is the right to entertain such religious beliefs as a person chooses, the right to declare religious beliefs openly and without fear of hindrance or reprisal, and the right to manifest religious belief by worship and practice or by teaching and dissemination.

53   *Ibid* at para 121. He went on to say that "the government may not coerce individuals to affirm a specific religious belief or to manifest a specific religious practice for a sectarian purpose" (*ibid* at para 123).

"[a]ttempts to compel belief or practice denied the reality of individual conscience and dishonoured the God that had planted it in His creatures."[54] Chief Justice Dickson, though, framed the protection of individual conscience in secular terms, tying it to respect for "human dignity" and to "our democratic political tradition."[55]

Locke's argument rested on a particular conception of religious truth and was intended to advance that truth. He viewed human conscience as a divinely endowed capacity to recognize religious truth. Chief Justice Dickson, however, recognized that, in the contemporary context, the protection of freedom of conscience and religion could no longer be based on religious values — as the most effective way to discover spiritual truth or as necessary to the individual's meaningful commitment to that truth. His "secularized" argument for religious freedom was based instead on the value of individual autonomy or liberty that underlies other fundamental rights. Freedom of conscience and religion protects the individual's choices, because it is through the exercise of choice or judgment that the individual lives an authentic life, a life that is their own.[56] When section 2(a) is understood in this way, as based on a commitment to individual autonomy, its protection will extend to both religious and non-religious beliefs.[57]

---

54   *Ibid* at para 120.

55   *Ibid* at para 122: "It should also be noted, however, that an emphasis on individual conscience and individual judgment also lies at the heart of our democratic political tradition. The ability of each citizen to make free and informed decisions is the absolute prerequisite for the legitimacy, acceptability, and efficacy of our system of self-government."

56   On this account, an individual's religious beliefs and practices should be protected not because they are true nor even because an individual must be given the freedom to judge, and possibly err, so that a meaningful or sincere commitment to the truth may be possible, but simply because an individual has chosen them or is committed to them. The religious adherent may view this understanding of the protection (or the civic value) of religion as trivializing their beliefs. Religious beliefs and practices matter to the adherent not because they have chosen them or have a preference for them, but because they are true. But, of course, any account of the value of religious belief that is external to the belief system — that rests on values that lie outside the belief system itself — is bound to be seen as trivializing.

57   For a similar view regarding art 18 of the *ICCPR*, above note 31, see UN Human Rights Committee, *CCPR General Comment No 22, Article 18 (Freedom of Thought, Conscience or Religion)*, 30 July 1993 (adopted at the Forty-eighth session of the Human Rights Committee), which provides that "[a]rticle 18 protects theistic, non-theistic and atheistic beliefs, as well as the right not to profess any religion or belief. The terms 'belief' and 'religion' are to be broadly construed. Article 18 is not limited in its application to traditional religions or to religions and beliefs with institutional characteristics or practices analogous to those of traditional religions." See, online: www.refworld.org/legal/general/hrc/1993/en/13375.

In *Big M Drug Mart*, the Supreme Court described freedom of conscience and religion as the liberty to hold, and live in accordance with, spiritual and other fundamental beliefs without state interference.[58] But, as I will discuss in the next chapter, there was implicit in *Big M Drug Mart* another understanding of religious freedom that became explicit in subsequent decisions.[59] Freedom of religion, on this other account, does not simply prohibit state coercion in matters of religion or conscience (state compulsion or restriction of a religious practice), but requires as well that the state treat religious belief systems or communities in an even-handed manner. The state must not support or prefer the practices of one religious group over those of another (religion, or at least religious contest, should be excluded from politics), and the state must not restrict the practices of a religious group unless it is necessary to protect a compelling public interest (religion should be insulated from politics).[60] Freedom of religion is, on this account, a form of equality right — a right to equal respect by the state without discrimination based on religious belief or association.

This shift in the courts' understanding of the freedom's justification has been accompanied by a narrowing of the freedom's scope. Despite the apparent breadth of section 2(a) and the courts' formal acknowledgment

---

58   Above note 42 at paras 94–95.

59   *Ibid* at para 134, Dickson CJ:

> In my view, however, as I read the Charter, it mandates that the legislative preservation of a Sunday day of rest should be secular, the diversity of belief and non-belief, the diverse socio-cultural backgrounds of Canadians make it constitutionally incompetent for the federal Parliament to provide legislative preference for any one religion at the expense of those of another religious persuasion.

Earlier (*ibid* at para 97) he stated:

> In proclaiming the standards of the Christian faith, the [Lord's Day] Act creates a climate hostile to, and gives the appearance of discrimination against, non-Christian Canadians. It takes religious values rooted in Christian morality and, using the force of the state, translates them into a positive law binding on believers and non-believers alike. The theological content of the legislation remains as a subtle and constant reminder to religious minorities within the country of their differences with, and alienation from, the dominant religious culture.

I have described this shift from liberty to equality in Richard Moon, "Liberty, Neutrality and Inclusion: Freedom of Religion under the *Canadian Charter of Rights*" (2003) 41 *Brandeis LR* 563.

60   The ban on state support is sometimes explained as simply a broad ban on coercion — that favouritism isolates or pressures individuals to conform to the preferred religion. But, as I will argue below, it seems more credibly tied to a conception of religion as a cultural identity and the view that to disfavour one religion is to suggest that it is less worthy or valuable than others.

that freedom of conscience and religion protects both religious and non-religious (fundamental) values and beliefs, the former have been at the centre of Canadian freedom of religion and conscience cases. The protection of nonreligious beliefs and practices (the freedom of conscience component of section 2(a)) appears to be limited to practices that resemble in content and structure familiar religious practices.

E. STATE NEUTRALITY AND ITS LIMITS: A RETURN TO PRAGMATISM

The requirement that the state remain neutral in religious matters was affirmed by Deschamps J, writing for the majority of the Supreme Court of Canada, in *SL v Commission scolaire des Chênes*: "Religious neutrality is now seen by many Western states as a legitimate means of creating a free space in which citizens of various beliefs can exercise their individual rights."[61] A few years later in *Mouvement laique quebecois v City of Saguenay*, the Supreme Court, in a judgment written by Gascon J, observed "[b]y expressing no preference, the state ensures that it preserves a neutral public space that is free of discrimination and in which true freedom to believe or not to believe is enjoyed by everyone equally, given that everyone is valued equally."[62]

This shift in the courts' understanding of religious freedom from a liberty right to a form of equality right—from a ban on state coercion in religious matters to a requirement of state neutrality or even-handedness—rests on a very different understanding of religion and

---

61 2012 SCC 7 at para 10 [*SL*]. Justice Deschamps observed that the "Canadian courts have held that state sponsorship of one religious tradition amounts to discrimination against others" (*ibid* at para 17). The commitment to the equal treatment of different religions, or state neutrality in religious matters, was earlier described by LeBel J in *Congrégation des témoins de Jéhovah de St-Jérôme-Lafontaine v Lafontaine (Village)*, 2004 SCC 48 at para 65: "This fundamental freedom imposes on the state and public authorities, in relation to all religions and citizens, a duty of religious neutrality that assures individual or collective tolerance, thereby safeguarding the dignity of every individual and ensuring equality for all." The concurring judgment of LeBel J in *SL* at para 54 expressed a similar view: "Moreover, in the modern Canadian political system, the state in principle takes a position of neutrality. And it is barred from enacting private legislation that favours one religion over another."

62 *Mouvement laïque québécois v Saguenay (City)*, 2015 SCC 16 at para 74: "[A] neutral public space free from coercion, pressure and judgment on the part of public authorities in matters of spirituality is intended to protect every person's freedom and dignity. The neutrality of the public space therefore helps preserve and promote the multicultural nature of Canadian society."

its place in public life. Religion, in this account, is viewed as a matter of personal or communal identity that should be both excluded and insulated from state action. If religious belief is central to the individual's identity, then a judgment by the state that a person's beliefs or practices are less important or less true than the beliefs or practices of others may be experienced as a denial of that person's equal worth and not simply as a rejection of their views and values.[63] Or if religious association is an important part of the individual's identity, then the differential treatment of religious groups may have the effect of marginalizing some groups, excluding them from full participation in public life. The inclusion of religion as a ground of discrimination under section 15 of the *Charter* lends support to this view of religion as an identity.[64]

Neutrality between different faiths can be achieved in a variety of ways. At an earlier time, it may have seemed possible to base public action on widely held religious beliefs and practices, although this "common religious ground" invariably excluded some individuals or groups. In any event, with the growth of religious diversity and the rise of agnosticism and spiritualism, state reliance on widely held religious beliefs can no longer be viewed as inclusive or neutral — if it ever was that. The state may also achieve a degree of neutrality by providing even-handed support to the different religious practices or institutions in the community as well as to nonreligious alternatives. Indeed, the Canadian courts have held that the *Charter* does not preclude the state from providing

---

63   State compulsion to engage in a religious practice as well as the restriction of such a practice may also be seen as deeply invasive once we recognize the strong connection between the individual and their religious beliefs. For a discussion of an equality-based conception of religious freedom, see Bruce Ryder, "The Canadian Conception of Equal Religious Citizenship" in Richard Moon, ed, *Law and Religious Pluralism in Canada* (Vancouver: UBC Press, 2008) 91; and Carissima Mathen, "What Religious Freedom Jurisprudence Reveals about Equality" (2009) 6 *JL & Equality* 163. As noted, this view of religion, as a matter of identity, is very different from the conception of religion that underlies the defence of religious freedom or tolerance in earlier times. Early defenders of religious tolerance or freedom in the West assumed the existence of religious truth, generally some form of Protestantism, and sought to protect the conditions necessary for the individual and collective realization of that truth.

64   But, of course, if s 2(a) is understood in this way, it will overlap significantly with s 15. This may explain why s 15 has played such a limited role in religion cases. As Sopinka J observed in *Adler v Ontario*, [1996] 3 SCR 609 at para 166, "It is evident that there is some overlap between the claims based on s. 2(a) and s. 15 of the Charter . . . During oral argument, it became increasingly difficult to identify whether a particular argument supported a claim under s. 2(a) or under s. 15." Yet, as will become apparent in the discussion of religious freedom in Chapter 3, the courts have adopted a weak standard of justification for limits on religious practice and avoided applying the more demanding s 15 equality standards.

financial support to religious schools or acknowledging the practices or celebrations of different religious groups as long as it does so in an even-handed way.[65] However, the commitment to state neutrality toward different religious belief systems is most often understood as requiring the privatization of religion, which involves both the exclusion and insulation of religion from political decision making.[66]

The difficulty in treating religion as a private matter, though, is that religious belief systems often say something about the way we should treat others and about the kind of society we should work to create. Because religious beliefs sometimes address civic concerns and are often difficult to distinguish from nonreligious beliefs, they cannot be fully excluded or insulated from political decision making. As will be discussed in the next chapter, the courts sometimes treat religion as a cultural identity toward which the state should remain neutral and other times (when it addresses civic matters) as a political or moral judgment by the individual that should be subject to the give-and-take of politics.[67]

Even when religious beliefs do not address civic issues, they may sometimes conflict with state policy (such as a police uniform requirement or a photo requirement for a driver's licence). I will argue that in such cases, the court's task is not to balance competing claims or interests but

---

65 See, for example, *Reference re Bill 30*, above note 14 at para 62. That case is examined in Chapter 6.

66 For a discussion of some of the problems with approaching religion as an identity (and with identity politics more generally), including the risk of "essentializing" the group or its belief system, see Avigail Eisenberg, "Rights in the Age of Identity Politics" (2013) 50 *Osgoode Hall LJ* 609.

67 The idea of religion as a form of cultural identity (that the state should treat with equal respect) fits some religious traditions and some elements of particular belief systems better than others. The shift to an equality-based conception of religious freedom may be in tension with the growth of spiritualism and other more individualized "systems" of belief and practice concerning the supernatural. The courts' uncertain or complex conception of religious commitment reflects larger questions about individual agency and the distinction often made between matters of identity, which are fixed or rooted, and matters of choice, which are open to revision. This is also apparent in the courts' s 15 jurisprudence, in which all grounds of discrimination are, on the face of it, treated the same—in the model of race or skin colour—as immutable traits that are generally irrelevant in political decision making. But the reality is that many of these grounds are not simply immutable and are, in part, a matter of choice or culture. I suspect that the inconsistent results in cases involving citizenship and marital status as grounds of discrimination reflect the courts' ambivalence about these grounds and a recognition that they involve an element of choice or control for which the individual may sometimes be seen as responsible. See, for example, the Supreme Court's judgment in *Lavoie v Canada*, 2002 SCC 23 (citizenship), and in *Quebec (AG) v A*, 2013 SCC 5 (marital status).

instead to define the scope of private or communal spiritual life that may be protected or exempted from state action. However, the line separating the spheres of private spiritual life and civic secular life is moveable and porous. And so the story of religious freedom in Canada may not be simply a linear progression from the pragmatic tolerance of religious minorities to the principled protection of individual liberty in religious belief and practice. The protection of religious freedom in the contemporary context involves the pragmatic reconciliation of civic action and spiritual life.[68]

---

68   The pragmatic account rested on a recognition that social stability might be more effectively achieved through religious tolerance than through the enforcement of religious uniformity. But, as the ban in Quebec on civil servants wearing religious symbols illustrates, this claim continues to be challenged as different political communities struggle with issues of identity and social cohesion. The ban is discussed in Chapter 3.

CHAPTER 2

GOVERNMENT SUPPORT FOR RELIGION

A. SUPPORT FOR RELIGIOUS PRACTICE

Religious freedom has two dimensions: the freedom to practise one's religion without state interference and the freedom from state compulsion to perform a religious practice — the "freedom to" and the "freedom from" religion. At an earlier time, when most individuals adhered to a particular religious belief system, these two dimensions were closely tied. In seeking to advance a particular conception of religious truth, a state might decide to both compel the "correct" or dominant religious practice and to prohibit "erroneous" practices. Compelling an individual to engage in a religious practice may sometimes also mean preventing them from engaging in their own practices.[1] In some cases, a religious adherent might consider their compelled (and formal) participation in "erroneous" practices to be a breach of their religious obligations or even to be blasphemous. However, with the growth in the community of non-religious or agnostic perspectives, the tie between these two dimensions of the freedom has been loosened. Indeed, as we shall see, most of the recent challenges against state support for a religious practice have been brought by nonbelievers, who object not to the preference of one religion over another but instead to any form of state support for religion.

---

1   See *Alberta v Hutterian Brethren of Wilson Colony*, 2009 SCC 37 [*Hutterian Brethren*] at para 92, McLachlin J: "To compel religious practice by force of law deprives the individual of the fundamental right to choose his or her mode of religious experience, or lack thereof."

In *R v Big M Drug Mart*,[2] the Supreme Court of Canada said that the test for determining whether section 2(a) has been breached is whether the state act in question amounts to "coercion" of the conscience. According to Dickson CJ, no one should "be forced to act in a way contrary to his beliefs or his conscience" except when necessary to protect an important public interest or individual right.[3] The individual must be free to practise their religion, and they must not be compelled to engage in other religious practices.

The issue in *Big M Drug Mart* was whether the federal *Lord's Day Act*,[4] which prohibited a variety of commercial activities on Sundays, breached section 2(a) of the *Charter*[5] and, if it did, whether this breach could be justified under section 1, the limitations provision of the *Charter*. Chief Justice Dickson said that, in deciding whether the law breached section 2(a), the Court had to consider both the law's effect and its purpose. In this case, he found that the *Lord's Day Act* breached section 2(a) because its "true purpose" was to compel a religious practice—"the observance of the Christian Sabbath."[6]

In defending the Act, the government had argued that the purpose of the Sunday ban, at least in the contemporary context, was to create a common pause day for workers. Chief Justice Dickson, though, noted that, at the time of its enactment, it was understood that the purpose of the law was to compel or support Sabbath observance. In his view, the law's "[p]urpose is a function of the intent of those who drafted and enacted the legislation at the time, and not of any shifting variable," and so the *Lord's Day Act* could not at this stage be held to have a secular purpose.[7] However, there was another reason the federal government could not now claim that the law's purpose was to create a common pause day. Before the enactment of the *Charter*, the *Lord's Day Act* had been viewed as a valid exercise of the federal government's power to enact criminal laws under section 91 of the *Constitution Act, 1867*.[8] The validity of the *Lord's Day Act* under the criminal law power was based on its religious purpose—and in particular its enforcement of the Sabbath. Since the provinces have exclusive jurisdiction under the Constitution to enact laws regulating business and trade activities within their territories, any

---

2   [1985] 1 SCR 295 [*Big M Drug Mart*].

3   *Ibid* at para 95.

4   *Lord's Day Act*, RSC 1970, c L-13, as repealed by SI/88-227, 12 December 1988.

5   *Canadian Charter of Rights and Freedoms*, Part 1 of the *Constitution Act, 1982*, being Schedule B to the *Canada Act 1982* (UK), 1982, c 11 [*Charter*].

6   Above note 2 at para 136.

7   *Ibid* at para 91.

8   *Constitution Act, 1867*, (UK), 30 & 31 Vict, c 3, reprinted in RSC 1985, App II, No 5.

attempt by the federal government to defend the law under the *Charter* on the basis that it advances a secular purpose, such as the creation of a common pause day for workers, would undermine its constitutionality under the federal division of powers.

Chief Justice Dickson went on to find that the law could not be upheld under section 1 because its purpose was religious: "The characterization of the purpose of the Act as one which compels religious observance renders it unnecessary to decide the question of whether s. 1 could validate such legislation whose purpose was otherwise."[9] A "religious" purpose could not be regarded as pressing and substantial, and so it was unnecessary for the Court to address the other elements of the section 1 test, as set out in *R v Oakes*.[10] The consequence of this determination by the Court is that section 1 may have no role in those section 2(a) cases in which the breach is based on state compulsion of (or support for) religion.[11]

While the Court in *Big M Drug Mart* formally described the wrong addressed by section 2(a) as coercion in spiritual matters, its finding that the *Lord's Day Act* breached section 2(a) seemed to rest on a broader understanding of the wrong. The Act did not require anyone to honour the Sabbath by attending church or reading the Bible or reflecting on their spiritual commitments. It prevented individuals from working but did not require them to worship or even rest.[12] Chief Justice Dickson, though, adopted a broad view of religious compulsion:

---

9   Above note 2 at para 142.

10   [1986] 1 SCR 103 [*Oakes*]. The *Oakes* test has several elements. A restriction on a right or freedom must have a substantial and pressing purpose. The restriction must be rationally connected to that purpose, and it must restrict the right or freedom no more than is necessary to advance that purpose. And, finally, the actual costs of the restriction to the right or freedom must not outweigh its benefits. A law that advantages the practices of one religious group, even if not intended to support or prefer that group, may sometimes be viewed as a restriction on the practices of other groups—a burden on their religious practice. See, for example, *R v Edwards Books and Art Ltd*, [1986] 2 SCR 713 [*Edwards Books*], which is discussed in Chapter 3.

11   See also McLachlin J in *Hutterian Brethren*, above note 1 at para 92: "To compel religious practice by force of law deprives the individual of the fundamental right to choose his or her mode of religious experience, or lack thereof. Such laws will fail at the first stage of *Oakes* and proportionality will not need to be considered."

12   This was the view of the majority of the Supreme Court in *Robertson and Rosetanni v The Queen*, [1963] SCR 651, a *Canadian Bill of Rights* case that considered whether the *Lord's Day Act* breached religious freedom. Justice Ritchie wrote at 657–58 (quoted by Dickson CJ in *Big M Drug Mart* at para 69):

My own view is that the *effect* of the Lord's Day Act rather than its *purpose* must be looked to in order to determine whether its application involves

> In my view, the guarantee of freedom of conscience and religion prevents the government from compelling individuals to perform or abstain from performing otherwise harmless acts because of the religious significance of those acts to others. The element of religious compulsion is perhaps somewhat more difficult to perceive (especially for those whose beliefs are being enforced) when, as here, it is non-action rather than action that is being decreed, but in my view compulsion is nevertheless what it amounts to.[13]

The chief justice recognized that the law did not compel the individual to perform a particular religious act but, rather, required that they refrain from performing an otherwise lawful activity.

The purpose of the law might have been simply to support those who wished to keep the Sunday Sabbath by removing the economic costs that would result from not working on Sunday when other people (and, more particularly, other retailers) were prepared to treat it as another business day. Or its purpose might have been to encourage all individuals to keep the Sunday Sabbath, without actually requiring anyone to do so. While it is true that support for a particular religious practice may in some circumstances put "pressure" on non-adherents to conform to the practice — for example, if there are significant advantages to following the practice — that does not seem to be the case here.[14] The Court, however, seemed prepared to find a breach of religious freedom simply

---

> the abrogation, abridgment or infringement of religious freedom, and I can see nothing in that statute which in any way affects the liberty of religious thought and practice of any citizen of this country . . .
>
> The practical result of this law on those whose religion requires them to observe a day of rest other than Sunday, is a purely secular and financial one in that they are required to refrain from carrying on or conducting their business on Sunday as well as on their own day of rest. In some cases this is no doubt a business inconvenience, but it is neither an abrogation nor an abridgment nor an infringement of religious freedom, and the fact that it has been brought about by reason of the existence of a statute enacted for the purpose of preserving the sanctity of Sunday, cannot, in my view, be construed as attaching some religious significance to an effect which is purely secular in so far as non-Christians are concerned. [emphasis added]

13   Above note 2 at para 133. In *S v Lawrence; S v Negal; S v Solberg*, 1997 (10) BCLR 1348 (CC), a majority of the South African Constitutional Court upheld a ban on the sale of liquor on Sundays and statutory holidays. The judges were divided on the question of whether the constitutional protection of freedom of religion simply prohibited state compulsion to engage in a religious practice or whether it also precluded the state from supporting the practices of a particular religion.

14   But see the discussion of *Edwards Books* above note 10.

because the law had a purpose that was religious in character.[15] And so the Court's objection to the *Lord's Day Act* may not have been that it compelled, or was intended to compel, individuals to keep the Sabbath but instead that it supported or favoured the practices of the dominant religious group. Indeed, near the end of his judgment, Dickson CJ indicated that it is "constitutionally incompetent for the federal Parliament to provide legislative preference for any one religion at the expense of those of another religious persuasion."[16] More specifically, about the law at issue in this case, he said:

> To the extent that it binds all to a sectarian Christian ideal, the Lord's Day Act works a form of coercion inimical to the spirit of the Charter and the dignity of all non-Christians. In proclaiming the standards of the Christian faith, the Act creates a climate hostile to, and gives the appearance of discrimination against, non-Christian Canadians. It takes religious values rooted in Christian morality and, using the force of the state, translates them into a positive law binding on believers and non-believers alike. The theological content of the legislation remains as a subtle and constant reminder to religious minorities within the country of their differences with, and alienation from, the dominant religious culture.[17]

In the later decision of *SL v Commission scolaire des Chênes*, the Supreme Court confirmed that the judgment in *Big M Drug Mart* was based on the requirement that the state remain neutral in religious matters. Referring to *Big M Drug Mart* (and other cases), Deschamps J observed that "Canadian courts have held that state sponsorship of one religious tradition amounts to discrimination against others."[18]

In *R v Edwards Books and Art Ltd*, the Supreme Court held that a *provincial* law that required stores to be closed on Sunday had a secular purpose — the creation of a common pause day for retail workers — and so did not compel a religious practice contrary to section 2(a).[19] Chief Justice Dickson thought that

---

15   See Shannon Ishiyama Smithey, "Religious Freedom and Equality Concerns under the Canadian Charter of Rights and Freedoms" (2001) 34 *Can J Pol Sci* 85 at 93.

16   Above note 2 at para 134. Section 15, the equality rights provision of the *Charter*, did not come into force until 1985, three years after the enactment of the *Charter*. Because its challenge was initiated before this date, the respondent in *Big M Drug Mart* was unable to make a direct equality rights claim.

17   *Ibid* at para 97.

18   2012 SCC 7 at para 17 [*SL*]. This case is discussed in Chapter 3.

19   Above note 10.

[religious freedom] is not necessarily impaired by legislation which requires conduct consistent with the religious beliefs of another person. One is not being compelled to engage in religious practices merely because a statutory obligation coincides with the dictates of a particular religion. I cannot accept, for example, that a legislative prohibition of criminal conduct such as theft and murder is a state-enforced compulsion to conform to religious practices, merely because some religions enjoin their members not to steal or kill. Reasonable citizens do not perceive the legislation as requiring them to pay homage to religious doctrine.[20]

As discussed in Chapter 3, the Court in *Edwards Books* went on to find that, even though the provincial Sunday closing law did not compel Sunday Sabbath observance, it had the effect of indirectly restricting the religious practice of those who kept a day other than Sunday as the Sabbath.[21] The Court, however, found that this restriction on religious practice was justified under section 1.[22]

---

20   *Ibid* at para 99. The US courts have similarly upheld Sunday closing laws on the basis that their purpose is no longer religious. In *McGowan v Maryland*, 366 US 420 (1961) at 450, the US Supreme Court found that the purpose of a Maryland Sunday closing law was "to set one day apart from all others as a day of rest, repose, recreation and tranquility ..." The Court noted that "[p]eople of all religions and people with no religion regard Sunday as a time for family activity, for visiting friends and relatives, for late sleeping, for passive and active entertainments, for dining out, and the like" (*ibid* at 451–52). The reason for this, said the Court, is now "irrelevant" and "[i]t would seem unrealistic for enforcement purposes and perhaps detrimental to the general welfare to require a State to choose a common day of rest other than that which most persons would select of their own accord" (*ibid* at 452). The Court concluded that the statute at issue was not a law "respecting an establishment of religion" (*ibid*). In *Braunfeld v Brown*, 366 US 599 (1961), the US Supreme Court held that if enacted for a secular purpose, a Sunday closing law did not breach either the establishment clause or the free exercise clause of the First Amendment.

21   As noted in the discussion of *Edwards Books*, above note 10, in Chapter 3, the law's favouring—or relative advantaging—of Christian practice played a role in the Court's finding that the law restricted the religious practice of Saturday Sabbatarians.

22   The courts in Canada have upheld statutory holidays that are based on Christian holy days such as Christmas and Easter as part of the school calendar, but have required state authorities to give paid days off for those who observe other religious holidays. See, for example, *Chambly (Commission scolaire régionale) v Bergevin*, [1994] 2 SCR 525. In *Islamic Schools Federation of Ontario v Ottawa Board of Education* (1997), 145 DLR (4th) 659 (Ont Div Ct), the court held that the provincial regulation that established school holidays did not breach s 2(a) simply because it included the major Christian holidays and not those of other religious communities. In the court's view, it was sufficient that Muslims, and the members of other religious groups, were not required to attend school on their religious holidays.

B. RELIGIOUS PRACTICES IN PUBLIC SCHOOLS

In *Zylberberg v Sudbury Board of Education*, the Ontario Court of Appeal ruled that the inclusion of the Lord's Prayer in the opening exercises of public schools in Ontario breached section 2(a) of the *Charter* and could not be justified under section 1.[23]

The court in *Zylberberg* found that the *purpose* of the law was religious and, following the Supreme Court of Canada in *Big M Drug Mart*, concluded that it breached section 2(a).[24] Yet the religious purpose of the law may not have been to compel or pressure students to engage in a religious practice but might instead have been simply to give students, who wished, the opportunity to participate in an important religious practice. However, the court also found that the *effect* of the practice was to compel students to participate in a religious ritual. The court determined that the prayer was coercive, even though the students could opt out of the practice, either by remaining silent or withdrawing from the classroom. The court recognized that in the public school context, children would feel significant pressure from their teacher and their peers to conform to the school-supported practices of the majority community. While students had a formal right to opt out of the prayer, those who exercised this right and declined to participate would feel isolated or stigmatized.[25] In the court's view, this was enough for the prayer to be regarded as coercive—as state compulsion to engage in a religious practice. In the school context, the line between state compulsion of religion and state

---

23 [1988] OJ No 1488 (Ont CA) [*Zylberberg*]. The same conclusion was reached in *Russow v BC (AG)* (1989), 62 DLR (4th) 98 (BCSC) and in *Manitoba Assn for Rights and Liberties Inc v Manitoba (Minister of Education)* (1992), 94 DLR (4th) 678 (Man QB). Over the course of the twentieth century, the Protestant character of the public school system had gradually been eroded. Nevertheless, in 1982 at the time of the *Charter's* introduction, many public schools still incorporated religious elements in the curriculum, as per provincial education policy. For a discussion, see RD Gidney and WPJ Millar, "The Christian Recessional in Ontario's Public Schools" in Marguerite Van Die, ed, *Religion and Public Life in Canada: Historical and Comparative Perspectives* (Toronto: University of Toronto Press, 2001) 275.

24 The Regulations under the Ontario *Education Act* provided: "28(1) A public school shall be opened or closed each school day with religious exercises consisting of the reading of the Scriptures or other suitable readings and the repeating of the Lord's Prayer or other suitable prayers" (Reg 262).

25 The majority judgment also thought it objectionable that students would have to identify themselves as different—as not part of the majority—to take advantage of the exemption. This objection, though, seemed to depend on the more fundamental claim that students should not be pressured to conform to the religious practices of the dominant group.

support for religion may be difficult to draw, because children are not yet independent agents and because the school represents a significant authority in their lives.

The Court of Appeal in *Zylberberg* went on to find that the law could not be justified under section 1 because its purpose was religious. The school board, though, argued that the law's purpose should be understood more broadly, as the affirmation of important values at the start of the school day.[26] The court, however, found that even if the law's purpose could be framed in more general (nonreligious) terms, the law did not interfere with section 2(a) rights as little as was necessary to advance this objective and so failed the *Oakes* test. The schools could advance this broader objective, said the court, other than by conducting a daily recitation of a Christian prayer. In holding that the law did not represent a minimal impairment of the religious freedom of non-Christians, the court referred to the practice of the Toronto School Board at the time, which involved daily readings, on a rotating basis, from a book of materials that drew from a wide range of spiritual and philosophical traditions. The court did not decide that the Toronto School Board's practice was constitutional but only that it offered a less intrusive way to affirm public values in the schools than the practice of reciting the Lord's Prayer.[27]

In *Canadian Civil Liberties Assn v Ontario (Minister of Education)*, the Ontario Court of Appeal held that a provincial regulation requiring

---

26   However, if this really was the law's purpose then there might have been no breach of s 2(a).

27   A system of rotating readings, drawn from different spiritual and moral traditions, might raise another problem. The use of different readings to create a moral or spiritual tone at the beginning of each school day could be seen as advancing a "relativistic" view of religion—that all traditions have merit. It does not appear that the roster of prayers and readings was being used to teach about religion, in a sociological sense, as occurred in the *SL* case, above note 18. For a discussion of the legislative response to this decision and some of the litigation that followed, see Robert Earl Charney, "The Limits of Religious Accommodation in Secular Public Schools" (2013) 7:2 *J of Parliamentary and Pol L* 247. In his partly dissenting judgment in *Zylberberg*, Lacourcière J noted the omission from the *Charter* of any provision resembling the establishment clause of the US *Bill of Rights* and argued that section 2(a) "does not prohibit all governmental aid to or advancement of religion per se" (para 113). According to Lacourcière J, it could not reasonably be said that either the purpose or the effect of the law was to compel participation in a religious practice, given the broad exemption granted to dissenters. However, Lacourcière J found that the particular practice of the Sudbury school board breached section 15 because "it gives preference to that tradition at the expense of all non-Christians" and could not be justified under section 1, because "there are other ways, which are less intrusive on the equality rights of religious minorities, to implement religious exercises which encourage respect for moral principles" (para 147).

public schools to devote two one-half hour periods each week to "religious education" had as its purpose the indoctrination of students into the Christian faith and therefore breached section 2(a) of the *Charter*, and that this breach could not be justified under section 1.[28] In reaching this conclusion, the court noted that the regulation permitted the use of clergy to teach the required course, even though uncertified instructors were not authorized to teach other parts of the school curriculum. The court thought that "in the absence of evidence that clergymen are better equipped to teach comparative religions than they are skilled at indoctrination, the conclusion has to be that the purpose was indoctrination."[29] The court also noted that the regulation referred to clergymen of "different denominations" rather than different religions, which suggested that the religious education was to be Christian in character. The regulation allowed students to be exempted from the religion classes, but the court noted that such an exemption would only be necessary if the instruction involved religious indoctrination. And, as in *Zylberberg*, the court found that the indoctrinating purpose or effect of the regulation was not altered by the fact that students who did not want to participate in the religious education classes could be granted an exemption. In the court's view, any students who requested an exemption would be stigmatized as "non-conformists" and set "apart from their fellow students who are members of the dominant religion."[30]

The court also considered the constitutionality of the particular form of religious instruction provided by the Elgin County School Board. The court recognized that the line between religious indoctrination, which is contrary to section 2(a), and education about religion, which is compatible with religious freedom, may sometimes be difficult to draw. Nevertheless, based on the "general themes, lesson plans, teaching and

---

28   [1990] OJ No 104. In *Bonitto v Halifax Regional School Board*, 2015 NSCA 80, the Nova Scotia Court of Appeal rejected Mr. Bonitto's claim that he should be permitted to distribute religious pamphlets at a public elementary school during school hours. The court found that the school's refusal to permit this was reasonable given the school's duty to remain neutral in religious matters.

29   *Ibid* at para 52.

30   *Ibid* at para 21. The court observed at para 55 that

> [s]tate-authorized religious indoctrination amounts to the imposition of majoritarian religious beliefs on minorities. Although s. 2(a) of the Charter is not infringed merely because education may be consistent with the religious beliefs of the majority of Canadians ... , teaching students Christian doctrine as if it were the exclusive means through which to develop moral thinking and behaviour amounts to religious coercion in the class-room. It creates a direct burden on religious minorities and non-believers who do not adhere to majoritarian beliefs ... [T]his amounts to violation of s. 2(a) of the Charter.

resource materials and the manner of presentation of the course of study," the court concluded that the curriculum constituted religious indoctrination.[31] The assumption made by the court — reflecting a more general view about religion — is that to teach from a particular religious perspective, or to teach a particular religion as true, is to engage in religious indoctrination.[32]

C. PRAYERS AT MUNICIPAL COUNCIL MEETINGS: *FREITAG V PENETANGUISHNE AND MLQ V SAGUENAY*

In *Freitag v Penetanguishene*, the Ontario Court of Appeal held that the practice of reciting the Lord's Prayer at the opening of town council meetings violated the religious freedom of non-Christians.[33] The court found that the practice was coercive — that it pressured individuals to conform to the tenets of a particular faith — even though no one was directly required to recite the prayer; even though some individuals, including the complainant, chose not to participate; and even though the meeting was composed of adults rather than children. The court acknowledged that "the nature and potential effect of the coercion are much different for an adult who wishes to attend Town Council meetings than for children, who are in the school environment all year with friends and teachers, and are subject to pressures that those important relations engender."[34] However, said the court, "[j]ust as children are entitled to attend public school and be free from coercion or pressure to conform to the religious practices of the majority, so everyone is entitled to attend public local council meetings and to enjoy the same freedom."[35] The difficulty with the court's claim, though, is that in *Zylberberg* the school environment was critical to the court's conclusion that the recitation of the Lord's Prayer was coercive. The practice in *Zylberberg* was seen as coercive because it involved children, who are vulnerable to peer pressure in a way that adults are not.

The court in *Freitag* found that the purpose of the practice was to "impose a specifically Christian moral tone on the deliberations of the

---

31   *Ibid* at para 71.

32   In *Loyola High School v Quebec (Attorney General)*, 2015 SCC 12, which is discussed in Chapter 5, the Supreme Court appeared to accept that religious instruction does not (necessarily) involve indoctrination.

33   (1999), 47 OR (3d) 301 [*Freitag*].

34   *Ibid* at para 33.

35   *Ibid* at para 34.

Town Council," contrary to section 2(a).[36] Yet it is unlikely that the council was trying to pressure non-Christians to say the prayer or adhere to the Christian faith. In all likelihood, the purpose was simply to signal the importance of the Christian faith in the community or to enable Christians attending the meeting to practice their faith. Nor is it even clear that a non-Christian adult attending the council meeting would experience the prayer as pressure to adopt the Christian faith and reject their own belief system. Recitation of the prayer may have caused the non-Christians present at the meeting to feel uncomfortable, embarrassed, and unfairly treated, but it put no tangible pressure on them.

It appears that the real objection to opening a council meeting with a Christian prayer was that it excluded non-Christians from full participation in a public meeting. More generally, it signalled to non-Christians that they were not full members of the political community. The court in *Freitag* recognized this when it described the practice of saying the prayer as "exclusionary."[37] The court went on to say that "the appellant ... feels intimidation when he attends the meeting of his local Town Council. This does not mean that he is so fearful that he does not participate. He does so, but as a citizen who is singled out as being not part of the majority recognized officially in the proceedings."[38] According to this view, state support for a religious practice is wrong because it sends a message of exclusion to non-adherents or because it treats some individuals less favourably than others on the basis of their religious membership.

In *Mouvement laïque québécois v Saguenay* the Supreme Court explicitly decided that the state has a duty to remain neutral in matters of religion and that the recitation of a prayer at the opening of a municipal council's public meeting breached this duty.[39] The Saguenay mayor, using a microphone, would recite the following prayer (along with council members and members of the public) at the opening of each council meeting:

> [TRANSLATION] O God, eternal and almighty, from Whom all power and wisdom flow, we are assembled here in Your presence to ensure the good of our city and its prosperity. We beseech You to grant us the enlightenment and energy necessary for our deliberations to promote

---

36 *Ibid* at para 25.

37 *Ibid* at para 36.

38 *Ibid*. The evidence showed that Mr Freitag and others sat quietly during the recitation of the prayer.

39 2015 SCC 16 [*MLQ*]. The case was decided under the Quebec *Charter of Human Rights and Freedoms*, CQLR c C-12. The court, however, was clear that the freedom of religion provision in the Quebec *Charter* should be interpreted in the same way as section 2(a), the freedom of religion section, of the *Canadian Charter of Rights and Freedoms*.

> the honour and glory of Your holy name and the spiritual and material
> [well-being] of our city. Amen.[40]

Just before reciting the prayer, the mayor would make the sign of the
cross and invoke the Christian Trinity: "in the name of the Father, the
Son, and the Holy Spirit." At the end of the prayer, he would again make
the sign of the cross. A number of others present at the meeting would
do the same. Mr. Simoneau, a member of the public who often attended
council meetings, objected to the mayor's practice of opening council
meetings with the prayer and brought a complaint under the Quebec
Charter of Human Rights. Before his complaint was considered by the
human rights commission, the municipal council passed a bylaw that
made minor changes to the wording of the prayer (the new prayer still
invoked the name of God in its opening line) and provided that the formal meeting would not begin until a few minutes after the conclusion
of the prayer. This delay in the start of the meeting was intended to give
those who objected to the prayer the opportunity to remain outside of
the council chamber until the prayer was completed and the formal
meeting began.[41]

The Court in *MLQ* decided that the prayer recited at the opening of
the council meeting breached the requirement of state neutrality, which
the court described as a "corollary" of the fundamental freedom of conscience and religion protected by the Quebec and Canadian *Charters*.[42]
The Court held "that the state may not consciously make a profession of
faith or act so as to adopt or favour one religious view at the expense of
all others."[43] In the Court's view, preventing the state from "expressing
a preference" in religious matters ensures the preservation of "a neutral
public space that is free of discrimination and in which true freedom to
believe or not to believe is enjoyed by everyone equally, given that everyone is valued equally"[44]: "[A] neutral public space free from coercion,
pressure and judgment on the part of public authorities in matters of
spirituality" serves to "protect every person's freedom and dignity" and

---

40   *Ibid* at para 7.

41   For the Court, this delay only contributed to the message of exclusion: "This
      solution adopted by the council of inviting citizens to physically leave the cham-
      ber for the duration of the prayer highlights the exclusive effect of the practice.
      Rather than limiting the religious nature of the By-law, the possibility so afforded
      accentuated it." (*Ibid* at para 101.)

42   *Ibid* at para 71.

43   *Ibid* at para 87.

44   *Ibid* at para 7.

to "preserve and promote the multicultural nature of Canadian society."[45] At the same time, the Court insisted that "the state's duty of neutrality does not require it to abstain from celebrating and preserving its religious heritage"; "The Canadian cultural landscape includes many traditional and heritage practices that are religious in nature," which the state may protect and maintain.[46]

According to the Court, the test for determining whether the neutrality requirement has been breached varies depending on whether the complaint relates to a legal rule (such as a statue, regulation, or bylaw) or to a state practice. A statutory or other legal provision "will be inoperative if its purpose is religious and therefore cannot be reconciled with the state's duty of neutrality ... The legislative objective cannot be to impose or favour, or to express or profess, one belief to the exclusion of all others."[47] However, in a case in which the complaint concerns a "state practice," the test has an additional step. The complainant must establish "that the state is professing, adopting or favouring one belief to the exclusion of all others [but also] that the exclusion has resulted in interference with the complainant's freedom of conscience and religion."[48] More specifically, it must be shown that the state practice impedes "the individual's ability to act in accordance with his or her beliefs."[49]

The Court found that the practice in this case, which included the mayor's genuflection and reference to the Trinity, had a religious purpose. The Court was helped to this conclusion by the mayor's public statements that the prayer was being used by the council because "we have faith." The mayor's comments confirmed that the prayer was not simply the "expression of a cultural tradition" but "was above all else a use by the council of public powers to manifest and profess one religion to the exclusion of all others."[50] Furthermore, said the Court, the practice amounted to a substantial interference with Mr Simoneau's freedom of religion. The practice effectively excluded Mr Simoneau (a self-described atheist and the complainant in the case) on the basis of religion and impaired "his right to full and equal exercise of his freedom of conscience

---

45   *Ibid* at para 74. The Court recognized that "[r]eligious belief orients the individual in the world, shapes her/his perception of the social and natural orders, and provides a moral framework for his/her actions and is often the central or defining association in her life"; *ibid* at para 73 quoting R Moon, "Freedom of Religion under the Charter of Rights: The Limits of State Neutrality" 45 *UBC L Rev* 497 (2012).

46   *Ibid* at para 116.

47   *Ibid* at para 83.

48   *Ibid*.

49   *Ibid* at para 85.

50   *Ibid* at para 118.

and religion."[51] The practice caused him to experience "a strong feeling of isolation and exclusion."[52]

This second element of the test, though, seems redundant. When a state actor engages in, or supports, a particular religious practice, it must always be the case that the nonbelievers who witness the practice will feel excluded or marginalized. State support for a particular religious practice can sometimes amount to pressure to conform to that practice, but the wrong is more basic than that. The wrong in this and similar cases is the differential treatment of community members because of their religion.[53] It is objectionable and harmful regardless of the subjective experience of individual members of the excluded group or the degree of offence or hurt experienced by the group's members. The Court's addition of this second element to the test suggests a reluctance to fully embrace the neutrality requirement and to see the wrong as unequal treatment rather than interference with liberty.[54] This second element may also reflect a confusion by the Court about the two different ways in which section 2(a) may be breached—state support for a particular religion and state restriction of religious practice.[55] State restriction of a religious practice is objectionable because it involves an interference

---

51   *Ibid* at para 64.

52   *Ibid* at para 121.

53   *Ibid* at para 64: "Sponsorship of one religious tradition by the state in breach of its duty of neutrality amounts to discrimination against all other such traditions (*S.L. v. Commission scolaire des Chênes*, 2012 SCC 7 at para. 17). If the state favours one religion at the expense of others, it imports a disparate impact that is destructive of the religious freedom of the collectivity (*R. v. Big M Drug Mart Ltd.*, [1985] 1 S.C.R. 295, at p. 337)."

54   It is also possible that in adding this element to the test the Court was anticipating the issue of civil servants wearing religious dress or symbols. Under the two-part test, the Court's response to a claim that a civil servant who wears a hijab, for example, is breaching the neutrality requirement might be that even though her practice indicates support for one religion over another, it does not interfere with anyone's religious freedom. Yet this response seems to get things backwards. Wearing a hijab at work, for example, is an act of personal religious expression, rather than a state act of religious favouritism that may "interfere" with the religious freedom of citizens. Chapter 3 considers the Quebec law that prohibits certain civil servants from wearing religious symbols.

55   It is noteworthy that the Court cites a number of religious restriction cases: "In *Syndicat Northcrest v. Amselem*, 2004 SCC 47, [2004] 2 S.C.R. 551, at paras. 56–59, the Court developed a test for determining whether freedom of conscience and religion has been infringed. To conclude that an infringement has occurred, the court or tribunal must (1) be satisfied that the complainant's belief is sincere, and (2) find that the complainant's ability to act in accordance with his or her beliefs has been interfered with in a manner that is more than trivial or insubstantial" (*ibid* at para 86).

with the individual's ability to practice their faith (measured by the effect of the law), while state support is objectionable because it involves the unequal treatment of different religious belief systems and communities, which has the effect of marginalizing the excluded group's members.[56] If the second subjective element of the test has any role, it can only be to give the courts some discretion to find that a religious practice does not breach section 2(a) without having to specify reasons for this conclusion.

The municipality in *MLQ* argued that because the preamble to the *Constitution Act, 1982*[57] includes a reference to God ("the constitution of Canada is founded on the rule of law and the supremacy of God"), the invocation of God in the town's prayer could not be unconstitutional — that the Constitution could not be read as prohibiting any reference to God by the state. The Court responded to this in two ways. First, according to the Court, the reference to God in a prayer may not itself breach the *Charter*. It will only do so if, as part of a religious practice, it has the effect of excluding some community members. The Court thought that "a single reference to God" in a prayer does not necessarily breach section 2(a) — although once again it is unclear why or when it would not do so. According to the Court: "The moral source of that practice, whether divine or otherwise, is but one of the contextual factors that make it possible to identify the practice's purpose and its effect."[58] But if the right to religious freedom requires the state to refrain from supporting one religion over another or religion over nonreligion, it is difficult to see how any reference to God by the state (unless hollowed of spiritual meaning) would not breach the right. If a Christian prayer excludes non-Christians, does not an ecumenical prayer that appeals explicitly to a divine creator in the same way exclude nonreligious individuals (agnostics or atheists) or the followers of polytheistic or nontheistic belief systems? Is the state not favouring the practices of those who believe in a divine creator over those who do not?

Secondly, said the Court, the preamble, including the reference to God, articulates the "political theory" behind the *Charter* and the rights

---

56   The distinction between the two branches of religious freedom — freedom to religion and freedom from religion — is clear in the Court's other judgments. In state compulsion/support cases, the Court has found no role for section 1. Once a court has decided that the state has compelled or supported a religious practice and so breached s 2(a), the breach cannot be justified under s 1 because its purpose is inconsistent with the right. On the other hand, as discussed in Chapter 3, any time the state restricts a religious practice in a nontrivial way, even if it is pursuing a legitimate public objective, the restriction breaches s 2(a), and the important issue for the court becomes whether this breach is justified under s 1.

57   *Constitution Act, 1982*, being Schedule B to the *Canada Act 1982* (UK), 1982, c 11.

58   *Ibid* at para 146.

it protects. The Court insisted that the reference to God should not be used to read down the proper scope of those rights.[59] But of course the scope or meaning of those rights is precisely what is at issue. The preamble might properly have been used by the courts in deciding how to interpret the right to freedom of religion. The better answer might be that the political community (or the court) is no longer willing to see the *Charter*, or the Constitution more generally, as founded upon a specifically monotheistic or divine order. The meaning of the word "God" in the preamble might instead be opened up or enlarged so that it is understood as referring more generally to an objective moral order that may or may not emanate from a divine will.[60] The rights and freedoms in the *Charter* are derived not from the will of man, but from a moral order that citizens in a democratic political community seek to understand, elaborate, and respect.[61]

D. *SERVATIUS V ALBERNI SCHOOL DISTRICT*

As part of a program to introduce elementary school students to the culture and history of the local Indigenous community, a school in Port Alberni conducted a smudging ceremony in which smoke from burning sage was used to "cleanse" a physical space. A parent objected to the ceremony, arguing that it breached the students' freedom of religion under the *Charter*, as well as the requirement in the BC *School Act*[62] that schools operate according to secular principles.

The parent claimed that the requirement or expectation that her child participate in the smudging ceremony amounted to a restriction on their (and her) freedom to practise their religion. She insisted that her faith requires that she (and her child) not participate in spiritual or supernatural ceremonies and rituals, such as a smudging ceremony, that

---

59   *Ibid* at para 147.

60   See the discussion of the preamble in Lorne Sossin, "The 'Supremacy of God', Human Dignity and the *Charter of Rights and Freedoms*" (2003) 52 *UNBLJ* 227. And Howard Kislowicz, "The 'Supremacy of God' Clause: A Surprisingly Empty Political Theory" in H Kislowicz et al, eds, *The Surprising Constitution* (Vancouver: UBC Press, 2024).

61   The two assertions in the preamble of the *Constitution Act, 1982* (that our political community is subject to God and to the rule of law) can be more easily reconciled once we recognize that laws can be based on both religious and nonreligious values. The reference to God may be a reminder that law must be grounded in deeper values that for many people are religious or that fundamental rights are not simply granted to citizens by the state but have a deeper foundation.

62   *School Act*, RSBC 1996, c 412.

are inconsistent with her beliefs. The other argument made by the parent was that the school had exposed her child to the practices of only one spiritual tradition (that is, that Indigenous practices were being given preference in the schools) in breach of the state neutrality requirement.

In *Servatius v Alberni School District No 70*, the BC Court of Appeal found that the smudging ceremony did not breach section 2(a).[63] The court relied on the trial judge's finding that the students had been observers rather than participants in an educational demonstration: "[T]he students' participation was limited to learning: observing, listening, and taking in the smell of the burning sage."[64] Evidence from the teachers and the elder who performed the ceremony confirmed that only a small amount of smoke was created and none of it was fanned on the students. The Elder also told the court that the demonstration performed in the school was not the same as the ceremony conducted in the community.[65]

But even if the children were not compelled or pressured to participate in the smudging ceremony, the school appeared to be favouring or supporting the practices of a particular religious tradition, contrary to the requirement under section 2(a) that it remain neutral in spiritual or religious matters. The parent argued that if it is objectionable and a breach of the *Charter*'s freedom of religion for a school to include the Lord's Prayer as part of its opening exercises, then surely it must also be a breach of the *Charter* when a school includes a smudging ceremony in its curriculum. The equation of these practices, though, is too simple and fails to understand why the recitation of the Lord's Prayer in the public schools is objectionable and why the smudging ceremony has been included in the school's curriculum.

The BC Court of Appeal in *Servatius* determined that the school was not affirming or supporting the smudging ceremony as a spiritually true practice and that the school's purpose was simply to introduce students to some of the practices of the local Indigenous community.[66] There

---

63 2022 BCCA 421.

64 *Ibid* at para 171.

65 *Ibid* at para 188. The elder also described the demonstration of the smudging ceremony as cultural rather than spiritual (*ibid* at para 171). If the demonstration to the students was simply a way of teaching them about the practice (and they were not being asked to participate), then it might be described as a lesson about Indigenous culture (an anthropological perspective), but if the Elder was describing the ceremony itself—as performed by members of her community—as cultural rather than spiritual, then this would seem to be emptying the ritual of its meaning or significance.

66 *Ibid* at para 218. The court accepted that "the purpose of these events was not to profess or favour Indigenous beliefs but, rather, to teach students about Indigenous culture and to introduce them to Indigenous perspectives and worldviews

were good reasons for this apparent preference.[67] The final report of the Truth and Reconciliation Commission has helped Canadians to see more clearly that the dominant culture in Canada did not simply ignore the cultural/spiritual practices of Indigenous Peoples, but actively sought to suppress those practices through residential schools and other means. Exposing public school students to a few of these practices is a small start in the process of acknowledging the presence of Indigenous Peoples in Canada and the injustices committed against them.

Even if the students were given the opportunity to participate in the practice, the result might have been no different. If a parent believes it is immoral or wrongful for their child to participate in an Indigenous spiritual ceremony, they should be able to request an exemption from participation. The parent, though, should not be able to prevent the school from introducing other students to the cultural and spiritual practices of the local Indigenous community. While a school prayer is objectionable, even if students are able to opt out, it is not obvious that the option to participate in a ritual—that the school does not endorse as spiritually true—involves the same kind of pressure.[68]

E. LEGISLATIVE IMMUNITY

Despite the Canadian courts' determination that the recitation of a Christian prayer in a public school or at a municipal meeting breaches section 2(a) of the *Charter*, the daily session in several provincial legislatures still begins with the Lord's Prayer. The same Mr Freitag who had challenged the constitutionality of the recitation of the Lord's Prayer at Penetanguishene town council meetings also brought a complaint under the Ontario *Human Rights Code*[69] against the Ontario legislature for its practice of opening its daily sessions with the Lord's Prayer.

In *Ontario (Speaker of the Legislative Assembly) v Ontario (HRC)*, the Ontario Court of Appeal held that the opening exercises of the provincial

---

as consistent with the curriculum." The courts have elsewhere said that a school may teach students about different spiritual traditions. In *SL*, above note 18, the Supreme Court confirmed that it was acceptable, even valuable, for schools to expose children to various religious belief systems provided they did not seek to indoctrinate children into a particular belief system.

67   The school also had a large number of Indigenous students, and the court accepted that the ceremony might help them feel welcome in the public school system.

68   However, the description of the practice as simply cultural rather than spiritual may be seen as lessening the significance of the practice.

69   *Human Rights Code,* RSO 1990, c H.19 [*Code*].

legislature, including the recitation of the prayer, were part of its internal operation and immune from review under the *Charter* and the *Human Rights Code*.[70] It followed then that the Ontario Human Rights Commission had no jurisdiction to consider whether the practice of opening the daily session in the legislature with a recitation of the Lord's Prayer was contrary to the *Code*.

In 2008 the premier of Ontario proposed that the legislature introduce a more inclusive opening to its daily session, involving a rotation of readings and recitations from different religious and other belief systems. The government, though, backed down from this plan following a public outcry. The Lord's Prayer continues to be part of the opening exercises of the Ontario legislature, although it is now supplemented with readings and prayers from other traditions. The province of Quebec some time ago adopted a moment of silence in place of a Christian prayer in its opening exercises. The crucifix that hung in the Quebec legislative assembly was only removed in 2019.[71]

F. IS SECULARISM NEUTRAL?

Secularism, understood as the ordering of public life on the basis of beliefs or practices that are not specifically religious, is generally treated as a neutral ground that lies outside religious differences. It provides the baseline for determining whether the state has compelled, supported, or restricted religious beliefs and practices. At an earlier time, when all or most community members adhered to some form of religion, the

---

70   [2001] OJ No 2180 at para 48: According to the court:

> [M]atters relating to the internal workings of the House must be subject to the exclusive jurisdiction of the House, since control over such matters is necessary to the independent existence of the House. The House must be absolutely free to set its own guidelines for how its legislative sessions will be carried out and the Standing Orders that detail the operation of parliamentary procedure must be considered privileged and insulated from outside review. Having made this determination, it is not open to this Court, nor to any other body associated with the executive or judicial branches of government, to question an individual exercise of conduct that falls within the protected sphere. As the recitation of the prayers is called for by the Standing Orders, it is encompassed as part of the Assembly's privilege relating to control of its internal proceedings, and is not susceptible to outside challenge.

71   Gérard Bouchard & Charles Taylor, *Building the Future: A Time for Reconciliation* (Quebec City: Government of Quebec, 2008) at 152. This report recommended the removal of the crucifix. This recommendation was initially rejected by all three parties sitting in the legislature.

exclusion of religious practices or rituals from the political or civic sphere could be viewed as neutral toward different religious belief systems. (In practice, of course, an imperfect form of neutrality was achieved in most Western democracies not by excluding religious practices but rather by relying on "non-sectarian" or shared Christian practices.)

However, the complainants in most of the recent state neutrality cases that have come before the courts have been agnostics or atheists.[72] Their complaint in these cases is not that the state is supporting one religion over another—the religion of the majority over a minority belief system—but rather that it is supporting religious belief or practice generally and imposing religion on citizens who are not religious or treating them unequally. If secularism is equated with agnosticism or atheism and understood as a worldview or cultural identity equivalent to religious belief, then its proponents may feel excluded or marginalized when the state supports even the most ecumenical forms of religious practice. But, by the same token, the complete removal of religion from the civic sphere may be experienced by religious adherents as the exclusion of their worldview and the affirmation of a nonreligious or "secular" perspective—the culture or identity of a particular segment of the community.[73]

To religious adherents, then, "secularism" may look less like a neutral or common ground that stands outside religious controversy and more like a particular worldview that dominates the political system simply because of the political power of its adherents.[74] Ironically, then, as the exclusion of religion from civic life in the name of religious freedom and equality becomes more complete, secular politics may appear less neutral and more partisan. With the growth of agnosticism and

---

72   See for example, *MLQ* above note 39 at para 120: "The prayer recited by the municipal council in breach of the state's duty of neutrality resulted in a distinction, exclusion and preference based on religion—that is, based on Mr. Simoneau's atheism—which, in combination with the circumstances in which the prayer was recited, turned the meetings into a preferential space for people with theistic beliefs."

73   The Supreme Court acknowledged but did not address this concern in *SL*, above note 18 at para 30: "We must recognize that trying to achieve religious neutrality in the public sphere is a major challenge for the state." See, for example, the recent decision of the Human Rights Tribunal of Ontario *RC and SC v District School Board of Niagara*, 2013 HRTO 1382, in which it was determined that "atheism" is a creed and that discrimination against atheists in the provision of services is prohibited under the Ontario *Human Rights Code*. The tribunal held that a school board policy that allowed the Gideon Society to distribute the Christian New Testament to Grade 5 students in public schools but prevented the distribution of an atheist tract amounted to discrimination contrary to the *Code*.

74   See Stanley Fish, "Mission Impossible: Settling the Just Bounds between Church and State" (1997) 97 *Colum L Rev* 2255.

atheism in the community, religious neutrality in the political sphere may have become impossible. What is for some the neutral ground upon which freedom of religion and conscience depends is for others a partisan, anti-religious perspective.

However, for several reasons this view is, I think, mistaken. The Supreme Court in *MLQ* emphasized that the state should remain neutral not just between religions but also between religion and atheism or agnosticism and not favour one over the other. It would be objectionable, said the Court, and a breach of the neutrality requirement if the state were to promote atheism by declaring that there is no God. The Court insisted that the exclusion of religious rituals from civic meetings "does not amount to taking a stand in favour of atheism or agnosticism" since it would also be unacceptable for the municipal council to "solemnly declare" that its "deliberations were based on a denial of God."[75] The state should abstain from taking any position on religious matters.

In any event, the courts have not excluded religion entirely from the public sphere. First, they have held that the state may support religious institutions and practices provided it does so in an even-handed way. The state may fund religious schools, for example, as long as it funds a range of such schools as well as secular shools. Second, the courts have said that because religious practices have shaped the traditions or customs of the community, they cannot simply be erased from the public sphere. In *MLQ*, the Supreme Court held that "the state's duty of neutrality does not require it to abstain from celebrating and preserving its religious heritage."[76] Governments cannot be expected to sandblast (literally or metaphorically) religious symbols and practices from physical and social structures, some of which were constructed long ago. The caveat to this is that it may often be difficult to determine when the use of a religious symbol or practice by the state is simply an acknowledgment or preservation of the country's religious history and when it amounts to a present affirmation of the truth of a particular religious belief system. Indeed, it may be that the acknowledgment of history or tradition always involves some form of contemporary affirmation.[77] Third, the courts have recognized that as long as religion remains an important part of

---

75   *MLQ* above note 39 at para 133.

76   *Ibid* at para 116.

77   This is the point made in *MLQ*, above note 39 at para 87: "[T]he Canadian cultural landscape includes many traditional and heritage practices that are religious in nature. Although it is clear that not all of these cultural expressions are in breach of the state's duty of neutrality, there is also no doubt that the state may not consciously make a profession of faith or act so as to adopt or favour one religious view at the expense of all others."

the private and communal lives of citizens, it will sometimes affect the shape of state action. If a large part of the population is Christian, it is difficult to see how the state could not take the practices of this group into account when, for example, selecting statutory holidays or establishing a "pause day" from work.[78]

The fourth and most significant exception to the neutrality requirement involves religious beliefs that address civic matters. Religious belief systems often say something about the way we should treat others and about the kind of society we should work to create. While the courts sometimes treat religion as a cultural identity toward which the state should remain neutral, at other times, when religion addresses or touches upon civic matters, the courts treat it as a political or moral judgment by the individual that may play a role in political decision making—and so may be accepted or rejected by political decision makers. In *Chamberlain v Surrey School District No 36*, the Supreme Court held that elected officials may draw on their religious values (or the religious values of their constituents) when making political decisions.[79] Chief Justice McLachlin recognized that "[r]eligion is an integral aspect of people's lives, and cannot be left at the boardroom door."[80] I will return shortly to the *Chamberlain* case and its broader implications for section 2(a).

G. THE US ESTABLISHMENT CLAUSE: CEREMONIAL DEISM AND HISTORICAL TRADITION

In judgments such as *Everson v Board of Education*, the US Supreme Court held that the establishment clause of the First Amendment precluded the state from supporting religious institutions or practices:

> The "establishment of religion" clause of the First Amendment means at least this: Neither a state nor the Federal Government can set up a church. Neither can pass laws which aid one religion, aid all religions, or prefer one religion over another. Neither can force nor influence a person to go to or to remain away from church against his will or force him to profess a belief or disbelief in any religion ... Neither a state nor the Federal Government can, openly or secretly, participate in the affairs of any religious organizations or groups, and vice versa. In the

---

78   *Edwards Books* above note 10.
79   *Chamberlain v Surrey School District No 36*, 2002 SCC 86.
80   *Ibid* at para 19.

words of Jefferson, the clause against establishment of religion by law was intended to erect "a wall of separation between church and State."[81]

To be compatible with the establishment clause, a government act must have a secular purpose, its primary effect must not be to promote or inhibit the practice of a particular religion, and it must not cause the state to become "excessively entangled" with religion (the *Lemon* test).[82] The US Supreme Court has since held that the state may provide aid to a religious organization, such as a school, provided it does so as part of a more general program that does not simply benefit religious organizations. For example, in *Agostini v Felton*, the Court held that a government program in which public school teachers delivered remedial education to disadvantaged children in private schools did not breach the First Amendment even though many of these schools were religious. Because the remedial education was secular and because it was provided to children in public and private, secular and religious schools, the program did not support or advantage religion or religious schools.[83] In the case of *Zelman v Simmons-Harris*, the US Supreme Court upheld a voucher program in the city of Cleveland that gave low-income parents money that was to be used to support their children's education costs.[84] The Court found that the program did not breach the First Amendment even though almost all of the money from the program was directed by parents to private religious schools.

The US Supreme Court has held that the state cannot display a religious symbol on public property unless the display serves a secular purpose.[85] Notably, the Court found that the posting of the Ten Commandments (the Decalogue) in public schools and other public buildings was unconstitutional.[86] However, the Court has permitted the posting of

---

81   330 US 1 at 15–16 (1947). The relevant part of the First Amendment of the US Constitution provides as follows: "Congress shall make no law respecting an establishment of religion, or prohibiting the free exercise thereof …" The Bill of Rights is the collective name for the first ten amendments to the US Constitution.

82   See *Lemon v Kurtzman*, 403 US 602 (1971) [*Lemon*], and *Agostini v Felton*, 521 US 203 (1997) [*Agostini*], in which the last two parts of the *Lemon* test were combined. In *Rosenberger v Rector and Visitors of the University of Virginia*, 515 US 819 (1995), the US Supreme Court held that the university breached the First Amendment's free speech protection when it distributed funds to secular student publications but declined to fund a student-run Christian publication.

83   *Agostini, ibid.* See also *Mitchell v Helms*, 530 US 793 (2000).

84   536 US 639 (2002).

85   *County of Allegheny v ACLU*, 492 US 573 (1989); *Salazar v Buono*, 559 US 700 (2010).

86   *Stone v Graham*, 449 US 39 (1980). Supporters of the public display of the Ten Commandments argue that it is an important historical document that helped to shape contemporary Western law. There is something to this claim — that the

the Ten Commandments in public buildings or on public grounds when it is displayed along with other historically significant documents and is not given pride of place and (or instead) if the structure in which it is incorporated was installed some time ago and so can be seen as a historical piece.[87] In *American Legion v American Humanist Society*, the US Supreme Court held that the presence on public land of a World War I memorial that took the form of a Latin cross did not breach the First Amendment because it had been erected many years earlier.[88] The majority of the Court in that case thought that the removal of the cross at this stage might even be perceived as an anti-religious act by the state.

The US courts have also held that references to God made during public events or proceedings do not breach the First Amendment, provided they are simply ceremonial, adding to the solemnity of the occasion, without advancing a particular religious perspective. Justice O'Connor in *Elk Grove Unified School District v Newdow* described the religious elements in public rituals, such as the reference to God in the Pledge of Allegiance, as "ceremonial deism":

> Given the values that the Establishment Clause was meant to serve . . . I believe that government can, in a discrete category of cases, acknowledge or refer to the divine without offending the Constitution. This category of "ceremonial deism" most clearly encompasses such things as the national motto ("In God We Trust"), religious references in traditional patriotic songs such as The Star-Spangled Banner, and the words with which the Marshal of this Court opens each of its sessions ("God save the United States and this honorable Court"). These references are not minor trespasses upon the Establishment Clause to which I turn

---

political community has a history, which the members of the community should know something about, if only to better understand their current circumstances. However, the problem with this attempt to link the Ten Commandments to the contemporary legal order is that the former does not appear to have had either a unique or even a significant role in shaping contemporary Western law. The Ten Commandments include several rules (the first four) that are exclusively about the duties of "man" to God. It also includes ideals that no legal system has sought to enforce, such as a ban on coveting the possessions of others. The few commandments that are included in modern legal systems, the bans on stealing and murder, are part of all moral and religious belief systems. The posting of the Ten Commandments in public spaces is clearly intended to link Christianity (or the "Judeo-Christian" tradition) to the US national identity.

87   *Van Orden v Perry*, 545 US 677 (2005); *McCreary County v ACLU of Kentucky*, 545 US 844 (2005).

88   588 US (2019). At the time the cross was erected, the land on which it was situated was privately owned; however, the land was later transferred to a public authority.

a blind eye. Instead, their history, character, and context prevent them from being constitutional violations at all.[89]

The US courts have held that the establishment clause forbids recitation of an ecumenical prayer as part of the opening exercises in public schools.[90] However, in *Marsh v Chambers* the Court held that the practice of opening the session of the state legislature with the recitation of an ecumenical prayer did not breach the First Amendment. In the Court's view, since this practice existed when the *Bill of Rights* was enacted, the "Founding Fathers" did not regard it as contrary to the First Amendment.[91] In *Town of Greece v Galloway*, the US Supreme Court again relied on an originalist interpretation of the First Amendment and held that the town's practice of inviting local clergy (all of whom were Christian) to deliver a Christian prayer at the opening of its council meetings did not breach the First Amendment.[92] The majority emphasized that the town's practice was longstanding and that no one attending the meeting was required or pressured to participate.

H. RELIGIOUS NEUTRALITY AND CHRISTIAN IDENTITY IN EUROPE

Article 9 of the *European Convention on Human Rights*[93] provides that "[e]veryone has the right to freedom of thought, conscience and religion," including the right to change one's religion, to practise "alone or in community with others" and in "public or private," and "to manifest" one's "religion or belief, in worship, teaching practice and observance."

---

89   542 US 1 at 37 (2004). A majority of the Court found that the plaintiff did not have standing and so did not express an opinion on the merits of the case.

90   *Engel v Vitale*, 370 US 421 (1962). See also *Abington Township v Schempp*, 374 US 203 (1963), which concerned Bible reading in public schools.

91   463 US 783 (1983). The Court also upheld the constitutionality of the state's employment of the chaplain who led the prayer.

92   572 US 565 (2014). More recently in *Kennedy v Bremerton School District*, 597 US (2022), the US Supreme Court held that a public high school coach's practice of reciting a prayer on the fifty yard line of the football field at the end of each game (and inviting team members to participate in the prayer) did not breach the First Amendment because it was a personal religious practice and that the school's attempt to prevent him from praying in this way amounted to a restriction on his religious practice. This decision ignores the location and timing of the prayer and more importantly the coach's authority over his players.

93   *Convention for the Protection of Human Rights and Fundamental Freedoms*, Rome, 4 November 1950, online (pdf): www.echr.coe.int/Documents/Convention_ENG.pdf [*ECHR*].

The *ECHR*, like the *Canadian Charter of Rights and Freedoms*, does not specifically preclude the establishment of religion or state support for religion. Indeed, several European countries, including the United Kingdom, continue to maintain, at least formally, an established church. In *Darby v Sweden*, the European Commission of Human Rights noted that a state church system existed in several of the contracting states when the *ECHR* was drafted and so accepted that such a system "cannot in itself be considered to violate article 9 of the Convention" provided it includes "specific safeguards for the individual's freedom of religion."[94] In many European countries, and not just those with an established church, Christianity is understood to be part of the country's national identity or its cultural heritage.

The cultural role of Christianity in civic life was recognized by the European Court of Human Rights in *Lautsi v Italy*.[95] The issue in that case was whether the state's practice of hanging crucifixes in public school classrooms was consistent with freedom of religion under the *ECHR*. The court in *Lautsi* affirmed the importance of state neutrality in matters of religion. Yet when considering whether the practice of hanging crucifixes in school classrooms was contrary to article 9, the court appeared to apply a more limited test—asking not whether the state's display of the crucifix was religiously neutral but, instead, whether it coerced students to engage in a religious practice or indoctrinated them into a religious belief system.

The court acknowledged that "by prescribing the presence of crucifixes in State-school classrooms—a sign which, whether or not it is accorded in addition a secular symbolic value, undoubtedly refers to Christianity—the regulations confer on the country's majority religion preponderant visibility in the school environment."[96] But, in the court's view, this did not in itself amount to coercion or indoctrination contrary to article 9. The court thought that, in contrast to the recitation of a prayer or the teaching of scripture, the hanging of a crucifix did not compel or pressure students to participate in a religious practice. According

---

94   Application no 11581/85, Commission Report, 9 May 1989, at para 45, online: www.strasbourgconsortium.org/common/document.view.php?docId=1960. See *ibid*.

95   Application no 30814/06, Eur Ct HR (Grand Chamber), 18 March 2011 [*Lautsi*]. The decision also considered art 2 of Protocol No 1 to the *ECHR*, above note 93, which protects the right to education and the right of parents "to ensure such education and teaching in conformity with their own religious and philosophical convictions." But see also the 12 May 1987 decision of the Federal Constitutional Court of Germany in *Crucifix Case (Classroom Crucifix Case)*, 1 BvR 1087/91 Kruzifix BVerfGE 93, in which the court held that crucifixes in the state schools of Bavaria breached art 4(1) of the German *Basic Law*.

96   *Lautsi*, *ibid* at para 71.

to the court, "a crucifix on a wall is an essentially passive symbol and . . . cannot be deemed to have an influence on pupils comparable to that of didactic speech or participation in religious activities."[97]

However, even if students are not required to participate in any ritual involving the crucifix, the crucifix is part of the environment within which they spend their days learning and interacting. It is an ordinary, normal part of their school life. In this way, the passive presence of the crucifix affirms, without argument or assertion, the central place of the Roman Catholic faith in Italian society.

In deciding that the placement of crucifixes in public school classrooms does not breach the state neutrality requirement, the court acquiesced in the Italian government's claim that the crucifix is a symbol of the national identity and Christian heritage of Italy and more substantially of the civic values of the Italian political community—values that the government claimed can be directly traced to Christian doctrine.[98] By tying religion and politics in this way, the government is able to make the crucifix into something more than a parochial symbol, something that transcends its religious origin. The crucifix becomes a symbol of the culture or civic identity of Italy—a "post-Christian" political community.[99]

---

97   *Ibid* at para 72. The court added at para 74 that

> the presence of crucifixes is not associated with compulsory teaching about Christianity . . . Italy opens up the school environment in parallel to other religions. The Government indicated in this connection that it was not forbidden for pupils to wear Islamic headscarves or other symbols or apparel having a religious connotation . . . [T]here was nothing to suggest that the authorities were intolerant of pupils who believed in other religions, were non-believers or who held non-religious philosophical convictions. . . . [T]he applicants did not assert that the presence of the crucifix in classrooms had encouraged the development of teaching practices with a proselytising tendency, or claim that the second and third applicants had ever experienced a tendentious reference to that presence by a teacher in the exercise of his or her functions.

> The court noted that it was presented with no evidence "that the display of a religious symbol on classroom walls may have an influence on pupils," and so it could not determine whether this "does or does not have an effect on young persons whose convictions are still in the process of being formed" (*ibid* at para 66).

98   But see Ian Leigh & Rex Ahdar, "Post-Secularism and the European Court of Human Rights: Or How God Never Really Went Away" (2012) 75:6 *Mod L Rev* 1064, which argues that the removal of the crucifix would breach the neutrality requirement. This claim rests on a conception of neutrality that encompasses religious and nonreligious perspectives. The crucifix was placed in the classroom long ago. It is part of the status quo, and so its removal would be a positive, anti-religious action.

99   It seems likely that many of the contemporary advocates of placing crucifixes in school classrooms believe that the crucifix symbolizes the sacrifice of Jesus and God's mercy and that these spiritual truths should be affirmed in the schools. Yet

It follows on this view that when the state hangs crucifixes in schools, it is not favouring or supporting Christianity as the true faith but is simply recognizing the historical and conceptual link between Christian doctrine and the national identity and civic values of Italy. The court thought "that the decision whether or not to perpetuate a tradition falls in principle within the margin of appreciation of the respondent State."[100]

This link between Christianity and politics, though, rests on the problematic claim that the values of democracy and tolerance emerged directly from Christianity (and are the logical, even necessary, outcome of Christian doctrine) and the disturbing claim that Christianity is uniquely tied to these values.[101] The civic values of modern liberal democracies, such as Italy, have other and more obvious precursors. The Italian government and courts conflate the plausible claim that certain elements of Christian doctrine made possible the separation of church and state in the West (the creation of a secular space) with the more problematic claim that tolerance and democracy are Christian values or values that arose directly or significantly from Christianity (and so may be symbolized by the crucifix). Indeed, the claim made by the Italian courts about Christianity, and more particularly Roman Catholicism, as the foundation of these values seems remarkable in light of the church's history and its relatively recent acceptance of religious tolerance. The Italian Administrative Court observed that "with the benefit of hindsight, it is easy to identify in the constant central core of Christian faith, despite the inquisition, despite anti-Semitism and despite the crusades, the principles of human dignity, tolerance and freedom, including religious freedom, and therefore, in the last analysis, the foundations of the secular State."[102] In making this claim about the link between Christianity and

---

support for the practice seems also to come from those who no longer formally adhere to Catholic practice.

100 *Lautsi*, above note 95 at para 68. Additionally, the court said at para 67:

> The Government, for their part, explained that the presence of crucifixes in State-school classrooms, being the result of Italy's historical development, a fact which gave it not only a religious connotation but also an identity-linked one, now corresponded to a tradition which they considered it important to perpetuate. They added that, beyond its religious meaning, the crucifix symbolised the principles and values which formed the foundation of democracy and western civilisation, and that its presence in classrooms was justifiable on that account.

101 The implicit message is that other religious traditions, most notably Islam, are incompatible with democratic values. Islam is assumed to lack the doctrinal resources to embrace the values of liberty and democracy and so is marked off as un-Italian or undemocratic.

102 *Lautsi*, above note 95 at para 15.

democratic values, the Italian courts eschewed an external, objective position and instead argued from a position within the faith community. When the Italian courts argued that there was a connection between Catholicism on the one hand and democracy and tolerance on the other, and when they dismissed past justifications for religious oppression as erroneous, they wrote as Christians who were engaged in debate about the best or proper understanding of their faith.

Behind the claim that the crucifix is not simply a religious symbol but also a symbol of the Italian identity and political culture is the draw of a thicker or richer form of national identity than that offered by civic nationalism.[103] The assumption is that Italians are connected not simply by their shared commitment to liberal values or democratic institutions but by a common culture rooted in a religious tradition—if not exactly a civil religion, then at least a Christian-inspired public morality. Religion and politics are joined at the core of national identity and the root of political obligation. The recognition of a link between Christianity and the identity and civic values of the Italian political community may serve to strengthen the civic bond and to create a sense of identity and connection among many Italians, but it also serves to exclude others from that community.

These identity-based arguments are unlikely to succeed in Canadian courts.[104] Although religion sometimes intersects with politics in Canada, it no longer plays a role in the definition of the country's national identity. Canada some time ago embraced multiculturalism as the defining feature of its national identity and liberal-democratic values as its political bond. While there is no doubt that Canada's moral and social culture has been shaped in different ways by the Christian faith of earlier generations, any attempt to formally link Canadian national identity to a particular religious tradition would run against the country's self-conception as a multicultural (multifaith) society. The critical difference, then, between Italy and Canada is not that Canada has had to negotiate cultural, linguistic,

---

103 See *ibid*, quoting from the decision of the Administrative Court: "Our era is marked by the ferment resulting from the meeting of different cultures with our own, and to prevent that meeting from turning into a collision it is indispensable to reaffirm our identity, even symbolically, especially as it is characterised precisely by the values of respect for the dignity of each human being and of universal solidarity."

104 The Canadian courts' view of the crucifix would also be different. In a country such as Canada that has a significant Protestant community, the crucifix (rather than a bare cross) is viewed as a distinctly Roman Catholic symbol, and not as a "Christian" symbol. Crucifixes hang in separate schools (Roman Catholic schools) and are the most obvious marker of the distinction between these schools and public schools.

and religious differences in a way that other countries have not. It is instead that Canada's identity has become tied to this diversity, although this is less clearly the case in Quebec. (See the discussion of Quebec's ban on civil servants wearing religious symbols in Chapter 3.) Multiculturalism has become part of Canada's self-understanding—a constituent part of the Canadian identity. This is why no serious English-Canadian politician would speak, as many European leaders have done, about the failure of multiculturalism. English-Canadian politicians may express concerns about religious accommodation going too far, but they will not be heard to question the basic commitment to religious and cultural pluralism.[105]

The *Lautsi* decision reflects the deep ambivalence in Western liberal democracies about religion and its relationship to politics. Like the Canadian courts, the European Court of Human Rights seemed to recognize that religion and politics should be separated but that this separation cannot be total. Where the European Court of Human Rights parts company with the Canadian courts is in its willingness to accept a formal link between religion, national identity, and political obligation. While both the European Court of Human Rights and the Supreme Court of Canada rely, at least formally, on a similar test for determining a breach of religious freedom, a test that emphasizes the state's obligation to remain neutral in spiritual matters, their application of the test is guided by different understandings of the public and political significance of religion and, more particularly, of the relationship between religion, civic values, and national identity.

I.   RELIGIOUS VALUES IN PUBLIC DECISION MAKING

It is sometimes argued that religious values should be excluded from political decision making because state law must be based on reasons that are

---

105   The Canadian political community is bound not by a common language, culture, or religion but by a shared commitment to civic values such as tolerance, equality, and liberty. The deficiencies and limitations of this "identity" are often noted. It may be complained that the Canadian commitment to multiculturalism is superficial, that it rests on a form of liberal individualism and does not, and indeed cannot, respect deep diversity, or that a shared commitment to liberal-democratic values is too thin a basis to sustain national unity and political loyalty, as the ongoing Canadian existential crisis may demonstrate. The point here is simply that any attempt to *formally* link Canada's national identity to a particular religious tradition would be inconsistent with the core understanding of that identity—Canada as a multicultural political community.

accessible to all members of the community.[106] Because religious beliefs rest on faith or familial and cultural socialization rather than reasoned judgment, they cannot provide a publicly acceptable basis for law making. To base state action on religious values would be to impose the beliefs of some members of the community on other members or to favour unfairly the beliefs of some over those of others. Political actors, then, must base their actions on nonreligious values or must be able to defend their actions on nonreligious grounds, even if their deeper motives are religious in character. That, at least, is the familiar argument. The debate on this issue has been particularly vigorous in the United States, where personal religious engagement is significant and the political commitment to state neutrality in matters of religion is well established.[107]

Two objections are often made to the exclusion of religious values from political decision making. The first is that preventing religious adherents from relying on their deeply held values and concerns when making political decisions will have the effect of excluding them from meaningful involvement in civic life. Because religion matters so deeply to its adherents and is often the foundation for their views about justice and the collective good, it is unreasonable or simply unrealistic to expect them to leave their beliefs behind when they participate in public life.[108]

The second and more substantial objection is that religious and secular values are not different in a way that can justify the exclusion of the former from political decision making. Fundamental secular values, such as respect for human dignity or equality, rest, no less than religious values, on a basic acceptance of their truth and are the premises rather

---

106 This position is associated with John Rawls, *Political Liberalism* (New York: Columbia University Press, 1993), although Rawls's argument is simply that constitutional essentials should not be based on a comprehensive belief system but instead on an "overlapping consensus" among such systems.

107 The literature on this issue is substantial, and I will make no attempt to address it directly. A sample of the different positions taken in the debate might include Robert Audi, *Religious Commitment and Secular Reason* (Cambridge, UK: Cambridge University Press, 2000); Christopher J Eberle, *Religious Conviction in Liberal Politics* (Cambridge, UK: Cambridge University Press, 2002); Kent Greenawalt, *Religious Convictions and Political Choice* (New York: Oxford University Press, 1988); and Michael J Perry, *Under God? Religious Faith and Liberal Democracy* (Cambridge, UK: Cambridge University Press, 2003).

108 See Benjamin Berger, "The Limits of Belief: Freedom of Religion, Secularism, and the Liberal State" (2002) 17 *CJLS* 39 at 67: "When religious conscience is properly understood as a pervasive claim upon the lives of believers, a liberalism that demands the severance of moral claims and political positions and a vision of secularism that requires an a-religious public space are irreconcilable with the freedom of the religion accorded by the *Charter*." See also David Blaikie & Diana Ginn, "Religious Discourse in the Public Square" (2006) 15:1 *Const Forum Const* 37.

than the conclusions of reasoned political debate. Religious values, particularly when they are framed in general terms, may be the subject of reasonable debate, no less than secular values. Charles Taylor argues that there is no clear distinction "in rational credibility between religious and non-religious discourse ... If we take key statements of our contemporary political morality, such as those attributing rights to human beings as such, say the right to life, I cannot see how the fact that we are desiring/enjoying/suffering beings, or the perception that we are rational agents, should be any surer basis for this right than the fact that we are made in the image of God."[109]

J. *CHAMBERLAIN V SURREY SCHOOL DISTRICT*

In *Chamberlain v Surrey School District No 36*, the Supreme Court of Canada held that elected officials could draw on their religious values (or the religious values of their constituents) when making political decisions.[110] According to McLachlin CJ, "[b]ecause religion plays an important role in the life of many communities, ... [the] views [of parents and communities] will often be motivated by religious concerns. Religion is an integral aspect of people's lives, and cannot be left at the boardroom door."[111]

In *Chamberlain*, a local school board rejected a proposal to include three books depicting same-sex parent families on the list of approved teaching resources for the primary grades. The appellants challenged the board's decision on two grounds: first, that the board had acted outside its mandate under the BC *School Act*, which provided that "[a]ll schools ... must be conducted on strictly secular and non-sectarian principles,"[112] and second, that the decision violated sections 2(a) and 15 of the *Charter*. A majority of the Court, in a judgment written by McLachlin CJ, agreed that the school board had "acted outside the mandate of the *School Act* ... and [its] own regulation for approval of supplementary material" when it had refused to include these three books on the list of approved teaching resources.[113] Having reached this conclusion, the majority did not have to consider whether the decision breached the *Charter*.

---

109 Charles Taylor, *Dilemmas and Connections: Selected Essays* (Cambridge, MA: Belknap Press of Harvard University Press, 2011) at 328–29.
110 2002 SCC 86 [*Chamberlain*].
111 *Ibid* at para 19.
112 RSBC 1996, c 412, s 76(1).
113 Above note 110 at para 2.

Chief Justice McLachlin accepted that the secularism requirement in the *School Act* did not preclude the school board from taking religious values and beliefs into account when making decisions, and in particular when making decisions about curriculum. What it did require, however, was that the board "conduct its deliberations on all matters, including the approval of supplementary resources, in a manner that respects the views of all members of the school community."[114] The board should not "prefer the religious views of some people in its district to the views of other segments of the community" and it should not "appeal to views that deny the equal validity of the lawful lifestyles of some in the school community."[115] The secularism requirement, said McLachin CJ, "simply signals the need for educational decisions and policies, whatever their motivation, to respect the multiplicity of religious and moral views that are held by families in the school community."[116] She found that the board, in acting on the concerns of some parents about the morality of same-sex relationships, had failed to take seriously the right of same-sex parents, and the children of such relationships, to be equally respected within the public school system. The board in this case had "failed to proceed as required by the secular mandate of the *School Act* by letting the religious views of a certain part of the community trump the need to show equal respect for the values of other members of the community."[117]

Chief Justice McLachlin agreed that religious values may play a role in political decision making; yet at the same time, she seemed to say that the state must remain neutral in matters of value. If the "secularism" requirement means that the schools should not favour one moral perspective over another in their teaching (that they should remain neutral on moral and religious issues), then religion (and indeed any value system) will have a role in board (and public) decision making only when it has no bite — only when it does not involve the repudiation of other values or viewpoints. Yet, if the board's rejection of the three books for use in the primary grades amounts to the improper exclusion of the "value" of gay and lesbian relationships, would not the inclusion of these books, by the same token, amount to the exclusion or rejection of the religious views of those parents who regard same-sex relationships as sinful? Can the schools affirm the equal value of same-sex relationships without, in effect, repudiating the religious belief that these relationships are immoral or unnatural?

---

114 *Ibid* at para 25.
115 *Ibid*.
116 *Ibid* at para 59.
117 *Ibid* at para 71.

Chief Justice McLachlin, though, thought that the inclusion of these books as teaching materials did not amount to the affirmation of same-sex relationships and the repudiation of contrary views. What the *School Act* demanded, she said, was tolerance:

> [T]he demand for tolerance cannot be interpreted as the demand to approve another person's beliefs or practices. When we ask people to be tolerant of others, we don't ask them to abandon their personal convictions. We merely ask them to respect the rights, values and ways of being of those who may not share those convictions. The belief that others are entitled to equal respect depends, not on the belief that their values are right, but only on the belief that they have a claim to equal respect regardless of whether they are right.[118]

Tolerance requires only that we respect the right of each individual to make their own judgments and, in this case, their choice of intimate partners or family arrangements. Teaching tolerance does not require that public actors, such as the schools, affirm a particular value or viewpoint. More specifically, it does not require that the schools teach or affirm that same- and opposite-sex relationships are equally valuable.

In the chief justice's view, the books would simply "expose" children to nontraditional family forms and encourage them to tolerate these forms. She thought that the use of the three books in the kindergarten classes would encourage "discussion and understanding of all family groups."[119] The problem with this view, however, is that at the kindergarten level, there is no way to simply expose children to same-sex relationships as a social reality or to engage them in an open discussion about such relationships. Including these stories in the kindergarten curriculum will normalize same-sex relationships and, in effect, affirm their value. To claim otherwise is to fail to recognize the authority of the school in the lives of students, particularly those in the primary grades.[120]

Chief Justice McLachlin stressed the importance of providing "a nurturing and validating learning experience for all children, regardless of

---

118 *Ibid* at para 66.

119 *Ibid* at para 72. And at para 23, quoting La Forest J in *Ross v New Brunswick School District No 15*, [1996] 1 SCR 825, she described the school as an "arena for the exchange of ideas" that "must, therefore, be premised upon principles of tolerance and impartiality so that all persons within the school environment feel equally free to participate."

120 For a critical discussion of the case and the chief justice's attempt to adopt a neutral stance, see Richard Moon, "The Supreme Court of Canada's Attempt to Reconcile Freedom of Religion and Sexual Orientation Equality in the Public Schools" in David Rayside & Clyde Wilcox, eds, *Faith, Politics and Sexual Diversity in Canada and the United States* (Vancouver: UBC Press, 2011) at 321.

the types of families they come from."[121] In her view, the school board should seek to affirm the personal circumstances of students from nontraditional families without imposing any views or values on other students in the school community. Yet it is not clear that affirmation can be segregated in this way, either practically or normatively. If the three books were used as teaching resources, then every student in the class would be exposed to them, regardless of their family situation or perspective. Chief Justice McLachlin recognized this but was not troubled by it:

> The number of different family models in the community means that some children will inevitably come from families of which certain parents disapprove. Giving these children an opportunity to discuss their family models may expose other children to some cognitive dissonance. But such dissonance is neither avoidable or noxious. Children encounter it every day in the public school system as members of a diverse student body. They see their classmates, and perhaps also their teachers, eating foods at lunch that they themselves are not permitted to eat, whether because of their parents' religious strictures or because of other moral beliefs. They see their classmates wearing clothes with features or brand labels which their parents have forbidden them to wear. And they see their classmates engaging in behaviour on the playground that their parents have told them not to engage in. The cognitive dissonance that results from such encounters is simply part of living in a diverse society. It is also part of growing up. Through such experiences, children come to realize that not all their values are shared by others.[122]

Once again McLachlin CJ's answer to concerns about "cognitive dissonance" is that the books will do no more than "expose" students to other perspectives or ways of life. But exposure to these books in the classroom is not the same as discovering that some of a student's classmates have same-sex parents. The books would be used by teachers, and (as the Court has elsewhere recognized) teachers are authority figures and role models.[123] More importantly, affirmation is not an individualized process. It is not particularly affirming to a child from a same-sex parent family when a teacher says to their class that same-sex parent families are fine for those who happen to be in them, but may not be fine for anyone else, or if a teacher informs the class that while some in the community feel this is an acceptable or valuable form of family, others regard it as immoral and that both views are entitled to respect. If what children need is affirmation of the equal value of their family

---

121 Above note 110 at para 49.

122 *Ibid* at para 65.

123 *Trinity Western University v British Columbia College of Teachers*, 2001 SCC 31.

arrangement, then the school must do more than indicate that there are such families and that this may or may not be a good thing. A child's sense of self, of value or worth, is tied up with the recognition they receive from others. To be meaningful, the acceptance or affirmation of same-sex relationships must involve a public statement or indication that such relationships are normal and valuable.

Chief Justice McLachlin seemed to accept that the schools should affirm the equal value of same-sex parent families. Yet, at the same time, she seemed to believe that the schools should remain neutral on religious or moral matters—that the state should neither affirm nor deny the value or truth of a particular religious belief. I suspect that the Court's reluctance to repudiate the religious belief that same-sex relationships are sinful rests in part on the view that religion is a deeply rooted part of an individual's identity that should be treated with equal respect. Yet however much the Court may wish to avoid repudiating a widely held religious value, (religious) value neutrality is not always an option. If equality, including sexual-orientation equality, is an important public value, it should be affirmed in the schools, even in the face of religiously based opposition from some parents. Indeed, the failure of the public schools to affirm clearly the equal value of same-sex relationships when opposite-sex relationships are constantly represented and affirmed in books and lessons will be experienced by same-sex families as discrimination.

We cannot include all "values" in the schools. If a school board or provincial government decides to advance or affirm a particular set of values, it must also reject other values—values that may be part of the religious commitment of some community members. Parents may have to live with the democratic consequence that their values are not included in the civic curriculum and perhaps even that their children are exposed to or taught views to which they are opposed. Of course, when affirming certain values, the schools should be sensitive to the dissonance younger students may experience when they are taught something different at home, but this is not the same thing as remaining neutral on questions of value. If religious values play a role in public decision making, they may be adopted or they may be repudiated. The public commitment to sexual-orientation equality involves a public repudiation of the view held by some religious adherents that same-sex relationships are immoral.

K. RELIGIOUS PRACTICES AND VALUES

In deciding that the commitment to religious neutrality does not preclude political actors from relying on religious values in public life, the court in *Chamberlain* relies, at least implicitly, on a distinction between the spiritual and civic elements of a religious belief system — between religious "practices" and religiously based "values." A religious belief should not play a role in political decision making (and will be treated as a matter of cultural identity) if the action it calls for is spiritual in character — that is, if it is concerned with the worshipping or honouring of God. However, when a religious belief addresses a political or civic matter, such as individual rights or collective welfare, the courts will treat it as a political or moral judgment that may play a role in political decision making.[124] Religiously grounded beliefs about civic issues may be adopted or rejected by law makers based on a public judgment about their contribution to human good or public welfare.

The courts then must draw a line between the spheres of spiritual and civic life (or between the spiritual and civic elements of a religious belief system), even if that line is contestable and porous. Where the line between the civic and spiritual elements of a religious belief system is drawn will reflect the courts' views about the nature of human welfare and the proper scope of political action. The claim that a religious belief or value may play a role in political decision making when there is a parallel secular argument (when the same or a similar position can be stated in nonreligious terms) points to this distinction between spiritual and civic. When a religious value or position (such as support for the eradication of poverty or for banning drug use) has a secular analogue, it will be seen as addressing a public or civic concern — as seeking to advance the public interest or to prevent harm to others. Even if these reasons are rooted in scripture and valued by adherents on that basis, they can be understood by non-adherents as concerned with public welfare, and so as civic values. However, when there is no parallel secular argument, non-adherents are bound to see the religious "practice" as simply the way in which adherents choose to honour God's will. In other words, a religiously motivated action will be viewed as a spiritual practice (as the

---

124 *Edwards Books*, above note 10 at para 99: "One is not being compelled to engage in religious practices merely because a statutory obligation coincides with the dictates of a particular religion. I cannot accept, for example, that a legislative prohibition of criminal conduct such as theft and murder is a state-enforced compulsion to conform to religious practices, merely because some religions enjoin their members not to steal or kill. Reasonable citizens do not perceive the legislation as requiring them to pay homage to religious doctrine."

worshipping or honouring of God) if non-adherents cannot understand it as relating to human welfare. If the state were to support Sunday Sabbath observance or a particular form of prayer or the wearing of a hijab or if it were to ban the consumption of pork, it would be seen as supporting a spiritual practice contrary to freedom of religion. These actions are viewed as exclusively spiritual, as acts of worship, because they cannot be understood by non-adherents as concerned with the advancement of human good.[125]

If law makers are permitted to draw on particular religious beliefs/values when formulating public policy, they should also be free to reject or repudiate those beliefs/values. In other words, (religiously grounded) civic values should be neither excluded nor insulated from political decision making. The state may remain neutral on spiritual matters, such as when or how to pray or what clothes to wear, but it cannot be neutral on civic issues, such as the recognition of same-sex marriage, the prohibition of gender discrimination, or the regulation of abortion.[126]

---

125 In the case of some (religiously based) state actions, such as a ban on public nudity, it may be more controversial whether the action should be viewed as relating to human welfare or as simply a matter of honouring God's will—depending on whether this is supported by other belief systems or can be defended on grounds that are more generally accessible.

126 See the discussion in Chapter 4 on "conscientious objection." The issue in conscientious objection cases is whether the individual's religiously based objection should be viewed as an expression of personal religious conscience that should be accommodated (if this can be done without noticeable harm to others) or whether it should be viewed as a (religiously grounded) civic position or action that may be the subject of legal regulation.

CHAPTER 3

THE RESTRICTION AND ACCOMMODATION OF RELIGIOUS PRACTICES

A. INTRODUCTION

Freedom of religion, when understood as a liberty, precludes the state from restricting a religious practice because it is believed to be errone-ous—because it is the wrong way to worship God. The state must have a public reason to restrict a religious practice, but any public reason may be sufficient. This was John Locke's position and also the position taken by the US Supreme Court in the case of *Employment Division, Department of Human Resources of Oregon v Smith*.[1]

In Locke's view, just "[a]s the magistrate has no power to impose by his laws the use of any rites and ceremonies in any Church, so neither has he any power to forbid the use of such rites and ceremonies as are already received, approved, and practised by any Church."[2] The govern-ment's role, according to Locke, "is only to take care that the common-wealth receive no prejudice, and that there be no injury done to any man, either in life or estate."[3] It is permissible, said Locke, for the government to prohibit a practice, such as animal slaughter, provided the prohibition

---

1   494 US 872 (1990) [*Oregon v Smith*].

2   John Locke, *A Letter Concerning Toleration* (1685; repr New York: Irvington Pub-lishers, 1979) at 197–98.

3   *Ibid* at 198.

has a civic purpose and is not enforced exclusively against those who engage in this practice for religious reasons.[4]

In *Oregon v Smith*, the US Supreme Court held that the free exercise clause of the First Amendment did not require the state to exempt individuals from a law that restricted their religious practice if the law was otherwise valid. In that case, two Indigenous men were dismissed from their employment with a drug rehabilitation program after it was learned that they had used peyote as part of a spiritual practice. Because the use of peyote was contrary to the state's criminal law, the state of Oregon's human resources department determined that the two men had been dismissed by their employer for cause and were therefore ineligible to receive unemployment insurance benefits. The men argued unsuccessfully that the legislative exclusion from unemployment insurance should not be applied to them because the reason for their dismissal was that they had engaged in a religious practice.[5] Justice Scalia thought that to

---

4   *Ibid* at 199: "Whatsoever is lawful in the Commonwealth cannot be prohibited by the magistrate in the Church. Whatsoever is permitted unto any of his subjects for their ordinary use, neither can nor ought to be forbidden by him to any sect of people for their religious uses. If any man may lawfully take bread or wine, either sitting or kneeling in his own house, the law ought not to abridge him of the same liberty in his religious worship; though in the Church the use of bread and wine be very different and be there applied to the mysteries of faith and rites of Divine worship. But those things that are prejudicial to the commonweal of a people in their ordinary use and are, therefore, forbidden by laws, those things ought not to be permitted to Churches in their sacred rites. Only the magistrate ought always to be very careful that he do not misuse his authority to the oppression of any Church, under pretence of public good."

    For an example of this, see *Church of the Lukumi Babalu Aye, Inc v Hialeah*, 508 US 520 at 553 (1993), in which the US Supreme Court held that a municipal ban on slaughtering "an animal in a public or private ritual or ceremony not for the primary purpose of food consumption" breached the free exercise clause of the First Amendment. The ban was put in place after the local council had learned that a group practising Santeria, which involves ritual animal slaughter, was planning to establish a church in the area.

5   The Court had to reconcile its conclusion in this case with earlier decisions in which it seemed to grant exemptions to religious groups from laws of general application, such as *Wisconsin v Yoder*, 406 US 205 (1972), in which the Court held that Amish children should be exempted from the requirement that they attend school until the age of sixteen. The Court in that case said at 220–21:

    > A regulation neutral on its face may, in its application, nonetheless offend the constitutional requirement for governmental neutrality if it unduly burdens the free exercise of religion ... The Court must not ignore the danger that an exception from a general obligation of citizenship on religious grounds may run afoul of the Establishment Clause, but that danger cannot be allowed to prevent any exception no matter how vital it may be to the protection of values promoted by the right of free exercise.

exempt the men from the ordinary law would be "to make the professed doctrines of religious belief superior to the law of the land, and in effect to permit every citizen to become a law unto himself."[6]

The US Congress responded to the *Oregon v Smith* decision, and its narrow reading of the free exercise clause, by enacting the *Religious Freedom Restoration Act of 1993*, which provides that the US government "shall not substantially burden a person's exercise of religion, even if the burden results from a rule of general applicability" unless "it demonstrates that application of the burden to the person (1) is in furtherance of a compelling governmental interest; and (2) is the least restrictive means of furthering that compelling governmental interest."[7]

The Canadian courts, at least formally, have adopted a different approach to the justification of limits on religious practice. According to the Canadian courts, section 2(a) of the *Canadian Charter of Rights and Freedoms*, which protects Canadians' right to freedom of religion, is breached any time the state restricts a religious practice in a nontrivial way.[8] Even when a law advances a legitimate public purpose, such as the prevention of drug use or cruelty to animals or violence in the schoolyard, the state must justify, under section 1 of the *Charter*, the law's nontrivial interference with a religious practice.

Yet, despite the Supreme Court of Canada's formal declaration that the state must justify any nontrivial restriction of a religious practice, the Court has given this requirement little substance. The Court appears willing to uphold a legal restriction if it has a legitimate objective (other than the suppression of an erroneous religious practice) that would be noticeably compromised if an exception were made. In other words, even though the courts have structured their approach to section 2(a) so that it has the form of an equality right (drawing on human rights code and

---

See also *Sherbert v Verner*, 374 US 398 (1963), the facts of which were similar to those in *Oregon v Smith*. Mrs Sherbert was dismissed from her sales job because she was unable for religious reasons to work on Saturdays. The Court held that the government could not ordinarily deny unemployment insurance to an individual who was dismissed from her employment because of a conflict between her religious practice and the formal requirements of the job.

6   *Reynolds v United States*, 98 US 145 at 167 (1879), quoted by Scalia J in above note 1 at 879.

7   Pub L No 103–141, 107 Stat 1488, s 3(a) & (b) (1993). A number of US states have enacted similar laws. In *Fulton v City of Philadelphia*, 593 US (2021), the US Supreme Court held that when an anti-discrimination rule allows for exceptions to be granted to its application (at the discretion of an administrative actor), the state cannot deny an exception to a religious actor without a compelling reason.

8   *Canadian Charter of Rights and Freedoms*, Part 1 of the *Constitution Act, 1982*, being Schedule B to the *Canada Act 1982* (UK), 1982, c 11 [*Charter*].

Charter equality jurisprudence), they have adopted in practice a very weak standard of justification under section 1 so that the right protects only a limited form of liberty—a standard not very different perhaps than that advocated by Locke or adopted by the US Supreme Court in *Oregon v Smith*.[9]

The Canadian courts have said that freedom of religion protects practices or activities that have for the individual "a nexus with religion" or "connect" the individual "with the divine" or stem from their spiritual faith.[10] These practices do not have to be part of an established belief system. Nor is it necessary that the individual or group understand them to be mandatory. A practice will fall within the scope of section 2(a) if it is spiritually significant to the individual. Section 2(a) protects different forms of religious worship or observance, including dress and diet requirements. It protects spiritual ways of life, such as living in an agrarian collective or living "separate and apart" from mainstream society. It protects proselytization activities—the teaching or promoting of one's faith to others.[11] It also protects the collective dimension of religious practice—the joining with others in worship or in advancing shared religious purposes.[12]

---

9   The differences between the US and Canadian approaches may simply reflect structural differences between the two bills of rights—specifically the inclusion of a separate limitations provision in the Canadian document. As described by Carolyn Evans, *Freedom of Religion under the European Convention on Human Rights* (Oxford: Oxford University Press, 2001) at 134, the approach of the European Court of Human Rights to art 9 may be similar to the Canadian courts' approach:

> While the Commission and the Court are prepared to scrutinize State action with some care in cases where there has been overt and intentional discrimination against members of a religious group, they have generally given States a wide margin of appreciation in determining whether or not a restriction on the manifestation of religion or belief is necessary. In most cases it seems to be sufficient in practice for the State to show that it has acted in good faith in order for it to be able to justify limitations on religion or belief under Article 9(2).

10   *Syndicat Northcrest v Amselem*, [2004] 2 SCR 557 at para 46 [*Amselem*].

11   The proselytization practices of the Jehovah's Witness community were the subject of several of the Supreme Court's pre-*Charter* freedom of religion decisions. See, for example, *Saumur v City of Quebec*, [1953] 2 SCR 299, which is discussed in Chapter 1. The European Court of Human Rights recognized a right to engage in proselytization in *Kokkinakis v Greece*, Application no 14307/88, Eur Ct HR (Chamber), 23 May 1993. In *Larissis and others v Greece*, Application nos 140/1996/759/958-960, Eur Ct HR, 24 February 1998, this right was found not to protect military officers seeking to convert those under their command.

12   The collective aspect of religious freedom was discussed by the Supreme Court in *Loyola High School v Quebec (Attorney General)*, 2015 SCC 12, and *Law Society of British Columbia v Trinity Western University*, 2018 SCC 32, and will be considered in Chapter 5.

According to the Canadian courts, "[t]he freedom to hold beliefs is broader than the freedom to act on them."[13] This is not so much an assertion as an observation that beliefs are less likely than practices to come into conflict with government action and so, as a practical matter, are less likely to be limited by such action. A practice involves outward behaviour (the externalization of belief) that may sometimes conflict with state law. Belief, though, is internal, personal. However, a restriction on religious belief may occur when the state denies a benefit to an individual because of their beliefs or when the state requires an individual to participate in an activity that they regard as immoral—that is contrary to their spiritual commitments—for example, when it requires a pacifist to serve in the military.[14]

B. *R V EDWARDS BOOKS AND ART LTD*

In *R v Edwards Books and Art Ltd*, several retailers challenged the constitutionality of an Ontario law that prohibited stores from operating on Sunday. The law permitted smaller stores to remain open on Sunday if they were closed on Saturday.[15] A majority of the Supreme Court, in a judgment written by Dickson CJ, accepted that the purpose of the law was not to enforce Sunday as the Sabbath (a religious practice) but was instead to create a common pause day, enabling retail workers to be with their families at least one day during the week. However, Dickson CJ held that even though the law did not compel anyone to engage in a religious practice, it restricted *indirectly* the religious practice of those who regarded Saturday as the Sabbath and so breached section 2(a). Chief Justice Dickson recognized that if a Jewish or Seventh-day Adventist

---

13　*Trinity Western University v British Columbia College of Teachers*, 2001 SCC 31 at para 36.

14　See Chapter 4 for a discussion of conscientious objections—cases in which an individual is compelled to act in a way that is contrary to their religious beliefs.

15　[1986] 2 SCR 713 [*Edwards Books*]. A number of other Supreme Court "accommodation" decisions are examined in later chapters, including *RB v Children's Aid Society of Metropolitan Toronto*, [1995] 1 SCR 315, in which the state was justified in overriding the parents' right to make decisions about the medical treatment of their infant child; *Young v Young*, [1993] 4 SCR 3, in which it was determined that the "best interests of the child" test in custody or access decisions did not breach s 2(a) or was a justified restriction under s 1; and *AC v Manitoba (Director of Child and Family Services)*, 2009 SCC 30, in which it was held that the "best interests of the child" test in cases concerning medical treatment of an older minor did not breach the *Charter*, particularly if the assessment of the minor's best interests took into account her religious views.

retailer was required by law to remain closed on Sunday, they would find it very costly, perhaps commercially unviable, to follow their religion and remain closed on Saturday as well.

The claim that the Sunday closing law *indirectly* restricted the religious practice of Saturday Sabbatarians raised two issues for the Court. The first concerned the type or degree of burden on religious practice that would breach section 2(a). If a law does not ban a religious practice outright but simply makes engagement in the practice more difficult, its interference with (or burden on) the practice might be either minor or substantial. As a practical matter, not every burden on a religious practice can be treated as a violation of section 2(a) that the government must justify under section 1. How significant, then, must the burden or impediment be before a court will decide that it breaches section 2(a)? Chief Justice Dickson accepted that "trivial or insubstantial" burdens on religious practice would not breach section 2(a): "Section 2(a) does not require the legislature to eliminate every minuscule state-imposed cost associated with the practice of religion. Otherwise the *Charter* would offer protection from innocuous secular legislation such as a taxation act that imposed a modest sales tax extending to all products, including those used in the course of religious worship."[16] A sales tax on Bibles or other items used in religious worship may have an impact on a religious practice, making it more costly, but not to such an extent that the tax should be seen as a restriction on freedom of religion that the government must justify. The chief justice accepted that the burden in this case was not trivial but said little about how, in future cases, a court would distinguish between different types of burden.[17]

The second, and more fundamental, issue concerned the state's responsibility for the "impact" on a religious practice of a law that advances an otherwise legitimate public purpose. When should the state be seen as responsible for the "burden on" a particular religious practice, and when should the disadvantage be seen simply as a "cost of" the practice, for which the state is not responsible?[18] The provincial government had argued that any harm to the business interests of Saturday Sabbatarians was the consequence of their religious practice rather than the law. Justice Beetz, in his dissenting judgment, accepted that religious commitment

---

16   *Edwards Books, ibid* at para 97.

17   This question (whether an interference with a religious practice is trivial) is connected to the issue raised in the s 1 analysis in later judgments, such as *Alberta v Hutterian Brethren of Wilson Colony*, 2009 SCC 37 [*Hutterian Brethren*], of whether the individual retains some choice or ability to practise their religion despite the restrictive state action.

18   *Edwards Books*, above note 15 at para 96.

sometimes involves costs or burdens for which the state should not be held responsible. He thought that while section 2(a) prohibits the state from restricting religious practices (from imposing burdens or penalties on particular practices), it does not require the state to facilitate or support such practices. And, in his view, state support for a religious practice was what the retailers in this case were seeking. He observed that if the government had not established a common pause day (Sunday or otherwise) and had permitted stores to remain open every day of the week, then anyone who wanted to keep either Saturday or Sunday as the Sabbath would have been at a competitive disadvantage. For religious reasons they would have to close on Saturday or Sunday, one day of the week, while other retailers could remain open for the whole of the week. For Beetz J, the fact that observant Jews (and others) would be at a relative disadvantage even if there were no Sunday closing law made clear that the disadvantage or burden at issue arose from their religious commitment and not from the law, which advanced a legitimate public policy.

Chief Justice Dickson acknowledged "that the state is normally under no duty under s. 2(a) to take affirmative action to eliminate the natural costs of religious practices."[19] However, he thought that in this particular case the "burden on" religious practice was the consequence of the Sunday closing law. The Act in question had the effect of creating a "purely statutory disadvantage" in that it required the Saturday observer to be closed for "an extra day relative to the Sunday observer": "Just as the Act makes it less costly for Sunday observers to practise their religious beliefs, it thereby makes it more expensive for some Jewish and Seventh-day Adventist retailers to practise theirs."[20] In his view, the Sunday closing law should be viewed as a source of disadvantage for Saturday Sabbatarians and not simply as part of the context in which they live their spiritual lives. The chief justice noted that the Sunday closing requirement did not simply impose a burden on the religious practice of those who would keep Saturday as the Sabbath; it also gave Christians, who honour Sunday as the Sabbath, an advantage over Saturday Sabbatarians. Even though Dickson CJ was unwilling to see the law as compelling a religious practice (or even as having a religious purpose), the Christian roots of the law and its favouring of Christian practice (its unequal impact on different religious groups) seemed to play a role in his decision that the law (indirectly) restricted the religious liberty of Saturday Sabbatarians. In the chief justice's view, the state should endeavour to advance its civic objective in a way that does not disadvantage one group of believers relative to another.

19   *Ibid* at para 111.
20   *Ibid*.

We can see in the chief justice's reasoning a link between the two dimensions of religious freedom. State support or preference for a particular religious practice may also be seen as disadvantaging the practices of other religious groups (or as excluding the members of other groups from a benefit). When the relative disadvantage is significant, it may be viewed as a restriction on the practice of the nonfavoured religious group. The Court in *Edwards Books* found that the Sunday closing law was not intended to compel or promote a religious practice, even though the choice of Sunday reflected the dominant religious practice in the community. The Court held instead that the law restricted religious freedom because it had the *effect* of disadvantaging the members of one religious group relative to another.

As in its earlier Sunday closing law case, *R v Big M Drug Mart*,[21] the Court in *Edwards Books* appeared to adopt a broader, equality-based conception of religious freedom that focuses less on individual liberty and more on the relative treatment of different religious groups in the larger community. But if section 2(a) is viewed as a form of equality right (requiring the accommodation of religious practices), then the distinction drawn by the chief justice between the "natural cost" of a religious practice and a state-imposed ("purely statutory") disadvantage is irrelevant. This distinction rests on the Court's formal or initial commitment to a liberty-based understanding of religious freedom—a commitment that the Court moves away from, more openly, in later judgments. If section 2(a) is concerned with the relative position of different groups in the community, and in particular with the systemic disadvantage of some groups, then a breach of the right can occur either when the state directly disadvantages one group relative to another or when it takes action that disproportionately disadvantages the members of a group that is already systemically disadvantaged. The state has an obligation to take account of the needs of a particular group when making decisions, so that the group is not further excluded or marginalized.

However, Dickson CJ, for the majority of the Court in *Edwards Books*, upheld the restriction under section 1 as reasonable and demonstrably justified. He accepted that the law had a substantial and pressing purpose and impaired the freedom no more than was necessary, since it permitted smaller retail operations to open on Sunday if they were closed on Saturday. The retailers had argued that the exception in the law (that enabled smaller operations to open on Sunday) should have included all stores, regardless of size, that were operated by Saturday Sabbatarians. In holding that the exception was not unduly narrow, the chief justice

---

21   [1985] 1 SCR 295.

indicated that the state should be given considerable latitude in deciding both the necessity and the scope of an exception. He noted that a larger exception would detract from the effectiveness of the law's policy, the creation of a common pause day.[22] In his view, it was not unreasonable for the state to decide that the interests of the "vulnerable employees" of larger retail operations "in securing a Sunday holiday" outweighed the interests of their employer in operating their business on a Sunday.[23]

Justice Wilson, dissenting in *Edwards Books*, found that the restriction was not justified under section 1 because, in her view, a partial exemption was unprincipled:

> [T]he legislature must decide whether to subordinate freedom of religion to the objective of a common pause day, one scheme of justice, or subordinate the common pause day to freedom of religion, the competing scheme of justice, and, having decided which scheme of justice to adopt, it must then apply it in all cases ... [The scheme] does not affirm a principle which is applicable to all. It reflects rather a failure on the part of the legislature to make up its mind which scheme of justice to adopt.[24]

Justice Wilson's dissent raised an issue that resurfaces in many of the Court's later "accommodation" decisions: the tension between the Court's commitment to resolve *Charter* issues on a principled basis and the unavoidably pragmatic character of religious accommodation.

Space should sometimes be made for religious practices not because they are intrinsically valuable but rather because they matter deeply to the believer and because their restriction may have the effect of marginalizing a religious group.[25] Under section 1, once the Court accepts that the state is advancing a legitimate policy, the question becomes what form or degree of accommodation, if any, should be made for the members of a religious group that is disadvantaged by the policy. This is a practical issue about which different judges can reasonably disagree, as they did in *Edwards Books*. Since the focus of judicial review for violations of a *Charter* right, such as equality, is on a particular law or other state act, and not on the entire system of distribution, the courts are not free to structure the system as they see fit, ensuring that certain rights and goals in addition to equality are protected. The courts can only look at

---

22   Chief Justice Dickson was not prepared to enlarge the legislative accommodation, nor can we be certain that he would have ordered the legislature to establish a narrow exemption if the legislature had not already done so.

23   Above note 15 at para 141.

24   *Ibid* at para 203.

25   More will be said about this later in the chapter.

the law before them and decide whether it should be struck down or an exception should be made to it. If a law that adds to a group's existing disadvantage is viewed as necessary to the advancement of an important social end, it will be upheld (without exception), despite its adverse effect and despite the failure of the state to improve, in some other way, the situation of the disadvantaged group. The courts are not in a position to alleviate the situation of a disadvantaged group by ensuring that other benefits are provided—adjusting other laws to ensure some compensation for the disadvantageous effect of the law in question.

C. *R V JONES*

The appellant in *R v Jones* was a pastor who educated his own and other children in the basement of his church.[26] The Alberta *School Act* permitted home schooling and private religious schools, but the Act required parents who wished to educate their children at home to apply for permission from the Department of Education.[27] Mr Jones refused to make such an application, arguing that he would be acting against his religious beliefs if he were to ask secular authorities for permission to educate his children according to "God's will."[28] He believed that when making decisions about the education of his children, he was answerable only to God.

A majority of the Supreme Court held that the requirement that Mr Jones apply to the Department of Education for permission to home school his children (which was separate from any educational or curricular standards established by the *School Act*) either did not interfere with his religious freedom or was a trivial interference and so did not amount to a breach of section 2(a). According to Wilson J, the pastor's freedom of religion was not breached simply because he "is required under the statute to recognize a secular role for the school authorities."[29] Justice Wilson went on to say that even if the legislation did affect Mr Jones's beliefs, "not every effect of legislation on religious beliefs or practices" breaches section 2(a).[30]

But was this only a trivial burden on his religious belief or practice? There are two ways in which the state's interference with an individual's religious belief or practice might be described as trivial. First, a state measure may be seen as a trivial interference when it limits

---

26   [1986] 2 SCR 284.
27   RSA 1980, c S-3, s 143(1)(a).
28   Above note 26 at para 3.
29   *Ibid* at para 63.
30   *Ibid*.

the individual's religious practice only partly or indirectly—when, as described in *Edwards Books*, it amounts to only a minor impediment. However, if Mr Jones believes that he is not answerable to state authorities, then the *School Act* requirement is directly at odds with his religious beliefs and is not simply a trivial interference with those beliefs. Second, an interference may be described as trivial when it restricts a belief or practice that is not a central or important part of the individual's religious belief system. But, as the Supreme Court has said on numerous occasions, this is not the sort of judgment a court can or should make when considering claims under section 2(a).[31] While a court may sometimes find it necessary to determine the sincerity of an individual's spiritual beliefs, it should generally refrain from making any judgment about the centrality of a belief or practice to a particular religious belief system. Of course, as I will argue later, it is not clear how a court is to balance competing civic and religious interests at the limitations stage of the analysis if it is unable to attach particular weight to the religious interest at issue.[32]

The problem with Mr Jones's claim was not that the state had interfered with his religious practice in only a trivial way or that the affected religious belief or practice was a trivial part of his belief system. The problem was that his claim amounted to a complete rejection of state authority. Mr Jones was not objecting to a state requirement that he teach his children things inconsistent with his religious beliefs, such as sex education or evolution. He was objecting to the very idea of state authority—to the state's claim to oversee his actions, or at least those actions that relate to the education of his children. Mr Jones believed that he was answerable to God and to no one else. The mere assertion of authority by the state in these matters is contrary to his religious belief in the supremacy of God.

Not surprisingly, the Court was unwilling to treat the rejection of state authority, regardless of how that authority is exercised, as a matter of religious freedom under section 2(a). When the state enacts a law that interferes with the religious practice of some members of the general community, it may be required under section 2(a) to accommodate that practice. But it is quite another thing for an individual to argue that any exercise of state power interferes with their religious freedom. While Mr Jones may have a right to home school his children, he does not have the

---

31   See, for example, the judgment of La Forest J, *ibid* at para 20.

32   In the more recent case of *R v NS*, 2012 SCC 72 [*NS*], which is examined later in this chapter, the Supreme Court seemed to say that the significance of the practice should be taken into account when a court is balancing competing interests. Yet, in that case the Court appeared to give the practice little or no weight and to give clear priority to the competing state interest.

right to do so free of any state oversight. This may be what Wilson J was getting at when she held (initially) that the law did not breach section 2(a), although formally her position was that the law did not restrict Mr Jones's religious belief or practice and not that his belief or practice fell outside the scope of section 2(a) protection.[33]

The plausibility of Mr Jones's argument rests on the widely held assumption that the actions of the secular state are based exclusively on nonreligious values or concerns. In Mr Jones's view, the secular state was intervening in a religious or spiritual matter — the education of his children. But if government action rests on the religious and nonreligious values of its citizens (if, as argued in the previous chapter, the commitment to public secularism does not require the exclusion of all religious values and concerns from political decision making), then Mr Jones is asserting the right to be free from any oversight of his actions, including actions affecting children and the larger society. He is not simply arguing for the right to live according to spiritual rather than secular (nonreligious) values. He is instead claiming a right to live according to his understanding of fundamental (spiritual) values rather than those of the political community, even when his actions affect others, including his children.[34] A democratic government, though, must sometimes take collective action based on judgments about what is right and just, adopting the views or values of some and rejecting those of others.

D. *SYNDICAT NORTHCREST V AMSELEM*

In *Syndicat Northcrest v Amselem*, the Supreme Court held that a condominium association's refusal to permit Orthodox Jewish unit owners to construct succahs on their balconies during the Jewish festival of Sukkot breached their freedom of religion under the Quebec *Charter of Human*

---

33   There is a parallel between Mr Jones's claim and the parents' claim in the later *SL v Commission scolaire des Chênes*, 2012 SCC 7 [*SL*] case. In both cases, the claimants described their belief or practice in very broad terms — not just as a particular activity, which they claimed was being interfered with by the state, but as a view, or belief, about their relationship to society and to the state, which challenged the prevailing assumptions of democratic politics.

34   Chapter 6 includes a longer discussion of the competing interests in education cases — the parents' interest in transmitting their faith to their child, the child's interest in developing the capacity to make their own judgments, and the state's related interest in the child's development as a community member who is tolerant of others and able to contribute to society.

Rights and Freedoms.[35] Because a nonstate actor imposed the restriction on religious practice, the *Canadian Charter of Rights and Freedoms* was not applicable. However, the majority judgment of Iacobucci J was clear that "the principles . . . applicable in cases where an individual alleges that his or her freedom of religion is infringed under the Quebec *Charter*" are also applicable to a claim under section 2(a) of the Canadian *Charter*.[36]

In deciding that the condominium association had violated the appellants' freedom of religion, Iacobucci J made two significant determinations concerning the scope of the freedom. First, he held that a spiritual practice or belief will fall within the protection of section 2(a) even though it is idiosyncratic and not part of an established or widely held religious belief system. Second, a practice will be protected under section 2(a) even though it is not regarded as obligatory by the individual claimant. The only question, according to Iacobucci J, is whether the individual has a sincere belief in the spiritual significance of a particular practice. He held that

> freedom of religion consists of the freedom to undertake practices and harbour beliefs, having a nexus with religion, in which an individual demonstrates he or she sincerely believes or is sincerely undertaking in order to connect with the divine or as a function of his or her spiritual faith, irrespective of whether a particular practice or belief is required by official religious dogma or is in conformity with the position of religious officials.[37]

The two rabbis who gave evidence at the *Amselem* trial gave different answers to the question of whether residing in a personal succah was a religious obligation. The Court, though, had no wish to arbitrate a dispute about religious doctrine. According to Iacobucci J, the Court should consider the sincerity of an individual's belief but not its validity—neither its objective truth nor the extent of its acceptance within a particular

---

35   *Amselem*, above note 10; CQLR c C-12 [Quebec *Charter*]. The condominium
     bylaws, to which all unit owners formally agreed before purchasing or occupy-
     ing their particular unit, prohibited decorations, alterations, and constructions
     on their balconies. However, the bylaws also provided that an individual owner
     might apply to the condominium association for an exemption from this general
     prohibition. For a discussion of the case, see Richard Moon, "Religious Commit-
     ment and Identity: *Syndicat Northcrest v Amselem*" (2005) 29 *Sup Ct L Rev* 201,
     and Robert E Charney, "How Can There Be Any Sin in Sincere? State Inquiries
     into Sincerity of Religious Belief" (2010) 51 *Sup Ct L Rev* (2d) 47.

36   *Amselem*, above note 10 at para 37. As will become apparent in the discussion
     that follows, I am not sure that the Court was correct in equating private and
     public sector restrictions on religious practice.

37   *Ibid* at para 46.

religious group. It is not for the courts, said Iacobucci J, to decide what is required by a particular belief system or which interpretation of that system is correct. Religion, he said, is a matter of "personal choice and individual autonomy and freedom."[38] And so even though not all of the appellants in this case regarded the practice of erecting a succah on their property as a religious obligation, the practice was protected because it had for them spiritual significance.

There was no doubt in this case that the claimants had a sincere belief in the spiritual significance of the succah. Erecting and "residing in" a succah is an established practice in Judaism, even if there are different views about whether this practice, or the practice of residing in one's own succah, is obligatory. Moreover, there is no obvious nonspiritual benefit to "residing in" a succah and so little reason to doubt the claimants' sincerity. However, Iacobucci J recognized that there may be cases in which the sincerity of the individual's claim is in dispute, and so he offered some general comments about the determination of sincerity in such cases. A court, he said, may hear expert evidence about religious practices but should not put any weight on the absence of such evidence, since section 2(a) protects beliefs and practices that are not part of an established or shared belief system.[39] He stressed that when a court is assessing sincerity, its role is "only to ensure that a presently asserted religious belief is in good faith, neither fictitious nor capricious."[40] According to Iacobucci J, a court may consider past practice but must be careful not to rely too much on such practice, since individuals often revise their beliefs or sometimes fail to live up to their religious ideals:

> Over the course of a lifetime, individuals change and so can their beliefs. Religious beliefs, by their very nature, are fluid and rarely static. A person's connection to or relationship with the divine or with the subject or object of his or her spiritual faith, or his or her perceptions

---

38   *Ibid* at para 40. He added that "[r]eligious belief is intensely personal and can easily vary from one individual to another" (*ibid* at para 54).

39   *Ibid* at para 54:

> A claimant may choose to adduce expert evidence to demonstrate that his or her belief is consistent with the practices and beliefs of other adherents of the faith. While such evidence may be relevant to a demonstration of sincerity, it is not necessary. Since the focus of the inquiry is not on what others view the claimant's religious obligations as being, but rather what the claimant views these personal religious "obligations" to be, it is inappropriate to require expert opinions to show sincerity of belief. An "expert" or an authority on religious law is not the surrogate for an individual's affirmation of what his or her religious beliefs are.

40   *Ibid* at para 52.

of religious obligation emanating from such a relationship, may well change and evolve over time. Because of the vacillating nature of religious belief, a court's inquiry into sincerity, if anything, should focus not on past practice or past belief but on a person's belief at the time of the alleged interference with his or her religious freedom.[41]

The adoption of a subjective test for belief presents challenges for the courts, not just in determining whether the claimant's beliefs are sincere but also in determining the content of the claimant's beliefs. A court must rely on the claimant's account of their beliefs and practices, but its ability to grasp the precise content or nuance of these beliefs may be limited.[42]

In some cases, past practice and religious tradition may determine the sincerity question. But in cases where an individual claims both that their spiritual belief is personal to them (that is, not part of an established belief system) and that it has only recently been adopted, the court must judge their sincerity simply on the basis of their claim. If the claimed practice has no obvious nonspiritual benefits for the claimant, then the court may accept that the belief is sincere. However, in other cases, the court may hesitate to find that the asserted belief is sincere. Consider, for example, the case of *MAB, WAT and J-AYT v Canada*,[43] in which the Human Rights Committee dismissed a claim made against Canada under the *International Covenant on Civil and Political Rights*.[44] In that case, a group of individuals claimed to be members of a religious association or church that regarded marijuana as spiritually significant—as a "sacrament." The committee decided that the practice did not fall within the scope of freedom of religion under the *ICCPR*: "a belief consisting primarily or exclusively in the worship and distribution of a narcotic drug cannot conceivably be brought within the scope of article 18 of the Covenant."[45] The committee did not directly comment on the sincerity of the complainants' beliefs, although it seems likely that

---

41   *Ibid* at para 53.

42   See, for example, the *SL* case, above note 33, discussed below, in which the Supreme Court decided that the claimants were mistaken in thinking that the law interfered with their religious beliefs or practices. Some of the difficulties with the sincerity test are discussed in Anna Su, "Judging Religious Sincerity" (2016) 5 *Oxford JL & Religion* 28.

43   Communication No 570/1993, UN Doc CCPR/C/50/D/570/1993 (1994) [*MAB*].

44   *International Covenant on Civil and Political* Rights, GA Res 2200A(XXI), 21 UNGAOR Supp (No 16) at 52, UN Doc A/6316 (1966) (entered into force 23 March 1976) [*ICCPR*], online: www.ohchr.org/en/instruments-mechanisms/instruments/international-covenant-civil-and-political-rights.

45   *MAB*, above note 43 at para 4.2.

the committee doubted their sincerity but was reluctant to make such a factual determination.

Justice Iacobucci in *Amselem* held that preventing the appellants from erecting succahs on their balconies amounted to a nontrivial interference with their religious practice and that this interference was not justified under the limitations provision of the Quebec *Charter*. In response to the safety concerns raised by the condominium association, Iacobucci J observed that the appellants had agreed to set up their succahs in a way that would not obstruct the fire escape routes. He regarded the association's interest in the aesthetic appearance of the building as a minor concern, noting that only a small number of succahs would be erected for nine days in the year. Moreover, the association could require that the succahs be constructed to blend in, as much as possible, with the general appearance of the building. Justice Iacobucci concluded that "the alleged intrusions or deleterious effects on the respondent's rights or interests under the circumstances are, at best, minimal and thus cannot be reasonably considered as imposing valid limits on the exercise of the appellants' religious freedom."[46]

Justice Iacobucci's focus on individual belief rather than community practice when defining the scope of religious freedom may have contributed in subsequent decisions to a weak standard of justification and accommodation at the limitations stage (even though the limitation in *Amselem* was struck down).[47] This is so for several reasons. First, the focus on individual belief raises the question of why religious or spiritual beliefs should be treated differently from nonreligious beliefs. All deeply held beliefs, religious and nonreligious, would appear to have the same claim to protection from state interference. Second, if the test for determining whether a practice is protected under section 2(a) is subjective (Does the individual have a sincere belief in its spiritual significance?), then it is not clear what weight should be given to the practice in the court's balancing of competing religious and public interests or even why the state should be expected to compromise its policy for a subjectively valued practice. The requirement of neutrality (that the state neither support a particular religious practice nor restrict such a practice without a compelling public reason) must rest to some extent on equality concerns—that identity groups not be socially excluded or politically marginalized. Third, the subjective test means that the scope of section

---

46   Above note 10 at para 84.

47   For a discussion of the problems raised by the Court's broad reading of the scope of s 2(a), see Louis-Philippe Lampron, "Pour que la tempête ne s'étende jamais hors du verre d'eau: Réflexions sur la protection des convictions religieuses au Canada" (2010) 55 *McGill LJ* 743. See also Moon, above note 35.

2(a) protection is uncertain or unstable. Any law may potentially breach section 2(a). And the number of individuals seeking exemption from a particular law is potentially unlimited. A decision to grant an exemption to a small number of individuals may not have a significant impact on a law's effectiveness; however, if more individuals seek exemption—and there is always the (theoretical) possibility that more may do so—then the law's purpose may be entirely undermined. Law makers can take account of established religious practices when formulating law, and they can assess the practicalities of reshaping the law or creating an exception to its application for an established religious group; but, as McLachlin CJ recognized in *Hutterian Brethren*, the legislature, when enacting a law, cannot be expected to anticipate every possible claim to exemption.[48]

The dissenting judgment of Bastarache J in *Amselem* adopted a much narrower approach to the scope of freedom of religion. In his view, an individual who claims their beliefs or practices fall within the protection of section 3 of the Quebec *Charter* (and section 2(a) of the Canadian *Charter*) must show a "nexus" between their personal beliefs and the precepts of their religion.[49] The individual claimant, said Bastarache J, must also show that they sincerely believe they are *obligated* to engage in a particular practice. He noted that in this case, only one of the applicants had claimed to be under an obligation to erect their own succah. He went on to say that even if there was a breach of religious freedom in this case, the condominium was justified in insisting on adherence to the bylaw.

Justice Binnie in his dissent thought that, since the appellants agreed to the condominium bylaws at the time they purchased their units, it was reasonable for the other unit owners to assume that the appellants' religious practice was compatible with the bylaws. "There is a vast difference," said Binnie J, "between using freedom of religion as a shield against interference with religious freedoms by the State and as a sword against co-contractors in a private building."[50] Justice Binnie noted that the appellants were in the best position to determine, before purchasing units in the building, what their religion required. They could have chosen to purchase units in another building if they were unhappy with the terms of the agreement. It was reasonable then to hold them to their agreement.

If religious commitment is, as the majority judgment described it, personal and individual, then Binnie J's response might be the right one. An individual's religious belief has no intrinsic value, at least from a perspective external to the belief system. It is valuable because the individual has chosen it or is personally committed to it. It is not obvious, though,

---

48   Above note 17 at para 69.
49   Above note 10 at para 118.
50   *Ibid* at para 185.

that others should be required to compromise their interests to make space for such a choice. And, as Binnie J recognized, who better to determine the content of an individual's personal religious commitment than the individual themself? When an individual undertakes not to perform a particular act or practice, others might reasonably assume they are not, or at least not deeply, committed to the particular practice. Since religion is a personal matter, others can rely only on the individual's statements about what is important to them—about what they think they can and cannot do without. More fundamentally, if religious practice is personal and protected as a matter of autonomy or liberty, then an individual should be free to decide that they do not need to take certain actions, or they should be free to bind themself contractually not to take such actions. Provided it is given voluntarily, an individual's undertaking not to act on a particular belief is also an expression of their autonomous judgment.

However, the issue of waiver or consent may be less straightforward if religious belief or practice is regarded as a matter of cultural identity that must be accommodated or treated with equal respect by both state and private actors. Justice Binnie seemed to assume that the condominium association could refuse to sell a unit to anyone who, for religious reasons, objected to the bylaws. In his view, prospective purchasers who were unwilling or unable to agree to the bylaws could choose to purchase a unit in another building. But if the condominium association is obligated to accommodate minority religious practices, then it cannot condition the sale of one of its units on the purchaser's agreement not to practise their religion, or more particularly not to erect a succah on the unit's balcony.

E. *REFERENCE RE SAME-SEX MARRIAGE*

In *Reference re Same-Sex Marriage*, several religious groups argued that the redefinition of marriage to include same-sex relationships breached their section 2(a) and section 15 *Charter* rights.[51] The groups opposed the legal change, arguing that the recognition of same-sex marriages "will have the effect of imposing a dominant social ethos and will thus limit the freedom to hold religious beliefs to the contrary."[52] Their claim seemed to be that the recognition of same-sex marriages would undermine traditional marriage or erode its value and meaning. The opponents

---

51   2004 SCC 79.
52   *Ibid* at para 47.

further argued that this change would also have "the effect of forcing religious officials to perform same-sex marriages."[53]

The Court rejected the first of these arguments, noting that "[t]he mere recognition of the equality rights of one group cannot, in itself, constitute a violation of the rights of another."[54] In response to the second argument, the Court said that if the state ever did enact a law requiring religious officials to perform same-sex marriages, it would breach the *Charter*. In the Court's view, "state compulsion on religious officials to perform same-sex marriages contrary to their religious beliefs would violate the guarantee of freedom of religion under s. 2(*a*) of the *Charter*," and "absent exceptional circumstances which we cannot at present foresee, such a violation could not be justified under s. 1."[55]

In most religious restriction cases, the claim made is that the state, through its actions, has made it impossible or more difficult for an individual or group to engage in a particular religious practice. The issue for the court in these cases is whether the restriction is justified in the public interest or whether an exception can be made to the law without significantly compromising its purpose. The law at issue in the *Same-Sex* marriage case, though, did not prevent anyone from practising their faith nor require them to perform an act that is inconsistent with their faith. The change in the definition of civil marriage meant only that some individuals must now live in a society that permits others to engage in an activity they regard as immoral — or that supports a moral view that is inconsistent with their own. The Court found that an individual's ability to practise their faith is not restricted merely because public policy is at odds with their beliefs.

The state's commitment to sexual-orientation equality, even though framed in secular or civic terms, involves a rejection of the belief that same-sex relationships are wrongful. While the state may avoid passing direct judgment on the truth of a particular religious belief (as religious truth), it cannot avoid doing so indirectly when determining public policy. When the legislature decides that a particular activity should be either supported or restricted, it does not frame its judgment in terms of what God has or has not commanded. But unless we hold on to some artificial distinction between public and religious morality, the

---

53   *Ibid.*

54   *Ibid* at para 46. The Court continued, "[t]he promotion of *Charter* rights and values enriches our society as a whole and the furtherance of those rights cannot undermine the very principles the *Charter* was meant to foster."

55   *Ibid* at para 58. The requirement that civil marriage commissioners perform same-sex marriages is discussed in Chapter 4.

legislature's judgment must be seen as a repudiation of a religious belief that is held by some in the community.

As we will see in the next chapter, the conflict between religious belief and public policy is more complicated when an individual who believes, for example, that same-sex relationships are sinful is required by law to act in a way that (in their view) supports or condones this "sinful" behaviour—for example, providing a cake or printing invitations for a same-sex wedding. While the individual may not be required to engage directly in an activity they regard as immoral, they are required to do more than simply live in a society that rejects their moral views. In these cases, the individual is required to take action that they believe supports or condones the immoral behaviour of others. The question the court must answer is whether the form or degree of the individual's involvement (as required by the state) with an activity they regard as immoral should be viewed as an interference with their religious belief.

F. *MULTANI V COMMISSION SCOLAIRE MARGUERITE-BOURGEOYS*

In *Multani v Commission scolaire Marguerite-Bourgeoys*, the Supreme Court held that a decision by a public school authority to prohibit a Sikh student from wearing a kirpan to school breached section 2(a) and was not justified under section 1.[56] The school had proposed, and the student's parents had agreed, that the kirpan be sewed into the student's clothing so that it would not fall out or be easily removed. However, the school's governing council refused to ratify this arrangement, taking the position that bringing the kirpan to school would breach the school's code of conduct, which prohibited carrying weapons.

It was accepted by all parties that the student had a sincere belief in the spiritual significance of the kirpan and, indeed, that he considered himself bound to wear it at all times. It followed then that the school authority's decision breached section 2(a). There was no question, said Charron J, that the school could establish a rule prohibiting weapons. The issue, however, was whether the school authority had applied this rule in

---

56   2006 SCC 6 [*Multani*]. The council of school commissioners interpreted the ban on weapons in its code of conduct as excluding the kirpan. For a discussion of the case, see Mahmud Jamal, "Freedom of Religion in the Supreme Court: Some Lessons from *Multani*" (2007) 21 *NJCL* 291. Dia Dabby, *Religious Diversity in Canadian Public Schools* (Vancouver: UBC Press, 2022) nicely sets out the context for this case as well as the *SL* case (above note 33), which is discussed later in this chapter.

a way that respected religious freedom and could be justified under the terms of section 1.

Justice Charron determined that the school's policy could do no more than ensure reasonable safety, since it was unrealistic to imagine that the school could ban all safety risks.[57] She noted that pens, scissors, and bats were all permitted despite their potential use as weapons. She found that the safety of the school would not be compromised if the student was permitted to wear the kirpan subject to certain conditions. Justice Charron observed that for Sikhs the kirpan was a religious symbol rather than a weapon: "while the kirpan undeniably has characteristics of a bladed weapon capable of wounding or killing a person ... for orthodox Sikhs [it] is above all a religious symbol."[58] The kirpan could, of course, be both a weapon and a religious symbol in the sense that its symbolic role is tied to its history or character as a weapon. Importantly, though, it is not carried by Sikh men as a weapon. Justice Charron rejected the school authority's claim that "kirpans are inherently dangerous" and noted that there were no recorded incidents in Canada of a Sikh student drawing his kirpan in a public school.[59] She further observed that in contrast to an airplane or a court house, where a ban on the kirpan might be justified, the school had an ongoing relationship with its students and so could monitor their actions and assess the risk of violent behaviour.[60] Finally, Charron J thought that if the kirpan was sewn into the student's clothes (something his family and the school administration had previously agreed to), there would be little risk of it falling out or being taken by anyone else and used as a weapon. She determined that the kirpan was a weapon in form only and presented no real risk to school safety.

G. *ALBERTA V HUTTERIAN BRETHREN OF WILSON COUNTY*

In 2003 the regulations in Alberta dealing with driver's licences were amended so that all licence holders had to be photographed.[61] The

---

57   Several years after this decision, the Court in *Dore v Barreau du Quebec*, 2012 SCC 12 set out a test for determining the constitutionality of administrative decisions affecting *Charter* rights.

58   *Multani*, above note 56 at para 37.

59   *Ibid* at 67.

60   See *Hothi v R*, [1986] 3 WWR 671 (Man CA) (kirpans banned in the courts); and *Nijjar v Canada 3000 Airlines Ltd* (2000), 36 CHRR D/76 (HRT) (kirpans banned on airplanes).

61   *Hutterian Brethren*, above note 17. For a discussion of the case, see Benjamin L Berger, "Section 1, Constitutional Reasoning and Cultural Difference: Assessing

licence holder's photo would appear on their licence and be included in a facial recognition data bank maintained by the province, which would allow the province to ensure that no one was able to apply for a second licence in another name or to renew or replace a licence that belonged to someone else.[62] Before this change, the regulations had permitted the registrar of motor vehicles to grant an exemption to an individual who, for religious reasons, objected to having their photo taken. Members of the Hutterian Brethren of Wilson Colony, who believed that the second of the Ten Commandments prohibited the making of photographic images, had been exempted from the photo requirement under the old regulations, but now under the new law were required to be photographed before a licence would be issued.[63] In *Alberta v Hutterian Brethren of Wilson County,* members of the colony challenged the photo requirement, arguing that it breached their section 2(a) and section 15 *Charter* rights and could not be justified under section 1. They claimed that no one from the colony would now be able to obtain a driver's licence and that this would affect the colony's ability to purchase goods and sell produce, activities that were necessary to the maintenance of its agrarian and communal way of life.

A majority of the Supreme Court, in a judgment written by McLachlin CJ, accepted that the photo requirement breached the section 2(a) rights of the members of the colony but found that the breach was justified under section 1. Chief Justice McLachlin was clear that "reasonable accommodation analysis" (the obligation to accommodate a practice unless it would cause undue hardship) is not the proper approach when the court is considering whether a *law* (rather than an administrative decision) that restricts a religious practice is justified under section 1.[64] According to McLachlin CJ, "[a] law's constitutionality under section 1 of the *Charter* is determined, not by whether it is responsive to the unique needs of every individual claimant, but rather by whether its

---

the Impacts of *Alberta v Hutterian Brethren of Wilson Colony*" (2010) 51 *Sup Ct L Rev* (2d) 25; Richard Moon, "Accommodation without Compromise: Comment on *Alberta v Hutterian Brethren of Wilson Colony*" (2010) 51 *Sup Ct L Rev* (2d) 95.

62   Driver's licences in Alberta are governed by the *Traffic Safety Act*, RSA 2000, c T-6, and the regulations made pursuant to the Act.

63   See *Hutterian Brethren,* above note 17 at para 29.

64   The chief justice, though, suggested that this might be an appropriate approach in the case of an individualized decision or restriction, as occurred in *Multani,* above note 56.

infringement of *Charter* rights is directed at an important objective and is proportionate in its overall impact."[65]

Chief Justice McLachlin found that the purpose behind the photo requirement (reducing the risk of identity theft by ensuring the integrity of the driver's licence system) is pressing and substantial. She accepted that the inclusion of the licence photos in a digital data bank will "ensure that each licence in the system is connected to a single individual, and that no individual has more than one licence," which in turn will help to prevent the fraudulent acquisition of driver's licences.[66] She also accepted that requiring *all* licence holders in the province to have their photo included in a digital data bank "will accomplish these security-related objectives more effectively than would an exemption for an as *yet undetermined number* of religious objectors [emphasis added]."[67]

At the final step of the *Oakes* test, McLachlin CJ decided that a religious exception to the photo requirement would detract from the effectiveness of the measure in preventing identity theft. She reached this conclusion even though, as she noted, there were adults in the province who did not have a driver's licence. At the same time, she emphasized that the photo requirement does not compel the colony members to have their photos taken. It is simply a condition for obtaining a driver's licence. Driving, she said, is a privilege and not a right. She suggested that the colony members might hire others to do their necessary driving, although she acknowledged that relying on outsiders might detract from the community's "traditional self-sufficiency."[68] She acknowledged the collective dimension of religious freedom, describing the freedom as "individual, but profoundly communitarian," but seemed to regard this dimension as simply a matter of individuals choosing to worship together.[69] She thought that it was reasonable to expect religious adherents who are affected by the law to compromise to some extent their nonreligious activities such as driving or engaging in certain kinds of

---

65   *Hutterian Brethren*, above note 17 at para 69. And in the same para:

> By their very nature, laws of general application are not tailored to the unique
> needs of individual claimants. The legislature has no capacity or legal obli-
> gation to engage in such an individualized determination, and in many cases
> would have no advance notice of a law's potential to infringe *Charter* rights.
> It cannot be expected to tailor a law to every possible future contingency, or
> every sincerely held religious belief. Laws of general application affect the
> general public, not just the claimants before the court.

66   *Ibid* at para 42.

67   *Ibid* at para 80.

68   *Ibid* at para 97.

69   *Ibid* at para 89.

work.[70] In her view, the costs of the regulation "do not rise to the level of seriously affecting the claimants' right to pursue their religion" and "do not negate the choice that lies at the heart of freedom of religion."[71] She concluded from this that the benefit of the law outweighed its negative impact on the religious practice.

The chief justice distinguished the claim in this case from that in *Multani*, "where the incidental and unintended effect of the law [was] to deprive the adherent of a meaningful choice as to the religious practice."[72] In *Multani*, "the adherent is left with a stark choice between violating his or her religious belief and disobeying the law."[73] It is unclear, though, when a constraint is so significant that it removes the individual's choice to practise their religion. Chief Justice McLachlin cited *Multani* as an example of a substantial constraint. But could it not be argued that there was an alternative available to the parents in that case, which was to send their child to a private school — the alternative they chose while their case moved though the courts? Is the cost of private schooling so great that the individual's "choice" is removed while the cost of hiring private transportation is not (without even taking account of any loss to the colony's self-sufficiency)?

In declining to grant an exemption in the *Hutterian Brethren* case, the chief justice made what is sometimes referred to in law as a "floodgates" argument: if the courts recognize a particular claim, they may be opening the floodgates to an overwhelming number of claims and may, as a consequence, undermine the effectiveness or predictability of the law.[74] There were very few claimants in this case, as Abella J noted in her dissenting judgment. Had they been granted an exemption, the impact on government policy would have been minor.[75] Chief Justice McLachlin, though, was concerned about the possibility of more

---

70 The British courts as well as the European Court of Human Rights have held that an individual may not have a right to accommodation when their religious obligations are incompatible with the ordinary requirements of a particular job. The individual, instead, should look for other work that is compatible with their religious practice. See, for example, *Stedman v UK*, (1997) 23 EHRR CD 168, in which an employer required an existing employee to work on Sundays. See also *R (On the application of Begum) v Headteacher and Governors of Denbigh High School*, [2006] UKHL 15, in which a student's religious dress did not conform with her school's particular dress code.

71 *Hutterian Brethren*, above note 17 at at para 99.

72 *Ibid* at para 96.

73 *Ibid* at para 94.

74 *Ibid* at para 36. Accommodating every religious claim "could seriously undermine the universality of many regulatory programs."

75 Justice Abella dissenting (with Lebel J agreeing on this point) (*ibid*) weighed the competing interests in this case differently, attaching greater weight to the

claimants coming forward at a later date. It is unreasonable, said the chief justice, to expect the state (when it is seeking to advance the public interest through law) to respond to or anticipate every possible claim for exemption on religious grounds. But on this reasoning no exemption could ever be given since the law's purpose might be significantly undermined if additional claimants were to come forward at some future time. Or, as in *Multani*, an exception could be made only if it was not truly an exception in the sense that its recognition (regardless of how many people sought "exemption") would not undermine the law's purpose.

The problem, in a case like *Hutterian Brethren*, is that the accommodation issue—the question of whether an exception should be made to an otherwise legitimate law—requires the Court to make a practical judgment about whether, and to what extent, the law's purpose should be compromised to make space for a religious practice. But an accommodation decision of this kind may need to be reversed or adjusted as circumstances change and so does not fit with the Court's self-understanding as a principled decision maker that is engaged in defining the scope of individual rights and determining the appropriate balance between competing rights or interests.[76] In seeking to follow a consistent and principled approach to religious freedom claims, the chief justice was led to reject any form of accommodation or exemption from the law. And so, while the Court approaches section 2(a) as a form of equality right, in *Hutterian Brethren* it reduces the section to a form of liberty right that protects a religious practice only if it does not interfere in a measurable way with public policy.[77]

---

community's self-sufficiency and downplaying the impact of a religious exemption on the objectives, noting that many adults in the province do not hold a licence.

76   *Ibid* at para 61: "governments may find it difficult to tailor laws to the myriad ways in which they may trench on different people's religious beliefs and practices."

77   The chief justice disposed of the section 15 claim very quickly: "Assuming the respondents could show that the regulation creates a distinction on the enumerated ground of religion, it arises not from any demeaning stereotype but from a neutral and rationally defensible policy choice ... The Colony members' claim is to the unfettered practice of their religion, not to be free from religious discrimination. The substance of the respondents' s. 15(1) claim has already been dealt with under s. 2(a)" (*ibid* at para 108).

Yet in other section 15 cases, dealing with other forms of discrimination, the courts have said that a law that has a disadvantaging impact on the members of a historically disadvantaged group will be found to breach the section. (See, for example, *Withler v Canada (AG)*, 2011 SCC 12 and *Fraser v Canada (AG)*, 2020 SCC 28.) The courts have found a breach in other s 15 cases, even when, as in *Hutterian Brethren*, the "distinction ... arises ... from a neutral and rationally

H. *SL V COMMISSION SCOLAIRE DES CHÊNES*

In *SL v Commission scolaire des Chênes*, the Supreme Court rejected a claim by a group of Roman Catholic parents who argued that their children should be exempted from a compulsory ethics and religious culture (ERC) course in the Quebec public school system.[78] The majority judgment of Deschamps J described the parents' objection to the course in this way:

> The principal argument that emerges from the reasons given by the appellants in their requests for an exemption is that the obligation they believe they have, namely to pass on their faith to their children, has been interfered with … The common theme that runs through the appellants' objections is that the ERC Program is not in fact neutral. According to the appellants, students following the ERC course would be exposed to a form of relativism, which would interfere with the appellants' ability to pass their faith on to their children.[79]

The Court, however, rejected the parents' claim. Justice Deschamps found no basis for thinking that the course (which had not yet been implemented) advanced a relativistic view of religion (that all religions were equally valuable or equally without merit). In her view, the course simply "exposed" children to a "comprehensive presentation of various religions."[80] It did not seek to indoctrinate the children into a particular faith or worldview and so did not infringe the parents' freedom of religion.

To establish a breach of section 2(a), said Deschamps J, a claimant must show not only that they sincerely believe in the spiritual significance of a particular practice (a subjective test) but also that this practice has been infringed by government action (an objective test). In this case, Deschamps J found that the mandatory course did not (objectively)

---

defensible policy choice" (at para 108). Here again we see the Court inclined to view religion as a personal commitment rather than a group identity.

78   Above note 33. The course was introduced following the reorganization of the state-funded schools in Quebec from a religion-based system to a language-based system. Benjamin L Berger, "Religious Diversity, Education, and the 'Crisis' in State Neutrality" (2014) 29 *CJLS* 103 at 106 notes that the claimants in recent cases are "[l]ess concerned with using the law to cleanse schools of religious traces … and are now deploying the logic of freedom of religion to resist a felt hegemony of secular ideals." See also *ET v Hamilton-Wentworth District School Board*, 2017 ONCA 893, in which the Ontario Court of Appeal rejected a parent's claim that his children be exempted from different elements of public elementary school curriculum.

79   *Ibid* at para 29.

80   *Ibid* at para 36.

interfere with the parents' ability to instruct their children in Roman Catholicism, which is understood by them to be the one true faith.[81] In their concurring judgment, LeBel and Fish JJ noted that at the time the complaint was made, the course had not yet been implemented in the schools. They found no breach of section 2(a) but left open the possibility that the course, once in place, might be shown to advance a relativistic view of religion, contrary to the parents' beliefs.

The majority in *SL* thought that the parents were mistaken in their belief (or at least had provided no evidence for their belief) that the ERC course taught a relativistic view of religion that was inconsistent with their belief that there is a true religion. However, the parents' objection to the course may have been more basic than this. Their objection may have been that their children would be taught about different belief systems without being told that one of these systems, Roman Catholicism, is true and the others are false. Or the parents may also have doubted that a distinction could be drawn in classroom teaching between exposure to and affirmation of a particular faith, and that religious education (or education about religion) should be left to parents. If this is what the parents thought, then the provincial course requirement could be seen as interfering with their religious beliefs and, more particularly, with their right to decide the religious education of their children. The problem with such a claim, though, is that it is fundamentally at odds with the public commitment to religious freedom and to the maintenance of a tolerant or respectful political community.[82] The majority said as much at the end of their judgment: "The suggestion that exposing children to a variety of religious facts in itself infringes their religious freedom or

---

81 A similar conclusion was reached in *Mozert v Hawkins County Board of Education*, 827 F 2d 1058 (1987), a decision of the US Court of Appeals for the Sixth Circuit. In that case, the parents of children enrolled in the Tennessee public school system argued that their children should be exempted from reading a series of books that depicted views and practices (such as gender equality and magic) that were contrary to their religious beliefs. The court held that the compulsory course did not breach the parents' free exercise rights under the First Amendment. The course simply "exposed" children to other views. It did not affirm views that were inconsistent with the parents' religious beliefs, and it did not require the children to participate in practices that were contrary to the parents' beliefs. In *Loyola High School v Quebec (Attorney General)*, 2015 SCC 12, the Supreme Court held that a private Roman Catholic high school should be exempted from teaching elements of the ERC course. The case is discussed in Chapter 5.

82 A similar view of the case is taken by Faisal Bhabha in "From *Saumur* to *L.(S.)*: Tracing the Theory and Concept of Religious Freedom under Canadian Law" (2012) *58 Sup Ct L Rev* 109; Richard Moon, "Freedom of Conscience and Religion" in Stéphane Beaulac and Errol Mendes, eds, *Canadian Charter of Rights and Freedoms*, 5th ed (Markham, ON: LexisNexis, 2013) 375; and Berger, above note 78.

that of their parents amounts to a rejection of the multicultural reality of Canadian society and ignores the Quebec government's obligations with regard to public education."[83]

I.   *R V NS*

The issue for the Supreme Court in *R v NS* was whether a witness in a criminal trial or hearing had a right under section 2(a) to wear a niqab when giving evidence.[84] The majority judgment of McLachlin CJ began by noting that two *Charter* rights were "potentially engaged" in the case: the witness's freedom of religion and the accused's right to a fair trial. In a case such as this, said the chief justice, a court must determine the "just and proportionate balance" between these two rights.[85] The issue, in her view, could not be resolved by a fixed rule that was applicable in all cases—either that the witness will always be required to remove her niqab when giving evidence or that she will never be required to do so—but must instead be resolved on a case-by-case basis.[86]

The chief justice set out the general approach that a trial judge should follow when deciding whether a witness should be permitted to testify wearing a niqab. The trial judge should take account of the particular circumstances of the case before them and ask the following questions. First, does the witness have a sincere religious belief that would be compromised if she were required to testify without the niqab? Second, "[w]ould permitting the witness to wear the niqab while testifying create a serious risk to trial fairness?"[87] The answer to this second question, said the chief justice, will depend on the nature of the witness's evidence. If, for example, the witness's evidence is uncontested so that credibility is not at issue, then wearing a niqab while testifying will not affect the fairness of the trial. Third, if both rights are "engaged" in the particular case, the judge should consider whether there is a way in which both can be "accommodated" so as to avoid any conflict or trade-off between them.[88]

---

83   Above note 33 at para 40.

84   Above note 32. The ruling under appeal concerned the right of a witness to wear a niqab in a preliminary inquiry.

85   *Ibid* at para 31.

86   See *ibid*: "Rather, the answer lies in a just and proportionate balance between freedom of religion on the one hand, and trial fairness on the other, based on the particular case before the Court." Justice Abella, in her dissenting judgment in *NS*, thought that the Court should adopt a rule permitting the witness to wear a niqab when testifying.

87   *Ibid* at para 9.

88   *Ibid*.

In other words, the judge must consider if there is a way in which the witness can give evidence while wearing a niqab that will not put the fairness of the trial at risk.[89] Finally, if accommodation is not possible, the issue becomes whether "the salutary effects of requiring the witness to remove the niqab outweigh the deleterious effects of doing so?"[90] In answering this final question, the judge should consider the importance of the religious practice to the witness, the degree of state interference with that practice, and the actual situation in the courtroom—most importantly, who will see the witness's face if she is not permitted to wear the niqab when giving evidence? The judge should also take into consideration "broader societal harms," most significantly whether requiring removal of the niqab will discourage women from reporting offences or otherwise participating in the justice system.[91] On the other side, the judge must consider whether the witness's evidence is peripheral or central to the case and whether her credibility is a significant issue in the case.

There are, however, a number of problems with the approach proposed by the majority in *NS*. First, the chief justice side-stepped the question of whether demeanour evidence is reliable or useful. She noted that the courts have long relied on such evidence and that, in this case, the Court had not been provided with any expert evidence refuting the assumption that demeanour evidence is useful when assessing witness credibility or conducting cross-examination. Because this assumption is so deeply embedded in the common law system, the chief justice thought that the burden fell on the witness (whose rights were being restricted) to demonstrate that it is unfounded:

> On the record before us, I conclude that there is a strong connection between the ability to see the face of a witness and a fair trial. Being able to see the face of a witness is not the only—or indeed perhaps the most important—factor in cross-examination or accurate credibility assessment. But its importance is too deeply rooted in our criminal justice system to be set aside absent compelling evidence.[92]

---

89   The chief justice used the term "accommodation" in a very limited way. A religious practice will be accommodated when it can coexist with the government's policy—with no trade-off or compromise to that policy (i.e., "minimal impairment" in the strictest or most formal sense).

90   Above note 32 at para 9.

91   *Ibid* at para 37. This seems like a general rather than a case-specific factor. Indeed, there are a variety of obvious reasons why it would not be appropriate to treat this as a case-specific consideration. I would note here also that the Court's approach seemed to assume that a witness might choose not to give evidence. But what if a witness was subject to a subpoena? Would a court compel her to give evidence?

92   *Ibid* at para 27. The use of the word "importance" highlights the Court's evasion of the issue. Earlier, McLachlin CJ said: "The common law, supported by

The chief justice's observation that the system has historically treated demeanour evidence as important substitutes for a judgment that demeanour is, in fact, important evidence of a witness's credibility. She appeared to reverse the ordinary requirement in *Charter* cases that the state demonstrate the need for a restriction on the right.

Second, in declining to establish a general rule and leaving the issue to be resolved by the trial judge, based on their assessment of the circumstances in a particular case, the majority has created a situation in which the trial judge's decision will be difficult to review. Review is made particularly difficult because, as I will suggest in a moment, the majority offered no real guidance about the factors the judge should be balancing in these cases or how this balancing is to be done. When the Court handed the issue back to the trial judge to decide whether, in the particular circumstances, a witness should be allowed to wear a niqab when giving evidence, it may have been doing one of two things. The Court might simply have been advancing a rule that a witness must testify without a niqab unless her credibility is not in issue. Indeed, the majority judgment was reasonably clear that the right to a fair trial should take precedence and that the religious practice should be accommodated only when it does not present an actual risk to a fair trial. The other possibility is that the Court was giving the trial judge the authority to decide the general issue of whether demeanour evidence has value — the issue that it was unwilling to directly address. The trial judge, in a particular case, is left to make their own decision on the general issue of the value of demeanour evidence based on their personal experience with or assumptions about such evidence.[93] I suspect that most trial judges believe that demeanour evidence has value and that they are capable of managing its problems or limits and so will decide that the witness must remove the niqab if her credibility is at issue.

Third, in the final stage of the approach proposed by the Court, the trial judge is required to balance the competing rights claims. However, many of the factors the Court said should be weighed in the balance

---

provisions of the *Criminal Code*, RSC 1985, c C-46, and judicial pronouncements, proceeds on the basis that the ability to see a witness's face is an important feature of a fair trial. While not conclusive, in the absence of negating evidence this common law assumption cannot be disregarded lightly" (*ibid* at para 21). If the evidence on the issue was inadequate, the Court might have called on the parties to bring forward more evidence.

93   The majority judgment suggested that expert evidence may be relevant in deciding whether, as a general matter, demeanour evidence is reliable or useful. But if the judge is making a contextual judgment about the relevance and risks of demeanour evidence (or the risks to a fair trial if a witness is permitted to wear a niqab), then the relevance of expert evidence may be limited.

have no clear content. For example, the majority thought that the most significant consideration weighing on the side of the religious freedom claim is the importance of the religious practice to the witness. But how is this to be measured? Indeed, the majority acknowledged that "[i]t is difficult to measure the value of adherence to religious conviction, or the injury caused by being required to depart from it. The value of adherence does not depend on whether a religious practice is a voluntary expression of faith or a mandatory obligation under religious doctrine: *Amselem*."[94] (Of course, when the Court in *Amselem* said that the practice's value did not depend on whether it is mandatory, the Court was considering the scope of section 2(a) protection and not the weight of the practice's value at the section 1 stage.)[95] The practice has no value from a secular perspective. A judge can determine that the practice matters deeply to the individual because the individual has told them so or has consistently adhered to this practice in the past. But it is not clear how a subjective commitment to a particular belief or practice (deep or shallow) is to be compared with the individual's right to (and the public interest in) a fair trial.

At the end of its analysis, the majority judgment seemed to say that the right to a fair trial must take precedence: "Where the liberty of the accused is at stake, the witness's evidence is central to the case and her credibility vital, the possibility of a wrongful conviction must weigh heavily in the balance."[96] Despite the chief justice's frequent references to balancing, it appears that a witness will be permitted to wear a niqab only when her credibility is not at issue, so that the niqab will have no impact on the fairness of the trial. The pretense that the issue will be resolved through "balancing" can be maintained only because the Court has given trial judges the authority to decide the matter based on their reading of the particular facts or circumstances of the case before them. The majority's unwillingness to create a general exception for witnesses who sincerely believe they must cover their faces in public settings is surprising given the other situations, described by the majority, in which

---

94   Above note 32 at para 36.

95   Above note 10.

96   Above note 32 at para 44. Furthermore, "[o]n an individual level, the cost of an unfair trial is severe. The right to a fair trial is a fundamental pillar without which the edifice of the rule of law would crumble. No less is at stake than an individual's liberty — his right to live in freedom unless the state proves beyond a reasonable doubt that he committed a crime meriting imprisonment. This is of critical importance not only to the individual on trial, but to public confidence in the justice system" (*ibid* at para 38).

witnesses may be excused from giving evidence in person.[97] The majority's refusal to recognize an exemption for the niqab seemed to rest on an assumption that wearing the niqab is a choice that lies within the witness's control and so is different from other situations in which a witness may be allowed to give testimony away from the courtroom or without being seen by the judge or lawyers.

J.   *KTUNAXA V BRITISH COLUMBIA*

In *Ktunaxa v British Columbia*, representatives of the Ktunaxa Nation argued before the Supreme Court that the decision of the BC government to approve a ski resort development on land with which the community had a spiritual connection breached their religious freedom under section 2(a) of the *Charter*.[98] The Ktunaxa believe that the Great Bear Spirit dwells in a section of Jumbo Valley in British Columbia, known to the community as Qat'muk, but that the construction and operation of a ski resort in the area would cause the spirit to leave. They argued that if the Bear Spirit was forced out of the area, many of their rituals would be emptied of meaning and their spiritual and material well-being would be harmed. The Court rejected the Ktunaxa's claim, although the two judgments, one by McLachlin CJ and Rowe J and the other by Moldaver J, followed different paths to this conclusion.

A majority of the Court's members, in a judgment written jointly by McLachlin CJ and Rowe J, accepted that the Ktunaxa have a sincere belief that the construction of the resort would lead to the departure of the Great Bear Spirit. However, the majority thought that, while section 2(a) protects the individual's (or group's) freedom to hold and manifest religious beliefs, it does not protect "the object of beliefs" or "the spiritual focal point of worship" from state action that might harm or undermine its spiritual significance.[99] In this case, said the majority, the Ktunaxa were seeking to "protect Grizzly Bear Spirit itself and the

---

97   See Natasha Bakht, "Objection, Your Honour! Accommodating *Niqab*-Wearing Women in Courtrooms" in Ralph Grillo et al, eds, *Legal Practice and Cultural Diversity* (Burlington, VT: Ashgate, 2009) 115 at 129: "it should not be forgotten that there are circumstances where judges will take evidence without being able to see the witness's face: for example, where evidence is taken over the telephone or where the judge is visually impaired."

98   *Ktunaxa Nation v British Columbia (Forests, Lands and Natural Resource Operations)*, 2017 SCC 54 [*Ktunaxa*]. The Ktunaxa also argued that the province had failed to fulfill its obligations to consult properly with the community under s 35 of the *Constitution Act, 1982*, before approving the development.

99   *Ibid* at paras 70–71.

subjective spiritual meaning they derive from it" and not simply their freedom to believe in the spirit or to pursue practices related to it.[100] In other words, the state's approval of the ski resort did not amount to an interference with the ability of the group to hold or manifest their beliefs, even though the development would nullify the spiritual meaning or significance of their practices.

The concurring judgment, written by Moldaver J, rejected this narrow reading of the scope of section 2(a) and held that the state's decision interfered with the Ktunaxa's religious freedom under section 2(a) because it made their spiritual rituals meaningless or empty.[101] The religious practice, said Moldaver J, must be understood from the perspective of the individual adherent or spiritual community if section 2(a) is to protect religious life and the vitality of religious community. Yet, at the limitations stage of the analysis, Moldaver J held that the minister's decision to approve the development was reasonable and amounted to a justified limit on the freedom.[102] He accepted that the minister had properly considered the competing claims and "reasonably" determined that the public interest in proceeding with the development (in accordance with the minister's statutory mandate) outweighed the religious interests of the Ktuxana.[103] In deciding that the minister's assessment of the competing civic and spiritual interests was reasonable,

---

100 *Ibid* at para 71.

101 *Ibid* at para 118: "[W]here state conduct renders a person's sincerely held religious beliefs devoid of all religious significance, this infringes a person's right to religious freedom. Religious beliefs have spiritual significance for the believer. When this significance is taken away by state action, the person can no longer act in accordance with his or her *religious* beliefs, constituting an infringement of s. 2(a)." The concurring judgment continued at para 118: "That is exactly what happened in this case. The Minister's decision to approve the ski resort will render all of the Ktunaxa's religious beliefs related to Grizzly Bear Spirit devoid of any spiritual significance. Accordingly, the Ktunaxa will be unable to perform songs, rituals or ceremonies in recognition of Grizzly Bear Spirit in a manner that has any religious significance for them."

102 The concurring judgment applied the test set out in *Dore*, above note 57, for administrative decisions affecting *Charter* rights.

103 Above note 98 at para 119: "[T]he Minister proportionately balanced the Ktunaxa's s. 2(a) right with the relevant statutory objectives: to administer Crown land and dispose of it in the public interest. The Minister was faced with two options: approve the development of the ski resort or grant the Ktunaxa a right to exclude others from constructing permanent structures on over 50 square kilometres of Crown land. This placed the Minister in a difficult, if not impossible, position. If he granted this right of exclusion to the Ktunaxa, this would significantly hamper, if not prevent, him from fulfilling his statutory objectives. In the end, it is apparent that he determined that the fulfillment of his statutory mandate prevented him from giving the Ktunaxa the veto right that they were seeking."

Moldaver J attached significant weight to the government's property interests. In his view, granting to the Ktunaxa "a power to veto development over the land" would be to give them "a significant property interest in Qat'muk—namely, a power to exclude others from constructing permanent structures" on land "the public in fact owns," which "is not a minimal or negligible restraint on public ownership."[104] And so, while Moldaver J did not deny section 2(a) protection to the objects of belief (and sacred sites), his approach to limits on the right under section 1—emphasizing the importance of property rights—had the same effect as the majority decision of denying protection to Indigenous claims involving spiritual sites that are not directly under their control.

In the background of the case was an unresolved land claim in relation to Qat'muk/Jumbo Valley. The negotiations concerning the ski resort sought to address this claim. However, the majority noted that in the case before them there was no evidence offered concerning the land claim and so accepted that they were not in a position to make a judgment about the merits of such a claim. And "with respect to the section 2(a) claim," the majority were clear that "the Ktunaxa stand in the same position as non-Aboriginal litigants" and that the Court could not take into account any claim the Ktunaxa might have to this land.[105]

---

104 *Ibid* at para 150. Justice Moldaver continues: "The public in this case includes an Aboriginal group, the Shuswap Indian Band, that supports the development—a fact which the Minister explicitly took into consideration in his reasons." And at para 152: "This power would permit the Ktunaxa to dictate the use of the land—namely, preventing any permanent structures from being constructed—so that it does not conflict with their religious belief in the sacred nature of Qat'muk. A religious group would therefore be able to regulate the use of a vast expanse of public land so that it conforms to its religious belief."

105 *Ibid* at para 58. Also in the background of the case was the dramatic shift in the Ktunaxa's position regarding the development after almost twenty years of negotiation. The Ktunaxa's stated priorities during this extended period of negotiation were to ensure that any disturbance of the grizzly bear population was minimal, to protect hunting and trapping rights, to acquire outright ownership (fee simple) of an area of land, and to receive payment in lieu of the transfer/recognition of property rights. Offers went back and forth between the parties during this period. Changes were made to the development plan to limit the impact on the bear population. An offer of land and money was also made. However, after years of negotiations, the community informed the developer and the minister that they could not consent to the project in any form. An Elder and knowledge keeper had told the community that he had had a dream several years before in which it had been revealed to him that the bear spirit would abandon the area if the development proceeded. After being informed of this revelation or vision, the Ktunaxa's representatives took the position that there could be no development on these lands. The Court described the change in the community's position without any hint of criticism or doubt about its sincerity and insisted that it played no role in

The two judgments follow, at least formally, the steps of the standard model of *Charter* adjudication: the court determines first whether there is a breach of the right and second, if there is a breach, whether the civic interest (that underlies the restriction) outweighs the religious interest. However, the majority and dissenting judgments, in different ways, are able to avoid engaging in any form of balancing of competing interests.

The concurring judgment, in its determination that the minister's balancing of the competing civic and religious claims was reasonable, attaches great, perhaps overwhelming, importance to property rights, including those of the state. The majority dismissed the Ktunaxa's claim at the first stage of the analysis because it found that section 2(a) does not protect the objects of worship from state regulation. The rule established by the majority only matters when the spiritual group does not have control over relevant spaces or properties. An individual or group may engage in religious rituals on land that they own but they ordinarily have no right under section 2(a) to do so on property owned by another or to require another to use their property in a particular way. Property rights (including those of the Crown) then serve as the baseline for section 2(a) claims, such that any claim that might directly affect the property rights of another will fall outside the scope of section 2(a) protection. The consequence of this is the denial of section 2(a) protection to important elements of Indigenous spiritual/cultural practices that are tied to privately owned land or land claimed by the Crown. The rule in the *Ktunaxa* case rests on a Christian or monotheistic understanding of religious practice, in which the central rituals are concerned with the worship of a divine power or being—an otherworldly spirit—and are not tied to the physical world.[106]

Property rights provide the infrastructure for the private sphere within which individuals are free to practise their faith. In this way

---

their decision. The late revelation of this belief, though, may have been relevant to the question of whether the minister's assessment of the competing claims was reasonable.

106 However, as John Borrows notes, "Ktunaxa people do not worship grizzly bears or the land"; "[t]hese objects are means to other ends, practicing and manifesting religious belief" (John Borrows, "Beyond Experience? Objectivity, Indigeneity & Freedom of Religion" in J Hewitt and R Moon, eds, *Indigenous Spirituality and Religious Freedom* (Toronto: University of Toronto Press, 2024). Borrows continues: "The land and grizzly spirit … are means of holding and manifesting commitments to a broader religious belief system. It is deeply offensive to decontextualize Ktunaxa's religious claims by primarily characterizing them through objects (land or spirits), rather than responsibilities to hold and practice that belief." Borrows's description of the practice exposes the difficulty with (and the artificiality of) the Court's attempt to distinguish the ritual or practice from the ritual's object.

property rights are essential to the separation of religion and politics that is central to the Anglo-American conception of religious freedom. Property rights are treated by the courts as a baseline for section 2(a) claims not simply because they are central to the liberal-democratic political order (tied to ideas of privacy and liberty), but because in a democratic society religious claims must be confined to that which can be treated as private—as personal to the individual or internal to the religious community. The priority given to property rights (and more generally to existing or recognized individual rights or interests) might have been uncontroversial had the claim been made by a non-Indigenous group that had no special relationship or claim to the land. Imagine, for example, if a religious group believed that skyscrapers were the modern equivalent of the Tower of Babel and objected to the construction of such buildings in their city because they believed it would bring God's wrath down upon the community. There can be little doubt that their religious freedom claim would fail because it would directly and significantly (and not just incidentally) impact the rights and interests of others and, in this particular example, would prevent the private property owner from making lawful use of its property.

The Court in *Ktunaxa* seemed to assume that the state's right to make decisions about the use of *its* property is the same as that of a private owner, and that neither owner can be required under section 2(a) to compromise its property use to accommodate the religious practices of others in the community. Yet when the state *owns* a particular property, its possession or control is meant to serve the public interest, and so its control over a particular area of land may be subject to different limits. The state may decide that it is in the public interest that private citizens be excluded from a particular state-owned property (such as a military facility or the office of a government employee), but this does not mean that, as a general matter, the government's decisions about its property use should be insulated from all religious accommodation claims under the *Charter*.[107] The majority's exclusion of "the object of worship" from the protection of section 2(a) appears to be a crude device to relieve the

---

107 The Court may be hesitant to second guess the choices made by the state about how it uses its property or the state's judgment about when accommodation might significantly impair that use, but that is not the same as saying that state ownership precludes any claim of access or accommodation. Under section 2(b) of the *Charter*, the freedom of expression right, the Canadian courts have said that individuals have a right to communicate on state-owned property that is ordinarily or traditionally open to the public, and that this right can be limited only for substantial and pressing reasons. In other words, ownership does not mean that state property is insulated from all claims of access under the *Charter*. See *Montréal (City) v 2952-1366 Québec Inc*, 2005 SCC 62.

Court from having to decide whether the spiritual practice should be accommodated on state-owned property.

The Court in *Ktunaxa* said that the section 2(a) claim should be addressed without taking any account of the particular circumstances of the Ktunaxa—of its traditional and spiritual connection to this land—since no land claim was before the Court. But even if accommodation can only be made for practices that are personal to the individual or internal to the group, the line between the personal (or communal) sphere of spiritual life and the civic/secular sphere of political action is neither firm nor bright and can be shifted in minor ways to protect the practices of religious minorities. Given the pragmatic character of accommodation (which is based on concerns about the status and vitality of religious/cultural communities), the Court's consideration of the Ktunaxa's claim should not have been shorn of context, including (1) the basis for the Crown's claim to land, which is about territorial sovereignty and the common good rather than private use; (2) the Indigenous community's connection to land; and (3) the historic role of the state in suppressing the community's cultural and spiritual practices.[108] Instead of excluding in advance a significant element of Indigenous spiritual/cultural life from the scope of section 2(a), the majority in *Ktunaxa* might have considered whether space should be made for these practices at the margins of law and policy (when they do not noticeably compromise the public interest or the rights of others) taking into account the group's particular circumstances, including its historical exclusion and marginalization and its spiritual connection to the natural world.[109]

At the same time, it is important to recognize that because section 2(a) can only require the state to make minor adjustments to public policy or land use, it cannot play a significant role in the larger project of reconciliation. Religious freedom can provide space for religious communities to operate according to their own norms; but it cannot support larger claims of sovereignty or autonomous governance and it cannot address disputes about the control of land. In *Ktunaxa*, the justices saw the section 2(a) claim not simply as a request for accommodation but as

---

108 Benjamin L Berger in "Is State Neutrality Bad for Indigenous Religious Freedom?" in Hewitt & Moon, above note 106, observes that "[a] contemporary call for even-handedness as amongst religions, and as between religion and non-religion, effaces the historic suppression of Indigenous religions."

109 As Natasha Bakht points out in "Indigenous Religious Rights: Reconciling Religious Views and Decolonizing Section 2(a) of the *Charter*" in Hewitt & Moon, above note 106, the Ktunaxa's claim would not have the effect of excluding others from the use or enjoyment of the land in its natural state.

a claim to control a particular area of land, or as a claim of sovereignty, that could not be reconciled with the authority of the state.

The failure of the courts to give religious freedom protection to important Indigenous practices may stem not from a narrow conception of religion but rather from a recognition of the limits of religious freedom in a democratic political community.[110] As a practical matter, religious freedom can protect only certain elements or dimensions of spiritual life — those beliefs/practices that can be viewed or treated as personal to the individual or as internal to the spiritual group. However, the line between the spiritual and civic spheres of life, or between civic and spiritual elements of a religious belief system, can be adjusted in small ways as the courts seek to make space for religious practices without interfering with the state's ability to advance the public interest. The separation of religion and politics involves a pragmatic reconciliation of civic action and spiritual life. It is important, though, not to expect too much from a constitutional right to religious freedom. The freedom cannot protect all practices, rituals, and ways of living from state interference. And it cannot do the significant work that is needed to advance reconciliation, settle land claims, or support self-government. However, if religious freedom (and the separation of the spiritual and civic spheres) is about ensuring space for personal and collective spiritual life within a democratic political community, then it should sometimes require the compromise of state policy, including the state's control or use of Crown land.[111]

---

110 In the past, the courts have sometimes limited the protection of Indigenous religious life by interpreting particular practices narrowly or by downplaying the importance of their communal character, as in the case of *Jack and Charlie v The Queen*, [1985] 2 SCR 332, in which the Supreme Court held that two Indigenous men, who were charged with hunting out of season, could have performed a particular ritual using frozen deer meat rather than fresh meat. For a discussion of this case see John Borrows, "Living Law on a Living Earth: Aboriginal Religion, Law, and the Constitution" in R Moon, ed, *Law and Religious Pluralism in Canada* (Vancouver: UBC Press, 2008) at 161.

111 The most frequently made criticism of the Supreme Court's decision in *Ktuxana* echoes a familiar and more general criticism of the Anglo-American understanding of religious freedom. The Court's narrow or "Protestant" conception of religious freedom, which is focused on the individual's belief or commitment and their personal relationship with a transcendent God, is said to have the effect of denying meaningful protection to Indigenous and other spiritual systems that emphasize ritual and community life and that recognize a spiritual presence in the natural world. See, for example, Winnifred Fallers Sullivan et al, *Politics of Religious Freedom* (Chicago: University of Chicago Press, 2015), which discusses and critiques the Christian/Protestant understanding of religion (as private and personal) that has shaped the Western commitment to religious freedom. See

K. THE QUEBEC BAN ON CIVIL SERVANTS WEARING RELIGIOUS SYMBOLS

In 2019, the Quebec government banned many civil servants, including police officers, prison guards, and teachers, from wearing religious symbols at work.[112] Several reasons were given for the ban. First, when a civil servant wears a religious symbol that is associated with a particular religious belief system, their actions may be ascribed to the state, which may then be viewed as religiously partisan. Second, when a civil servant wears a religious symbol, they may be seen as promoting their faith, which is incompatible with the requirement of state neutrality. Third, when a civil servant displays their religious affiliation, they may be perceived by others as non-neutral or partial in the performance of their duties.

The arguments in support of the ban are at best weak and at worst disingenuous. To begin with the first claim, religious symbols are worn as an expression of personal faith or group identity. When a civil servant wears a religious symbol, it is very unlikely that citizens will think that the government is supporting a specific religion, particularly since relatively few civil servants wear religious symbols and the few who do come from a variety of religious groups.

As to the second reason, it is not obvious that simply wearing a religious symbol will promote a particular religion. If a civil servant

---

also John Borrows, above note 110 at 168: "the Constitution will have difficulty protecting Anishinabek religious beliefs and practices if they are outside the law's central commitments to individual choice, autonomy, privacy, and personal conviction. Unfortunately, when it comes to beliefs about the Earth, Anishinabek religion is largely outside the Constitution's informing commitments—they are alien to Western law, politics, and religion."

112 *An Act respecting the laicity of the State*, SQ 2019, c 12. A number of European countries have banned the wearing of religious head coverings in a variety of settings. Many of these restrictions have been challenged under the *European Convention on Human Rights*. However, in each case the European Court of Human Rights [ECtHR] has upheld the ban, often relying on "the margin of appreciation," which gives state law makers some leeway in determining the need for a particular law within the cultural context of the particular political community. See, for example, *Dahlab v Switzerland*, ECtHR (February 15, 2001), upholding a restriction on elementary school teachers wearing the hijab. The court held that because a teacher is a representative of the state and because elementary students are impressionable, the limit on religious practice was reasonable. Other judgments upholding restrictions on face or head coverings include *Leyla Sahin v Turkey* (Application no 44774/98), ECtHR; *Kervanci v France* (Application no 31645/04), ECtHR; *Kurtulmuş v Turkey* (Application no 65500/01), ECtHR; *R Singh v France*, (Application no 27561/08), ECtHR.

wears a religious symbol, others will know that they belong to a particular group or faith tradition, but as long as a civil servant does not actively promote their faith (which they could do without the display of a religious symbol), their form of dress should be viewed simply as a personal practice—an expression of their religious identity or membership. As the *Bouchard-Taylor Report* observed: "Successful cohabitation in a diversified society demands that we learn to perceive as normal an array of identity-related differences."[113]

The idea that wearing a religious symbol involves promoting a religion may reflect a Christian perspective on symbols and symbol wearing. While the crucifix and the cross are important symbols in Christianity of the suffering and resurrection of Jesus, in most versions of Christianity the believer is not required to wear a symbol of any kind. And so, when a Christian chooses to wear a visible symbol of their faith, they may be seen not just as signalling a personal faith commitment but also as advertising or even promoting their faith to others. In other faith traditions, however, individuals are required or expected to wear religious dress as an expression of their faith. Those who wear these "symbols" (or adhere to these practices) do so not to promote their faith but to fulfill a personal obligation or to signal their membership in a particular religious community.

The other reason offered in support of the ban is that civil servants who wear religious symbols will not be, or at least will not appear to be, impartial in the exercise of their civic responsibilities. The wearing of a turban or kippa makes visible the individual's commitment to a particular spiritual belief system. The assumption is that a devoutly religious individual may be inclined to favour other members of their religious group or to apply the tenets of their faith, rather than state law when performing their duties. But does wearing a religious symbol mean that the individual is more likely to ignore their legal responsibilities and rely on religious law? There is no reason to think so. The most that can be said is that some in the community might think there is a link; but this perception rests on prejudice rather than experience. According to the *Bouchard-Taylor Report*:

> Why should we think that the person who wears a religious sign would be less likely to display impartiality, professionalism and loyalty to the institution than the person who does not wear such a sign? Why, therefore, dwell on external displays of faith? Should we not also demand of State employees that they relinquish any conviction of conscience? It would obviously be absurd to do so. Why think *a priori* that people

---

113   Gérard Bouchard & Charles Taylor, *Building the Future: A Time for Reconciliation* (Quebec City: Government of Quebec, 2008) at 150.

who display their religious affiliation are less likely to take things into consideration than those who do not externalize their convictions of conscience or who externalize them in a much less visible manner (the wearing of the Catholic cross comes to mind)? Why refuse one person the presumption of impartiality and grant it to the other one?[114]

There are also practical challenges in enforcing a ban on religious symbols. A court must decide whether an item of clothing or jewellery is religious or symbolizes a religious commitment. Would the traditional dress of the Old Order Mennonites be seen as religious dress? Mennonites are required to dress in a manner that is plain and not ostentatious. However, the fulfillment of this obligation has taken a particular form that is now identified with the religious community. The simple dress of the Old Order Mennonites, which is based on peasant dress styles in the eighteenth and nineteenth centuries, has become a marker of membership in the group. Does this style of clothing amount to a religious "symbol," or is it simply the particular way in which the members of the community satisfy a more general religious duty? What about the wig worn by an Orthodox Jewish woman, who is forbidden to expose her hair? Is her wig a form of religious dress or simply the established way in which she fulfills her duty of modesty? It seems unlikely that her wig would be classified as religious dress, because it is not the only way in which Orthodox Jewish women fulfill their duty of modesty (they may also wear scarves or hats) and because wigs are worn for many nonreligious reasons—and most often for reasons other than modesty. The hijab, like many other forms of religious dress, is worn to fulfill a duty of modesty. It has become the established or conventional way in which this duty is fulfilled, and as a result it has also become a marker of group identity for those inside and outside the group. However, because wigs and headscarves are worn for nonreligious reasons, it may be necessary, in applying the *laïcité* law, to determine why a wig or headscarf is being worn in a particular case—whether it is for religious or other reasons.[115]

The significant and often regressive political role of the Roman Catholic church in Quebec prior to the Quiet Revolution in the 1960s may have contributed to a general wariness in the province about the visibility of religion in the public sphere. However, at least some of the support for the *Laïcité Act* seems to rest on concerns about the growth of religious minorities in the province. As long as anxiety about national identity

---

114 *Ibid.*

115 As noted earlier, Locke, above note 2, argued that religious freedom is breached when an activity that is otherwise lawful is banned when it is performed for religious reasons.

and the cohesiveness of the cultural community remains significant in Quebec, the presence of identifiable minority groups, which are thought to be resistant to integration into the larger civic culture or committed to values that are incompatible with that culture, will be regarded as a threat to civil society.

While the proposed ban focuses on the visibility of religion in the public sphere, its appeal is based on anxieties about religious pluralism in the province. It seems likely that the main purpose of the ban on conspicuous religious symbols is to limit Muslim visibility or practice and that the ban is framed in general terms to avoid the complaint that it is discriminatory. The concern most often expressed by non-Muslims about the hijab is that it represents a particular form of Islam that is reactionary or austere in character. In other words, the concern behind the ban is not the religious or spiritual nature of religious symbols but rather the civic meaning or significance of particular symbols. According to this view, when a woman covers her head in this way, she is signalling to others her submission to the men in her community—even though there is plenty of evidence that women in the West who wear the hijab most often do so for reasons such as modesty and identity.[116] If the goal is to protect women from male domination, a law that excludes these women from different forms of employment will be entirely counterproductive.

While the ban on religious symbols focuses on the visibility of religion in the public sphere and claims to be about defending state neutrality, it is a repudiation of religious freedom that stands only because of the Quebec government's use of section 33, the notwithstanding clause, of the *Charter* to insulate the law from *Charter* review.[117]

---

116 See Joan Wallach Scott, *The Politics of the Veil* (Princeton: Princeton University Press, 2007).

117 Section 33 provides as follows: (1) Parliament or the legislature of a province may expressly declare in an Act of Parliament or of the legislature, as the case may be, that the Act or a provision thereof shall operate notwithstanding a provision included in section 2 or sections 7 to 15 of this Charter. (2) An Act or a provision of an Act in respect of which a declaration made under this section is in effect shall have such operation as it would have but for the provision of this Charter referred to in the declaration. (3) A declaration made under subsection (1) shall cease to have effect five years after it comes into force or on such earlier date as may be specified in the declaration." In *Hak v Attorney General of Quebec*, 2021 QCCS 1466, a Quebec Superior Court judge rejected a challenge brought against the Act. Just prior to the publication of this book, the Quebec Court of Appeal, in *Hak v Attorney General of Quebec*, 2024 QCA dismissed the appeal from the Superior Court decision.

L. BALANCING AND LINE-DRAWING

Under section 2(a), religious beliefs/practices are sometimes insulated from political contest not because they are intrinsically valuable but instead because they are a source of meaning and duty for their adherents. Religious commitment connects the individual to a community of believers and orients them in the world. The ties of religious community can sometimes be as deep and significant to the individual as the ties of family. This is what is meant when religious practices are described as deeply held or rooted. The separation of religion and politics rests on the idea that religion is a matter of cultural identity rather than contestable political opinion and that the restriction of a religious group's practices, and more generally the marginalization of the group, whether intended or not, can harm individual adherents and undermine social stability.

The courts have said that section 2(a) is breached any time the state restricts a religious practice in a nontrivial way. According to the courts, the state must justify the restriction under section 1 of the Charter (using the *Oakes* test),[118] which involves a balancing of competing interests: the individual's freedom to practise their religion weighed against the state's ability to advance what it understands to be the public good. However, when deciding whether a particular limit on religious practice is justified or whether accommodation should be made for a particular practice, it is not clear how the courts are to balance these competing religious and civic interests.

From a secular or public perspective, a religious belief/practice has no necessary value; indeed, it is said that a court should take no position concerning its value—that the court should remain neutral on the question of religious truth. The belief/practice is significant, from a civic-secular perspective, because it matters "deeply" to the group and its members or because it is part of their cultural identity. But there is no way to balance this value against the purpose or value of the restrictive law. The secular concern is not with the belief/practice itself but rather with its importance and meaning to the group's members and with the potential impact of its restriction on the position of the group in the larger society.

The requirement that the state make some accommodation for religious practices (and treat these practices as the equivalent of group traits) is intended to prevent or limit the marginalization of minority religious

---

118 *R v Oakes* [1986] 1 SCR 103.

groups.[119] While a religious group will think that its practices should be protected because they are true, in making its case before the courts the group must adopt a detached perspective and argue that its practices should be protected because it *believes* them to be true—because their beliefs and practices are important to them. Yet it is unclear the extent to which this belief—its significance to the religious believer or group—can justify limiting the state's ability to pursue a particular objective. This may account for the courts' unwillingness to accommodate religious beliefs/ practices except in very minor ways. In the cases discussed in this chapter and in Chapter 5, the courts go through the motions of applying the *Oakes* test and balancing the competing religious and civic interests, but invariably find ways to discount the importance of the religious practice or the impact of the restriction on the practice.

Religious practices (forms of worship) that are "personal" in character are sometimes indirectly or incidentally limited by state action. In such cases, the courts may require the state to compromise in a minor way its pursuit of a particular objective to make space for the religious practice, without directly challenging the state's authority to govern in the public interest and to establish public norms.[120] For example, the government may have decided on a particular route for a new highway only to discover that its preferred route runs through an area that is sacred to an Indigenous group.[121] In such a case it may be possible for the state to advance its purpose as (or almost as) effectively in a different way, through different means, so that it does not interfere with the religious practice or interest. If that is so, then it may be said that the law makers should have taken into account the interests and circumstances of the different religious (and other) groups in the community and designed the law (selected a highway route) so as to avoid unnecessary interference with a religious belief or practice. Indeed, it may reasonably be asked whether the state would have enacted the same law (adopted the same means) had the religious practices of a more politically influential group been similarly affected.[122] It is important to recognize, though,

---

119   In this way religious freedom is different from rights, such as freedom of expression, which is protected because there is value in the activity of expression (its contribution to democracy, knowledge, individual agency).

120   In the discussion that follows I have drawn a distinction between indirect and direct restrictions on religious practice. I recognize, though, that these two categories are sometimes difficult to distinguish and might more accurately be viewed as part of a continuum.

121   Such a claim was rejected in the US Supreme Court judgment of *Lyng v Northwest Indian Cemetery Protective Association*, 485 US 439 (1988).

122   See Christopher L Eisgruber & Lawrence G Sager, *Religious Freedom and the Constitution* (Cambridge, MA: Harvard University Press, 2010). However, they

that even in the case of what might be described as an indirect conflict between law and religion, the adoption of different means will often detract to some extent from the law's ability to advance a particular policy. In the example given, an alternative highway route may add to construction costs or detract from ideal road conditions.[123] The issue for the court in cases involving an indirect or incidental conflict between law and religious practice is whether the state can pursue its objective as (or almost as) effectively in another way that will not interfere to the same extent with the religious practice. When applying this test and determining whether a religious practice should be accommodated, there can be reasonable disagreement about the extent to which government policy should be compromised.

Sometimes, however, the conflict between law and religious practice is more direct, in the sense that the law is pursuing a policy (a public value) that is directly at odds with a religious practice. In such a case the conflict between the law and the religious practice cannot be avoided or reduced by the state simply adjusting the means it has chosen to advance its civic purpose. If law makers have decided, for example, that corporal punishment of children is wrong and should be banned or that sexual-orientation discrimination is wrong and ought to be prohibited, how is a court to decide whether an exception to these norms should be granted to a religious individual who believes that corporal punishment is mandated by God or that same-sex relationships are sinful and should not be supported?

The issue for the court in the corporal punishment example is not whether physical discipline is effective or whether the value or utility of physical discipline outweighs its physical and emotional harm to children. Nor is the issue whether parents should have the right to make judgments about the welfare of their children without state interference, which if resolved in favour of parental autonomy would result in the striking down of the ban and not just the creation of an exception for some parents. In other words, the court is not questioning the public norm and considering whether physical discipline is, in fact, sometimes right or justified. Instead, the issue is whether some parents—*religious*

---

mistakenly believe that this test can be applied in a way that does not depend on the special character or value of religion. For an effective critique of their position, see Jeremy Webber, "Understanding the Religion in Freedom of Religion" in Peter Cane, Carolyn Evans, & Zoë Robinson, eds, *Law and Religion in Theoretical and Historical Context* (Cambridge: Cambridge University Press, 2008) 26.

123 Conflict may occur more frequently in the case of "lived" religions that put greater emphasis on public ritual or that govern significant elements of the individual's life. For a discussion, see Lori G Beaman, "Is Religious Freedom Impossible in Canada?" (2010) 6 *Law, Culture and Human* 1.

parents—should be exempted from an otherwise justified ban on physical discipline because they believe that God has mandated them to discipline their children in a way that the law has forbidden. The court must decide whether space should be given to a different normative view—a view that the legislature has rejected. In such a case, then, the court's task is not to decide the proper balance or trade-off between competing interests or values (in accordance with the ordinary justification process under section 1 of the *Charter*) but is instead to determine if certain beliefs or practices should be treated as personal to the adherent or internal to the religious group. However, in the case of a ban on corporal punishment or a ban on sexual-orientation discrimination in the provision of market services, the conflicting religious belief/practice cannot be viewed as simply a private matter, given the significant impact of these actions on others—on children or retail customers.

Despite their formal commitment to "reasonable accommodation" or "proportionality" analyses, the Canadian courts have been unwilling to require the state to compromise its policies in any significant way. While the courts do not engage in anything that could properly be described as the "balancing" of competing public and religious interests (in which the state's objectives might sometimes be subordinated to the claims of a religious community), they have sometimes sought to create space for religious practices at the margins of law, by adjusting the boundary between spheres of religious life and civic action. The courts, in seeking to protect religious life, may sometimes carve out "private" space for a religious practice (that is viewed as personal to the individual) by drawing the line between spiritual and civic life so that the practice is exempted from the application of an otherwise justified law. A police uniform requirement may have the effect of excluding individuals who wear head coverings for religious reasons, or a school schedule may not take account of the holidays of some religious groups. An exemption to a uniform requirement made for an individual who wears a turban or hijab as an expression of their faith or identity will have an impact on state policy, but only a minor one. Allowing a government employee to take a day off work for a religious holiday that is not included in the list of statutory holidays will not disrupt the unit's operations in any significant way. These practices may be viewed as personal and treated as private since they are not concerned directly with public policy and do not noticeably compromise the state's objectives.[124] Accommodation, though, cannot be extended to beliefs or practices that explicitly address

---

124 Moreover, we know that police and other official uniform requirements or statutory holidays often reflect, or already take account of, the cultural and religious practices of historically dominant groups.

civic matters (the rights or welfare of others in the community) and are directly at odds with democratically adopted public policies.[125]

Because there is no principled way for the courts to determine the appropriate "balance" between democratically selected public values or purposes and the spiritual beliefs or practices of a religious individual or community (an alternative normative system), the insulation of religion from public decision making will be at best minor. However, this pragmatic response to the competing claims of state policy and religious practice does not fit well with the court's commitment to resolving issues in a principled way, a commitment that underpins the legitimacy of judicial review.

---

125 A much-publicized and highly controversial accommodation dispute arose several years ago at York University in Toronto. A male student, doing an online course, informed the instructor that for religious reasons he could not participate in a required group project that involved meeting and interacting with female students. The response to the student's claim seemed to depend on whether one saw his refusal to meet with female students as simply a personal spiritual practice—like praying at certain times or refusing to eat pork—or instead as a position about gender equality—that women are a source of temptation or that women should not participate in university programs. Those who saw it as a personal spiritual practice thought it should be accommodated, since accommodation would have no significant impact on others. Those who saw it as a moral/political position thought that no accommodation should be granted, even though accommodation would have only a minor impact on others in the course. For a discussion of the case see R Moon, "Religious Accommodation and Its Limits: The York University Case" (2014) 23 *Const Forum* 1.

CHAPTER 4

CONSCIENTIOUS OBJECTIONS

A. INTRODUCTION

The term "conscience" is used in two different ways in discussions about freedom of conscience and religion. Sometimes conscience is contrasted with religion and refers to fundamental beliefs or commitments that are not part of a religious or spiritual system.[1] "Freedom of conscience," in this sense, is the subject of Chapter 7. Other times the term refers to a particular kind of accommodation claim. In most religious accommodation cases an individual (or group) asks to be exempted from a law that prevents them from engaging in a religious practice — for example, from wearing religious dress or keeping religious holidays. In conscientious objection cases, however, the individual asks to be exempted from a law that requires them to *perform* an act that they regard as immoral or sinful. In many of these cases the claimant wishes to be excused from performing an act that is not itself immoral but that supports or facilitates (what they see as) the immoral action of others, and so makes them complicit in this immorality.[2]

---

1   The term "freedom of conscience" was once used interchangeably with "freedom of religion" to refer to the individual's freedom to hold beliefs that were spiritual or moral in character. At this earlier time, the moral beliefs of most individuals were rooted in a religious system. Freedom of conscience, though, is now viewed as an alternative to, or extension of, religious freedom.

2   The two uses of the term are easily confused since many "conscience" claims, in the first sense of the term, involve conscientious objections. Conscience (in

The issue in conscientious objection cases is not, as the courts sometimes claim, the reasonable balance between the individual's religious interests and the interests of others in the community but is instead whether the individual's religiously based objection to performing a particular act should be viewed as an expression of personal religious commitment that ought to be accommodated, provided this can be done without noticeable harm to others, or instead as a (religiously grounded) civic position or action that falls outside the scope of religious freedom protection and may be the subject of legal regulation. An individual's spiritual practices are both insulated and excluded from political decision making. However, their beliefs concerning civic issues, such as the rights and interests of others or the just arrangement of social relations, even if grounded in a religious system, must be subject to the give-and-take of ordinary politics.[3]

In determining whether a particular (conscientious) objection should be viewed as a personal/spiritual matter or instead as a civic/political position, two factors may be relevant. The first is whether the individual is being required to perform the particular act (to which they object) because they hold a special position not held by others, notably some form of public appointment. For example, when the definition of civil marriage was changed to enable same-sex couples to marry, a number of civil marriage commissioners objected on religious grounds to performing such marriages.[4] While some provinces agreed to accommodate the commissioners' religious objections and excuse them from performing same-sex marriage ceremonies, other provinces were unwilling to do so and instructed their commissioners to perform these marriages or face dismissal. The objecting commissioners claimed that in performing this role they would be facilitating the "immoral" actions of others. However, the commissioners were required to take such action

---

the first sense), in contrast to religion, does not ordinarily involve practices or rituals—manifestations of belief. Laws sometimes restrict the manifestation of (religious) belief, but for obvious reasons they do not simply or directly restrict the holding of belief. However, belief may be interfered with when the state compels an individual to act in a way that is contrary to their beliefs. For this reason, most freedom of conscience cases involve a conscientious objection to performing an act required by the state—such as serving in the military.

3   See the discussion in Chapter 2 of the role of religious values in public decision making.

4   Marriage and divorce, including the definition of marriage, falls within the jurisdiction of the Government of Canada, under the *Constitution Act, 1867* (UK), 30 & 31 Vict, c 3, reprinted in RSC 1985, Appendix II, No 5, s 91(26). However, the solemnization of marriage falls within provincial jurisdiction under s 92(12).

only because they held a special public position and could avoid any "complicity" simply by giving up this position.

The other factor is the relative remoteness/proximity of the act that the objector is required to perform from the act they consider to be inherently immoral. When the act the objector is required to perform is far removed from the "immoral" act, we are more likely to see their objection as a political position rather than an expression of personal religious commitment. An obvious case of remoteness is the objection to paying taxes on the grounds that some of the government's revenue is used to fund the military or to support abortion services. The courts have invariably rejected such claims.[5] In contrast, the courts have generally viewed the objection to compulsory military service during war (on the grounds that it is morally wrong to kill another person) as an expression of personal conscience that should be accommodated, because it requires the individual to engage directly in acts they regard as immoral.[6] The courts have taken this view, even though the objector, presumably, believes that it is wrong for anyone to go to war, and even though the exemption may place a greater burden of public service on other members of the community.

---

5   See, for example *R v Prior*, [1988] 2 FC 311, in which the court dismissed the claim of a member of the Quaker faith who sought to withhold a portion of her income tax. A complaint was later made by Dr Prior to the Human Rights Commission under the Optional Protocol to the *International Covenant on Civil and Political Rights: Dr JP v Canada*, Communication No 446/1991. Another example of this might be the argument made by opponents of same-sex marriage in *Reference re Same-Sex Marriage*, 2004 SCC 79, which is discussed in Chapter 3. A number of religious groups argued that the recognition of same-sex marriages would breach religious freedom under the *Charter of Rights and Freedoms*, Part I of the *Constitution Act, 1982*, being Schedule B to the *Canada Act 1982* (UK), 1982, c 11 [*Charter*] because it would undermine the value and meaning of marriage for religious individuals and communities. State recognition of same-sex marriage, it was claimed, would interfere with their religious beliefs and practices and therefore with their *Charter* rights. The Supreme Court of Canada's answer to this was that the redefinition of civil marriage to include same-sex marriage did not interfere with anyone's religious beliefs or practices. The consequence of the change was simply that some individuals had to live in a society that permits others to engage in an activity that they regard as immoral. The individual's ability to practise their faith (their religious freedom) is not restricted merely because public policy is at odds with their beliefs. The individual does not have the "right" to live in a society that accepts all their moral positions.

6   As will be discussed in Chapter 7, governments sometimes have their own, more political, reasons for exempting conscientious objectors from military service. They may be concerned, for example, that conscription will result in acts of civil disobedience, which in times of war may be particularly destabilizing.

In several recent conscientious objection cases, a public official or market service provider objected to serving a same-sex couple and sought to be exempted from anti-discrimination requirements. The claim to exemption in these cases signals a shift in the public role of religious opposition to same-sex relationships. The religious claim that same-sex relationships are immoral or wrongful was, until not long ago, a political position in debates about the restriction of sexual-orientation discrimination and the legal recognition of same-sex relationships. This position, though, was rejected by legislatures and courts, which decided first that same-sex relationships should be protected as a matter of liberty and later that they should be respected or recognized as a matter of equality. In the religious exemption cases, those who consider same-sex relationships to be sinful or immoral now assert the right to be exempted from the application of ordinary law (most often anti-discrimination law). The claimants in these cases are not "directly" challenging the legal recognition of same-sex marriages or sexual-orientation equality but are instead "personally" opposing the law's recognition of such relationships. The public debate about same-sex marriage did not go as they wanted, and so they are now seeking to opt out of the legal ban on sexual-orientation discrimination or to personally reject the legal recognition of same-sex relationships.[7]

B. MARRIAGE COMMISSIONERS AND SAME-SEX MARRIAGES

The question of whether a province can require marriage commissioners to perform same-sex marriages, despite their religious objections, has been addressed by the courts (and tribunals) in a number of cases.

In Saskatchewan, a couple that wishes to be married in a civil ceremony must approach a commissioner in their geographic area to request their services. As noted by the Saskatchewan Court of Appeal, "commissioners are the route—the only route—by which individuals who wish

---

7   Richard Moon, "Why Indiana's 'Anti-Gay' Law Might Sound Familiar," *National Post* (13 April 2015), online: https://nationalpost.com/opinion/richard-moon-why-indianas-anti-gay-law-might-sound-familiar; Douglas NeJaime & Reva Siegel, "Conscience Wars: Complicity-Based Conscience Claims in Religion and Politics" (2015) 124 *Yale LJ* 2516; Richard Moon, "Conscientious Objections by Civil Servants: The Case of Marriage Commissioners and Same-Sex Civil Marriages" in B Berger and R Moon, eds, *Religion and the Exercise of Public Authority* (London: Hart/Bloomsbury, 2016).

to be married by way of a non-religious ceremony may have their union solemnized."[8]

Mr Nichols had been a civil marriage commissioner in Saskatchewan for more than twenty years when the definition of marriage was amended to include same-sex relationships.[9] Following the change, the province's Department of Justice informed all commissioners that they would be required to perform such marriages. Mr Nichols responded by bringing a human rights complaint against the province, in which he argued that the requirement that he perform same-sex marriages amounted to religious discrimination. Mr Nichols considered it morally wrong to officiate the marriage of a same-sex couple and argued that he should not be forced to solemnize such marriages.

Mr Nichols's complaint was dismissed by the Saskatchewan Human Rights Commission (HRC). This dismissal was upheld by the provincial Human Rights Tribunal.[10] Despite the tribunal's insistence that the issue must be resolved through balancing, its judgment did not seem to involve any comparison or weighing of the competing interests of religious freedom and sexual-orientation equality. The tribunal appeared to give complete priority to the same-sex couple's right to equality. In the tribunal's view, even if a same-sex couple could easily find another commissioner to perform their civil marriage, the initial refusal was objectionable and amounted to a significant breach of the right to equality. When the commissioner, in his official capacity, expressed his religious belief to a same-sex couple (and directed them elsewhere), he was considered to have caused them injury.[11]

Mr Nichols's human rights complaint against the Saskatchewan government was still under review by the HRC when he was approached by a same-sex couple who wished to engage his services. Mr Nichols declined to perform the couple's civil ceremony and instead directed them to another commissioner who he thought would be willing to perform the

---

8 *Reference re Marriage Commissioners Appointed Under the Marriage Act*, 2011 SKCA 3 [*Re Marriage Commissioners*]. The provincial Marriage Unit did not assign commissioners to perform particular marriage ceremonies, but instead provided the names and contact information of local commissioners to any couple inquiring about civil marriage services.

9 *The Marriage Act, 1995*, SS 1995, c M-4.1, s 30.

10 *Nichols v Department of Justice, Government of Saskatchewan* (25 October 2006, Sask HRT).

11 According to the tribunal, *ibid*, while Mr Nichols "is free to practice his religion as he chooses, he cannot 'infringe on the rights of others'." However, it appears that the rights of others (of a same-sex couple) are breached whenever a commissioner openly refuses, for religious reasons, to perform a same-sex marriage ceremony.

ceremony. The couple brought a complaint against Mr Nichols under the *Saskatchewan Human Rights Code*,[12] arguing that his refusal to perform the ceremony amounted to sexual-orientation discrimination. The tribunal decided that Mr Nichols had breached the *Code*. This decision was upheld on review by the Saskatchewan Court of Queen's Bench.[13]

In this second case, Mr Nichols argued that his religious beliefs could be accommodated without any impact on the ability of same-sex couples to access the services of a civil marriage commissioner, since there were other commissioners willing to perform same-sex marriages. If a commissioner's personal decision not to perform the marriage had no practical impact on the couple (as long as they were able to quickly find someone else to perform the ceremony), then the "competing" interests of equality and religious freedom did not appear to be in conflict, at least not in any significant way. Nevertheless, the court in this case held that even if a same-sex couple could easily find another commissioner to perform their civil marriage, the initial refusal was objectionable and amounted to a significant breach of the couple's right to equality—an affront to their dignity. This was so even though the refusal was based on the commissioner's sincerely held religious belief—a belief that the court agreed fell within the scope of section 2(a) of the *Canadian Charter of Rights and Freedom*[14] (freedom of religion) protection.[15] When the marriage commissioner told the same-sex couple that he was opposed on religious grounds to their marriage and sent them to another commissioner, he was considered to have caused them injury, even though his refusal to perform the ceremony rested on a protected religious belief. The courts also attached no significance to the fact that other provinces had decided not to require civil marriage commissioners to perform same-sex marriages and instead had introduced a "single entry system," in which those seeking the services of a commissioner applied to a central office, which then assigned a commissioner to perform the marriage. Under such a system, the couple seeking a commissioner would never know if one of the commissioners on the roster had refused to perform their ceremony and so would not experience any harm to their dignity.[16]

---

12   *Saskatchewan Human Rights Code*, SS 1979, c S-24.1 [*Code*].

13   *Nichols v MJ*, 2009 SKQB 299 [*Nichols*].

14   *Canadian Charter of Rights and Freedoms*, Part 1 of the *Constitution Act, 1982*, being Schedule B to the *Canada Act 1982* (UK), 1982, c 11 [*Charter*]

15   *Nichols*, above note 13 at para 57.

16   In the United Kingdom, the claim of a registrar in the London Borough of Islington to be excused from conducting civil partnership ceremonies for same-sex couples ("a purely secular task") was rejected by the courts (and later by the European Court of Human Rights) even though the borough operated a single-entry point system (so that any accommodation of an objecting registrar

In both of these cases the issue of whether a marriage commissioner (who has religious objections) can be required to perform same-sex marriages was framed by the courts as a contest between religious freedom and sexual-orientation equality that must be resolved through the balancing of these competing interests. Yet in both cases the court seemed to give no weight to the marriage commissioner's religious freedom interest and instead gave complete priority to the same-sex couple's equality right, even though the denial of service by the objecting marriage commissioner had no practical effect on the couple's ability to obtain this service. Despite the court's/tribunal's claim that it must balance the competing religious freedom and equality interests, the issue in these cases was not the correct or fair balance between religious freedom and the right to equality but was instead whether the commissioner's claim deserved any protection under section 2(a).

The objecting marriage commissioner in these two cases argued that his refusal to perform same-sex marriages was simply an expression of his personal conscience. Yet he wanted to be excused from performing the duties attached to his civic role, because he believed that same-sex marriage is immoral and should not be recognized by the state.[17] The commissioner's religiously based refusal to perform a same-sex couple's civil marriage was viewed by the courts as an act of state discrimination—as a political or civic act (that should not be insulated from democratic judgment and legal duty) rather than an expression of personal conscience. As a private citizen, the marriage commissioner can refuse to attend (participate in) a same-sex wedding. But the commissioner is a public official who has been granted special rights and powers. If a commissioner objects to performing their duties because they disapprove of the conduct of others and the law's acceptance or affirmation of that conduct, they can step down from their position.

In *Re Marriage Commissioners Appointed Under the Marriage Act*, the Saskatchewan Court of Appeal held that a legislative proposal that would

---

would occur behind the scenes and be unknown to couples seeking to enter into a civil partnership). In the courts' view, her request to opt out was disruptive to the "rota" and caused offence to fellow registrars who are gay (*Eweida and others v UK*, 48420/10 36516/10 51671/10 59842/10, HEJUD [2013] ECHR 37 (15 January 2013).

17   The distinction between a civil servant's personal religious expression and the performance of their public role or duty is erased to opposite effect in the province of Quebec's Bill 21 (*An Act respecting the laicity of the State*), which treats the wearing of religious dress or symbols, such as a hijab or turban, by certain civil servants as a political act—a state act—that is incompatible with the requirement that the state remain neutral in matters of religion. The Quebec ban is discussed in Chapter 3.

allow provincially appointed civil marriage commissioners to refuse on religious grounds to perform same-sex marriage ceremonies violated the section 15 equality rights of gay and lesbian couples and was not be justified under section 1.[18]

A majority of the court recognized that if the government enacted such a law, a same-sex couple who approached a marriage commissioner could be told by the commissioner that they are unable to perform the couple's marriage because of their sexual orientation. This, said the majority, will have the effect of "drawing a distinction based on sexual orientation," a ground the Supreme Court of Canada has identified in earlier cases as "analogous" to those specifically listed in section 15.[19] The majority accepted that the harm from such a denial would be significant:

> It is not difficult for most people to imagine the personal hurt involved in a situation where an individual is told by a governmental officer "I won't help you because you are black (or Asian or First Nations) but someone else will" or "I won't help you because you are Jewish (or Muslim or Budd[h]ist) but someone else will." Being told "I won't help you because you are gay/lesbian but someone else will" is no different.[20]

Moreover, said the majority, a significant number of commissioners might decide that they are unable to perform same-sex marriages, and the law provides no assurance that a "minimum complement of commissioners will always be available to provide services to same-sex couples."[21] The majority concluded that the legislative proposal would have "the effect of creating a negative distinction based on sexual orientation" and that given the "historical marginalization and mistreatment of gay and lesbian individuals," the proposal would be discriminatory contrary to section 15.[22]

In its section 1 analysis, the majority accepted that a requirement that all marriage commissioners solemnize same-sex marriages would breach the religious freedom of those commissioners who objected on religious grounds to performing such marriages. The issue "at bottom,"

---

18   *Re Marriage Commissioners*, above note 8. The proposed exemption provided that "[n]otwithstanding *The Saskatchewan Human Rights Code*, a marriage commissioner is not required to solemnize a marriage if to do so would be contrary to the marriage commissioner's religious beliefs": *ibid* at para 17. A second version of the exemption put before the court "grandfathered" the current group of commissioners, allowing them not to perform same-sex marriages, but did not extend this exemption to newly appointed commissioners: *ibid* at paras 17–18.

19   *Ibid* at para 39.

20   *Ibid* at para 41.

21   *Ibid* at para 42.

22   *Ibid* at paras 44–45.

said the majority, is "managing the intersection of the freedom of religion of marriage commissioners on the one hand, and the equality rights of gay and lesbian individuals on the other."[23] The majority found that the proposed restriction on the section 15 rights of gay and lesbian couples failed both the minimal impairment and proportionality components of the *Oakes* test.[24] There were, said the majority, other ways in which the state might protect the commissioners' religious freedom without impairing, at least to the same degree, the right to equality.

The majority identified as a less restrictive measure "a 'single entry point' system under which a couple seeking the services of a marriage commissioner would proceed, not by directly contacting an individual commissioner, but by dealing with the Director of the Marriage Unit or some other central office."[25] Such a system would ensure that no couple would be denied services because of their sexual orientation. Any accommodation for marriage commissioners would occur "behind the scenes" and would not be apparent to the couple.[26] The majority did not decide whether a single entry point system would restrict the equality rights of gay and lesbian couples or, if it did, whether it would be a reasonable limit on those rights. They decided only that such a system would be "less restrictive of s. 15 rights" than the proposed law.[27]

The majority also found that the "freedom of religion interests" accommodated by the proposed law "do not lie at the heart of s. 2(a)," because they concern only the ability of the commissioners "to act on their beliefs in the world at large" and not their freedom "to hold the religious beliefs they choose or to worship as they wish."[28] Moreover, said the majority: "Persons who voluntarily choose to assume an office, like that of marriage commissioner, cannot expect to directly shape the office's intersection with the public so as to make it conform with their personal religious or other beliefs."[29]

Justice Smith, in a concurring judgment, suggested that the requirement that the commissioners (who are public officials) perform same-sex civil marriages might not interfere with their religious beliefs or practices. The marriage commissioners are not "compelled to engage in the sexual activity" to which they object; rather, "[t]heir objection

---

23   *Ibid* at para 66.

24   *R v Oakes*, [1986] 1 SCR 103.

25   *Re Marriage Commissioners*, above note 8 at para 85.

26   *Ibid*.

27   *Ibid* at para 89.

28   *Ibid* at para 93.

29   *Ibid* at para 97.

is that it is sinful for *others* to engage in such activity."[30] "It is far from clear," said Smith J, "that officiating at a civil marriage ceremony carries any implication or connotation at all that the marriage commissioner who officiates necessarily *approves* of the particular union."[31] According to Smith J, any "interference with the right of marriage commissioners to act in accordance with their religious belief … is [at most] trivial or insubstantial, in that it is interference that does not threaten actual religious beliefs or conduct."[32] In the judge's view, then, the decision of a marriage commissioner not to perform a same-sex marriage (based on the commissioner's belief that it would be wrong to perform such a marriage) falls outside the scope of section 2(a), and so its "restriction" requires no justification under section 1.

More recently, in *Kisilowsky v Manitoba*, the Manitoba Court of Appeal rejected the *Charter* claim of a marriage commissioner whose commission had been cancelled by the province when he indicated that he would only perform "Christian" weddings and would not perform same-sex weddings.[33] The court noted that in Manitoba there were two ways in which an individual could be authorized to perform a marriage ceremony. First, an individual could be registered as a religious official under *The Marriage Act*,[34] which would enable the individual to solemnize marriages "of his or her choice." They would not be required to solemnize a same-sex marriage. In the alternative, an individual could be registered under the Act to perform civil marriages on behalf of the province. These "provincial" marriage commissioners are required to perform all forms of lawful marriage, including same-sex marriages. In the court's view, even if the cancellation amounts to an infringement of the applicant's freedom of religion, "[i]t reflects a proportionate balancing of the applicant's section 2(a) rights and the section 15 equality rights of same-sex couples," particularly since the province "has made available sufficient options that would accommodate the applicant's section 2(a) rights and allow him to solemnize marriages for who he chooses."[35]

The marriage commissioners in these cases present their objection to performing same-sex civil marriages as a personal or private position that should be insulated from state action. Yet their religious beliefs relate to the actions and status of others in the community. The objecting commissioners believe that same-sex relationships should not be permitted.

---

30   *Ibid* at para 148.
31   *Ibid* at para 142.
32   *Ibid* at para 148.
33   2018 MBCA 10 [*Kisilowsky*].
34   *The Marriage Act*, CCSM c M50.
35   *Kisilowsky*, above note 33 at para 3.

They think that the law is wrong to recognize these relationships. Their claim to exemption amounts to a rejection of the law (a law one may presume they opposed in political debate) and its recognition of the equal worth of same-sex relationships.

The commissioners are free to live their personal lives in accordance with their views about sin and virtue. They are also free to associate with those who share their views. But when they enter the public sphere, their interactions with others should be subject to public norms. If the state has decided that sexual-orientation discrimination should be prohibited (that gays and lesbians should be treated as full members of the community), those who hold a different view (and believe that gays and lesbians are sinners) should not be exempted from their public obligation to treat sexual minorities in a nondiscriminatory manner when acting in an official capacity. A public official, such as a marriage commissioner, should not be excused from performing their duties simply because they disapprove of the conduct of others and the law's acceptance or affirmation of that conduct.

A province may choose to accommodate the religious objections of marriage commissioners, as several provinces have done, provided it establishes a system that does not have a discriminatory impact on same-sex couples. The province, though, does not have an obligation under the *Charter* to accommodate the moral beliefs of a civil servant when those beliefs relate to the rights and interests of others—and are better understood as a political position rather than an expression of personal conscience.[36]

The protection of religious freedom, and more particularly the requirement that the state remain neutral in matters of religion, depends on a distinction between the religious and the political—between the sphere of personal or communal religious life and the sphere of political or civic life. Views and actions that relate to civic concerns (to the rights and interests of community members), even if rooted in a religious belief system, may be subject to the give-and-take of political decision making. In contrast, the religious or spiritual life of the individual or church community may be viewed as a personal or internal matter that should be both excluded and insulated from politics. The role of courts

---

36   For a different view see Bruce Ryder, "The Canadian Conception of Equal Religious Citizenship" in Richard Moon, ed, *Law and Religious Pluralism in Canada* (Vancouver: UBC Press, 2008) at 101: "Governments have obligations to affirm both religious rights and equal access to civil marriage ... [which] can be met by taking steps to the point of undue hardship to accommodate religious beliefs and to ensure that a sufficient number of public officials are willing and available to perform civil marriages for same-sex couples."

in religious freedom cases is not to strike a balance between competing religious and civic interests, but rather to draw the line between the spheres of religious and civic life.

C. THE OBJECTION OF MEDICAL PRACTITIONERS TO PROVIDING A REFERRAL

Doctors in Ontario are not required to perform medical procedures, such as assisted death or abortion (except in emergency situations), if they have moral or religious objections to doing so. However, the College of Physicians and Surgeons of Ontario (CPSO), which licenses and regulates doctors in the province, requires that they provide an "effective referral" to another doctor or health care professional when they are unwilling to perform a particular procedure themselves. The CPSO's policy defines an effective referral as a "referral made in good faith, to a non-objecting, available, and accessible physician, other health-care professional, or agency."[37]

In *The Christian Medical and Dental Society of Canada v CPSO*, a group of doctors who identify as Christian challenged the effective referral policy, arguing that if they were to provide a patient with a referral, they would be complicit in acts they regard as immoral.[38] The referral requirement,

---

37 CPSO, "Professional Obligations and Human Rights," Policy Statement #2-15, and CPSO "Medical Assistance in Dying," Policy Statement #4-16. See also the Divisional Court's description of the requirement in *The Christian Medical and Dental Society of Canada v College of Physicians and Surgeons of Ontario*, 2018 ONSC 579 at para 26:

> First, the Policies do not require that a referring physician provide a formal letter of referral to, and arrange an appointment for a patient with, another physician. The CPSO says that the intent of the Policies is to ensure only that patients are not left to finding a willing physician on their own without any assistance from the physician from whom they first sought care. Accordingly, the spirit of the requirements is that the physician take "positive action" to connect a patient with a physician, another health-care professional or an agency. Second, referral may be made to any of a physician, another health-care professional or an agency provided the party to whom a patient is referred provides the requested medical services and is "non-objecting, available and accessible." In the case of an agency, a referral may be made to an agency that is charged with facilitating referrals for the health care service.

38 *Christian Medical and Dental Society of Canada v College of Physicians and Surgeons of Ontario*, 2019 ONCA 393 [*Christian Medical*].

they said, breached their freedom of conscience and religion under section 2(a) of the *Charter* and could not be justified under section 1.

The doctors' claim was rejected by the Ontario Court of Appeal, which held that the referral requirement restricted the objecting doctors' section 2(a) rights but was nevertheless necessary to protect the interests of patients. The court stressed that in a publicly funded system "which is structured around patient-centered care . . . the interests of patients come first, and physicians have a duty not to abandon their patients."[39] The court described family doctors as "advocates" and "navigators" for their patients in the public health care system.[40] Furthermore, said the court, because patients are dependent on their doctors, they may experience shame or humiliation when their doctor explains their religious objections to a procedure they want or require and declines to provide them with a referral to another doctor.[41]

At the same time, the court thought that the referral requirement did not interfere in a significant way with the doctor's religious freedom. In the court's view, the doctors had no right to practise medicine and "[a]s members of a regulated and publicly-funded profession they [were] subject to requirements that focus on the public interest rather than their interests."[42] The court also noted that physicians may adopt "other practice structures that will insulate them from participation in actions to which they object," including changing their specialization or subpractice.[43] If the doctors are unable to do this, said the court, "they will have to seek out other ways in which to use their skills, training and commitment to patient care," even though this may involve some sacrifice.[44] The court concluded that "the burden of these sacrifices did

---

39   *Ibid* at para 185.

40   *Ibid* at para 43.

41   *Ibid* at paras 132 and 141.

42   *Ibid* at para 187.

43   *Ibid* at para 186. At para 50:

> For those physicians whose religious objections could not be addressed by the options identified in the Fact Sheet, the physicians could change the nature of their practice to a specialty or sub-specialty that did not engage the same moral and ethical issues. Given the options available to comply with the Policies, the potential for a conflict between a physician's religious beliefs and the Policies, and any resulting psychological concern, results from a conscious choice of the physician to practice in circumstances in which such a conflict could arise. The deleterious effects of the Policies, while not trivial, are less serious than outright exclusion from the practice of medicine.

44   *Ibid* at para 186.

not outweigh the harm to vulnerable patients that would be caused by any reasonable alternative."[45]

There are several troubling aspects to the court's assessment of the competing factors. The first is the suggestion that a doctor can always alter the nature of their practice or specialization if they want to avoid situations in which they might be complicit in acts they consider to be immoral. Doctors are not public officials, even though they are members of a regulated profession and are paid for their services through a publicly funded medicare system. Unlike a marriage commissioner, a doctor is not acting as an agent of the state and is not exercising any special or public powers delegated to them by the state.[46] The second concern is the court's emphasis on the "stigma and shame" a patient will experience when told by their doctor the reasons the doctor will not assist them in accessing a particular service. The court had decided that the doctor's refusal to make an effective referral rested on a sincere religious belief that was protected under section 2(a). Should the shame experienced by a patient, when a doctor exercises their right to religious freedom, be a basis for limiting that freedom? The doctor's refusal to provide an effective referral will cause harm to the patient's dignity only if we think that the refusal amounts to a judgment about the morality of the patient and is not simply an expression of the doctor's personal conscience. Finally, the court did not require the state to establish other processes or channels that would enable a patient to access medical procedures or referral processes, without compromising the doctor's religious commitments.

Because the court framed the issue before it as the proper balance between conflicting doctor and patient interests, it had to find ways to discount the doctor's interest—at least if it was to uphold the effective referral requirement. However, the issue in this and other conscientious objection cases is not what the objector sincerely believes or whether the state has struck a reasonable balance between the individual's religious interests or commitments and the interests or rights of others in the community.[47] Rather, the issue is whether the objector's sincerely

---

45   *Ibid.*

46   I am aware of, but entirely unconvinced by, the argument that doctors are engaging in state action subject to the *Charter* because they are implementing a specific state policy: *Eldridge v British Columbia (Attorney General)*, [1997] 3 SCR 624. Ryder, above note 36, at 129, observes that individual doctors "do not have an obligation to provide all medical services; that obligation is borne by the public health care system as a whole, not by individual doctors."

47   The Divisional Court of Ontario in *Christian Medical*, above note 38 at para 108: "the notion that the Court should determine what constitutes 'complicity' or 'participation' in an act that a physician regards as immoral or sinful is inconsistent with the Court's role in matters involving religious belief." The court then

held religious belief should be viewed as an expression of their personal morality or spiritual commitment that should be accommodated if this can be done without noticeable harm to others or instead as a religiously grounded civic position that falls outside the scope of religious freedom protection and may be subject to legal regulation. The doctors present their objection to the effective referral requirement as a personal position—as an expression of personal conscience. However, the action the objecting doctors are required to perform (a referral) is so remote from the act they regard as inherently immoral that it is better viewed as a political position rather than an expression of personal conscience. While the doctor's objection is framed as a belief about their personal practices or actions, it is really about the immorality of the actions of others and the error of law makers in permitting (and even facilitating) these actions.

The religious belief that medical assistance in dying (MAID) is immoral—a belief that played a role in public debate but was rejected by courts and legislators—now becomes the basis for a rights' claim by the objecting doctors—a claim to be exempted from their obligation to refer patients to doctors who can provide the particular medical services. In other words, a religious belief or value that was treated as political—as something that might influence public policy but was rejected by policy makers—is converted by the objecting doctors into a private or personal practice or belief (a matter of personal religious conscience) that should be protected from political judgment.

The doctors may continue to oppose such laws in the political sphere, although constitutional requirements may limit the state's political options. However, the state should not be required to "accommodate" the doctors' beliefs about what others should and should not do and their personal opposition to a law that permits these activities.

---

points to the statement of Iacobucci J in *Syndicat Northcrest v Amselem*, [2004] 2 SCR 557, that the state is in no position to be "the arbiter of religious dogma." Yet the Supreme Court of Canada in *SL v Commision scolaire des Chênes*, 2012 SCC 7 [*SL*], said that the question of whether the law actually interferes with the religious practice is an objective test—and that the religious adherent in that case was mistaken in thinking that the law interfered with their religious belief/practice. The sincerity test, though, enables the objector in conscientious objection cases to blur the distinction between a religious belief about how one should live one's life, which should sometimes be accommodated, and a (religiously grounded) moral or political belief about how others should act or about the public interest, which must remain subject to political debate, and which political decision makers may either accept or reject.

D. CONSCIENTIOUS OBJECTION AND ANTI-DISCRIMINATION LAWS

In two recent cases, one in the United States and the other in the United Kingdom, the courts have considered conscientious objection claims made by cake bakers who objected to producing a cake for the celebration or promotion of same-sex marriage, a relationship they believe to be immoral or sinful.

In *Masterpiece Cakeshop v Colorado Civil Rights Commission*, a baker refused, on religious grounds, to provide a cake for a same-sex wedding reception and argued that he (and his business) should be exempted under the First Amendment from the state's ban on sexual-orientation discrimination in the provision of market services.[48] The Colorado Civil Rights Commission decided that there were reasonable grounds to believe the baker had discriminated against a same-sex couple and that the case should therefore be referred to an administrative law judge for adjudication. The commission's decision, though, was set aside by the US Supreme Court. In the Court's view, the commission had shown anti-religious bias in its deliberations, contrary to the First Amendment requirement that the state remain neutral in religious matters.

Justice Kennedy, writing for the majority of the Court, acknowledged that "[t]he Court's precedents make clear that the baker, in his capacity as the owner of a business serving the public, might have his right to the free exercise of religion limited by generally applicable laws."[49] However, Kennedy J did not find it necessary to address "the delicate question of when the free exercise of [the baker's] religion must yield to an otherwise valid exercise of state power"[50] because, in his view, the commission's assessment of the competing claims had been tainted by hostility to religion that "was inconsistent with the First Amendment's guarantee that our laws be applied in a manner that is neutral toward religion."[51] The commission, said Kennedy J, was required to weigh the competing civic

---

48   *Masterpiece Cakeshop v Colorado Civil Rights Commission*, 584 US __ (2018) [*Masterpiece*]; *Colorado Anti-Discrimination Act (CADA)*. Concurring judgments were written by Kagan J, Thomas J, and Gorsuch J, with a dissenting judgment by Ginsburg J.

49   *Ibid* at 2.

50   *Ibid* at 3. According to the majority, the commission adjudicated the bakery's religious objection based on a "negative normative 'evaluation of the particular justification' for his objection and the religious grounds for it."

51   *Ibid* at 17. In Kennedy J's view, the government does not have a "role in deciding or even suggesting whether the religious ground for Phillips' conscience-based objection is legitimate or illegitimate."

and religious interests in a way that respected its obligation to remain neutral in religious matters.[52]

When considering the discrimination complaint against the owner of the bakery, one of the commissioners made the following observation:

> Freedom of religion and religion has been used to justify all kinds of discrimination throughout history, whether it be slavery, whether it be the Holocaust, whether it be—I mean, we—we can list hundreds of situations where freedom of religion has been used to justify discrimination. And to me it is one of the most despicable pieces of rhetoric that people can use to—to use their religion to hurt others.[53]

To Kennedy J this was a shocking expression of hostility to religion:

> To describe a man's faith as "one of the most despicable pieces of rhetoric that people can use" is to disparage his religion in at least two distinct ways: by describing it as despicable, and also by characterizing it as merely rhetorical—something insubstantial and even insincere.[54]

However, Kennedy J's reading of this comment by a single commissioner seems entirely unjustified.[55] The commissioner appeared only to be making the point that just because someone offers a religious reason to explain their discriminatory action does not make that action right or just or something that should be accommodated. Justice Kennedy saw the commissioner's remark as a dismissal of religion, when it was more reasonably understood as a rejection of a particular religious view—in this case a view about the immorality of same-sex relationships.[56]

---

52   *Ibid* at 18: "The official expressions of hostility to religion in some of the commissioners' comments—comments that were not disavowed at the Commission or by the State at any point in the proceedings that led to affirmance of the order—were inconsistent with what the Free Exercise Clause requires."

53   *Ibid* at 13.

54   *Ibid.*

55   Justice Kennedy dismissed the claim instead of sending it back to the commission for reconsideration. For a discussion of the requirement that the decision making by the state must be "neutral and respectful" toward religion, see Leslie Kendrick & Micah Schwartzman, "The Etiquette of Animus" (2018) 132 *Harv LR* 133.

56   Nor does it seem likely that the commissioner was equating the refusal to bake a cake with the imposition of slavery or the murder of six million Jews. He was simply pointing out that in the past, religion has been used to justify all sorts of immoral action, a point that seems plainly true. Justice Kennedy was critical not only of the commissioner who described the use of religion to justify immoral actions but also of another commissioner who suggested that the owner of the bakery "can believe 'what he wants to believe', but cannot act on his religious beliefs 'if he decides to do business in the state'" (*ibid*). To Kennedy J, the implication of this statement was that "religious beliefs and persons are less than fully

According to Kennedy J, the state is forbidden to "impose regulations that are hostile to the religious beliefs of affected citizens and cannot act in a manner that passes judgment upon or presupposes the illegitimacy of religious beliefs and practices."[57] The state should not prefer the religious practices of one group over those of another or religious beliefs over nonreligious beliefs and vice versa.[58] However, the state is not required to remain neutral toward religious beliefs that address the rights and interests of others in the community. Indeed, it is hard to see how the state could remain neutral in these matters. In recognizing same-sex marriage, the state (in Colorado and elsewhere) has rejected the view that same-sex relationships are immoral, even if it has not done so in religious terms, employing the language of sin or making an argument about the best understanding of Christian scripture or doctrine. While the state has not limited the individual's freedom to hold or express such beliefs, it has limited their ability to act on those beliefs and has done so because it recognizes that those who believe that same-sex relationships are immoral or unnatural are mistaken.[59] The state can remain neutral toward a religious belief/practice only if that belief/practice can be viewed as personal or communal (and bracketed off from politics).

---

welcome in Colorado's business community" (*ibid*). But the commissioner is correct, surely.

57   *Ibid* at 17:

> The Free Exercise Clause bars even 'subtle departures from neutrality' on matters of religion. Here, that means the Commission was obliged under the Free Exercise Clause to proceed in a manner neutral toward and tolerant of Phillips' religious beliefs. The Constitution "commits government itself to religious tolerance, and upon even slight suspicion that proposals for state intervention stem from animosity to religion or distrust of its practices, all officials must pause to remember their own high duty to the Constitution and to the rights it secures.

58   *SL*, above note 47 at para 17.

59   In a more recent US Supreme Court decision, *303 Creative LLC et al v Elenis et al*, 600 US __ (2023), the operator of a graphic design business argued that she should not be required under the state's anti-discrimination law to create wedding sites for same-sex couples. The state agreed with the business owner that her activity—designing a website—could be considered speech and so the issue for the Court was whether, in offering her services to the public, she should be required to conform to anti-discrimination norms, even though this would mean compelling her to speak. Justice Gorsuch, writing for the majority, held that the First Amendment precludes the state from forcing the business owner "to create websites endorsing same-sex marriage or expressing any other message with which she disagrees" (15). The case is discussed and critiqued in Richard Moon, *The Life and Death of Freedom of Expression* (Toronto: University of Toronto Press, 2024), c 8.

The baker was seeking to convert his belief that same-sex relationships are immoral and ought not to be permitted or recognized in law, which had initially been treated as a political position on a matter of public policy, into a personal expression of religious conscience that should be insulated from politics. Because the individual (or the business) was providing market services and was not compelled to engage directly in action he regarded as immoral, his objection was better seen as a (political) view about the morality of the actions of others and the justice of the law that permits those actions. The baker's view that same-sex marriage should not be permitted—that no one should be allowed to enter such a relationship—did not prevail in the political sphere, and so now he is seeking to resist the law by claiming exemption from the legal ban on sexual-orientation discrimination.

In the UK case of *Lee v Ashers Bakery Co Ltd*, a bakery had refused to prepare a cake that had the words "Support Gay Marriage" iced on to it.[60] Mr Lee had ordered the cake for a pro-same-sex marriage event at the QueerSpace in Belfast. The bakery's owners, though, said that preparing such a cake would be contrary to their Christian belief that same-sex intimacy and marriage are unacceptable to God. The UK Supreme Court decided that the bakery's refusal to make the cake did not constitute sexual-orientation discrimination under the law in Northern Ireland. Baroness Hale, writing for the Court, accepted that the bakery owners' "objection was to the message and not to any particular person or persons."[61] According to Hale PSC, "[s]upport for gay marriage is not a proxy for any particular sexual orientation" since straight people may also support gay marriage and so might also order a cake with such a message.[62]

---

60   [2018] UKSC 49.

61   *Ibid* at para 34. While the anti-discrimination law prohibited both direct and indirect discrimination, Mr Lee argued before the Court that the bakery's refusal to make the cake amounted to direct discrimination. Christopher McCrudden notes that while indirect discrimination "depends on the 'adverse impact' of an ostensibly neutral practice" on the members of a particular group, direct discrimination "requires 'exact equivalence'"—that the law explicitly excludes all the members of a group (and only the members of that group) from its benefit. As McCrudden further notes, there was no "exact equivalence between the bakery's refusal to bake a cake with a message supporting same-sex marriage and the sexual orientation of any person." (Christopher McCrudden, "The Gay Cake Case: What the Supreme Court Did, and Did Not, Decide in Ashers" (2020) 9 *Oxford JL & Religion* 238.) As this case illustrates, these two forms of discrimination (direct and indirect) may sometimes overlap—when a service provider intends to exclude the members of a particular group, or to deny their equal worth, even though they have not denied service to every member of that group in all circumstances.

62   *Ibid* at para 23.

However, the distinction drawn by the Court between objection to (discrimination against) the group and objection to the message associated with the group may be too simple, even in the case of direct discrimination. What about a message on a cake that said, "Congratulations John on coming out" or "Congratulations Bill and John on your wedding"? Would the refusal to produce such a cake not be viewed as (direct) discrimination against gays and lesbians, even if the person ordering the cake was not gay? The bakery was unwilling to produce the cake because its owner believed that same-sex relationships are immoral and that gay people should not live according to their orientation or identity, and more particularly that they should not be able to marry.

At the time this case arose, same-sex marriage had not yet been recognized in Northern Ireland. In this context, Mr Lee's message could be viewed as a political position — a form of advocacy — on a (then) current political issue, a position with which the owners of Ashers Bakery disagreed. This reading of Mr Lee's message (as advocacy rather than celebration of same-sex marriage) and the labelling of Ashers's refusal (as the expression of a political position rather than an act of discrimination) might be different in a different political/legal context — in a context in which the state has recognized same-sex marriage.

In support of her conclusion that the bakery's action did not amount to discrimination, Hale PSC argued that if the anti-discrimination law were interpreted as requiring a bakery to produce a cake with a particular message, it would be compelling it to communicate a particular political position contrary to its right to freedom of expression. Once again, it may be that this argument had particular force for the Court because there was an ongoing debate in Northern Ireland about the recognition of same-sex marriage. Yet compelled expression is objectionable because it is experienced by the individual as a personal invasion, or as an interference with their "freedom of mind."[63] It follows, then, that an artificial entity such as a corporation does not have the same claim as an individual to freedom from compulsion to communicate. Asher's Bakery was not a large company, but it did operate six shops with a staff of sixty-five who were employed to bake and sell cakes. The owners of the bakery, Mr and Mrs McArthur, did not have to write the words on the cake themselves. Indeed, the messages on the cakes were generated mechanically by bakery employees. It is difficult then to see how the obligation to place these words on a cake could be an invasion of the bakery owners' personal sphere.

---

63   Moon, above note 59, c 8.

E. SOME CANADIAN ANTI-DISCRIMINATION CASES

There have been a number of cases in Canada in which market providers objected to serving same-sex couples and sought to be exempted from anti-discrimination laws. The claims in these cases have generally been unsuccessful.

In *Brockie v Brillinger (No 2)*, the Canadian Lesbian and Gay Archives (CLGA), a registered charity "with a mandate to acquire, preserve, organize, and give public access to publications, information, records and artifacts by and about homosexuals in Canada," ordered letterhead and business cards from a small printing business.[64] The owner of the business, Mr Brockie, refused to do the work because he believed same-sex relationships are sinful and that "he must not assist in the dissemination of information intended to spread the acceptance of a gay or lesbian ... lifestyle."[65] Mr Brockie indicated that he was willing to provide printing services to gay and lesbian customers, but not to an organization that "was involved in furthering and supporting the homosexual 'lifestyle.'"[66] The CLGA responded by bringing a *Human Rights Code*[67] complaint against Mr Brockie's business.

The Human Rights Tribunal of Ontario held that Mr Brockie's refusal to provide printing services (which were otherwise available to the public) to a 2SLGBTQ+ group amounted to discrimination under the Ontario *Human Rights Code*. The case was appealed to the Divisional Court of Ontario, which upheld the tribunal's decision. The court rejected as "specious" the distinction proposed by Mr. Brockie "between discrimination because of the presence of, or association with, a human characteristic referred to in s. 1 [of the *Code*] per se and discrimination because a person engages in the political act of promoting the causes of those who have such characteristics."[68] The court thought that even if Mr Brockie's objection was to the "Archives' objects and political purposes" rather than to "its mere association with people who bear such characteristics," the purpose of the *Code* is to create "a climate of understanding and mutual respect."[69] In the court's view, "efforts to promote an understanding and respect for those possessing any specified characteristic should

---

64   2002 CanLII 63866 (Ont SCDC) at para 4.
65   *Ibid* at para 3.
66   *Ibid* at para 15.
67   RSO 1990, c H.19 [*Code*].
68   *Ibid* at para 29.
69   *Ibid*.

not be regarded as separate from the characteristic itself."[70] The court found that although the tribunal's order breached Mr Brockie's section 2(a) rights under the *Charter*, it was nevertheless justified under section 1. According to the court, claims to religious freedom "in the commercial marketplace" are "at the fringes" of section 2(a) and carry little weight.[71]

Yet, in its section 1 analysis, the court also said that if the tribunal's order were read as requiring Mr Brockie to print not just the CLGA's letterhead and business cards but also "brochures or posters with editorial content espousing causes or activities clearly repugnant to [his] fundamental religious tenets," it would fail the section 1 proportionality requirement.[72] In the court's view, the *Code* prohibits only "discrimination arising from denial of services because of certain characteristics of the person requesting the services."[73] More particularly, said the court:

> If any particular printing project ordered by Mr. Brockie (or any gay or lesbian person, or organization/entity comprising gay or lesbian persons) contained material that conveyed a message proselytizing and promoting the gay and lesbian lifestyle or ridiculed his religious beliefs, such material might reasonably be held to be in direct conflict with the core elements of Mr. Brockie's religious beliefs. On the other hand, if the particular printing object contained a directory of goods and services that might be of interest to the gay and lesbian community, that material might reasonably be held not to be in direct conflict with the core elements of Mr. Brockie's religious beliefs.[74]

The court seemed to distinguish between material that assists group members and material that proselytizes or promotes a gay "lifestyle" or ridicules religion. Yet such a distinction is imaginable only when sexual orientation is viewed or treated as a choice. If sexual orientation is seen as an identity, then "promotion of homosexuality" will be indistinguishable from support for the gay and lesbian community. The purpose of the CLGA's activities, whether described as support or promotion, is to protect or advance the interests of sexual minorities. On the other hand, if homosexuality is viewed, in the way Mr Brockie views it, as a "lifestyle choice," then any support for or advocacy of the interests of sexual minorities will amount to the promotion of this "lifestyle." The court's reference to "proselytizing" this lifestyle suggested some sympathy for Mr Brockie's view, or at least an ambivalence about sexual orientation

---

70 *Ibid* at para 31.
71 *Ibid* at para 54.
72 *Ibid* at para 49.
73 *Ibid*.
74 *Ibid* at para 56.

as an identity or a choice, and a troubling uncertainty about how to fit sexual orientation into the framework of anti-discrimination laws.

In *Smith v Knights of Columbus*, a Roman Catholic organization that made its hall available for rental to the general public cancelled an existing rental arrangement after discovering that the renters were a same-sex couple who intended to use the hall for their wedding reception.[75] The couple brought a complaint against the Knights of Columbus under the British Columbia *Human Rights Code*,[76] arguing that the organization had discriminated against them on the grounds of their sexual orientation. The tribunal found that a *prima facie* case of discrimination had been made out against the organization. Under the *BC Code*, a religious organization that was primarily engaged in serving the members of its group would not be considered to have breached the discrimination ban simply because it gave preference to the members of that group.[77] The tribunal, though, found that the exemption was not applicable in this case, because the organization rented its hall to members of the general public. However, the tribunal went on to find that the organization had a bona fide and reasonable justification for its action. While the Knights of Columbus did not limit the rental of the hall to Roman Catholics, it had an informal policy of not renting the hall for events that were inconsistent with the Roman Catholic faith or would compromise the organization's relationship with the Roman Catholic church. The tribunal accepted that the organization should not be required to rent the hall for a function that was contrary to its "core" religious beliefs and to "indirectly condone" activities it regards as sinful.[78]

The tribunal, though, held that the organization, having initially agreed to rent the hall to the couple, had an obligation to help the couple find another location:

> Although we have accepted that the Knights could refuse access to the Hall to the complainants because of their core religious beliefs, in the

---

75 2005 BCHRT 544 [*Knights of Columbus*].

76 RSBC 1996, c 210 [*BC Code*].

77 *Ibid*, s 41(1):

> If a charitable, philanthropic, educational, fraternal, religious or social organization or corporation that is not operated for profit has as a primary purpose the promotion of the interests and welfare of an identifiable group or class of persons characterized by a physical or mental disability or by a common race, religion, age, sex, marital status, political belief, colour, ancestry or place of origin, that organization or corporation must not be considered to be contravening this Code because it is granting a preference to members of the identifiable group or class of persons.

78 *Knights of Columbus*, above note 76 at para 113.

Panel's view, in making this decision they had to consider the effect their actions would have on the complainants ... [T]he Knights could have taken steps such as meeting with the complainants to explain the situation, formally apologizing, immediately offering to reimburse the complainants for any expenses they had incurred and, perhaps offering assistance in finding another solution. There may have been other options that they could have considered without infringing their core religious beliefs ... In the circumstances of this case, including the fact that the Hall was not solely a religious space, and the existence of the agreement between the parties for its rental, the Panel finds that the Knights should have taken these steps, which would have appropriately balanced the rights of both parties.[79]

In seeking to balance the competing interests at stake without giving priority to one over the other, the tribunal made several determinations that do not sit easily together. The tribunal found that an organization linked to the Roman Catholic faith that rented its hall to members of the general public for a wide range of purposes could refuse to rent the hall to individuals who intended to use it for a purpose that was lawful but inconsistent with Roman Catholic teaching. The scope of this "exemption" or justification is unclear. Would the "exemption" allow the organization to refuse to rent the hall to a couple for a wedding reception following a civil or Protestant ceremony? Or will this "exemption" or justification apply, in practice, only to events involving same-sex couples or 2SLGBTQ+ organizations? At the same time, the tribunal also found that the Knights of Columbus, having initially but mistakenly rented the hall to a same-sex couple, had an obligation to help that couple find another location for their reception—an activity that the organization considered to be immoral. There seems to be little justification for this compromise. Either the organization has a duty not to discriminate on the grounds of sexual orientation in the rental of its hall or it does not, because it should not be required to support activities it regards as immoral.

In *Eadie and Thomas v Riverbend Bed and Breakfast (No 2)*, a couple operating a bed and breakfast cancelled a reservation after discovering that the double room had been reserved by a gay couple, because they were opposed on religious grounds to same-sex relationships.[80] A human rights tribunal found that even though the business was run by individuals who sincerely believed that same-sex relationships were sinful, and even though the business was operated out of a portion of their personal residence, it was still a commercial activity and therefore subject to the

---

79   *Ibid* at paras 120 and 124.
80   2012 BCHRT 247 [*Eadie*].

BC *Human Rights Code* ban on sexual-orientation discrimination in the provision of services. This case, said the tribunal, "falls more toward the commercial end of the spectrum" (in contrast to the *Knights of Columbus* case).[81] The owners had made the choice to start up a business in their personal residence. The state had not compelled them to act in a way that was inconsistent with their religious beliefs.

A similar issue came before the UK Supreme Court in *Bull v Hall*.[82] The Court in that case found that the cancellation amounted to unlawful discrimination and noted that "[s]exual orientation is a core component of a person's identity which requires fulfilment through relationships with others of the same orientation."[83] The Court considered both the *Eadie* and the *Knights of Columbus* decisions, but said "[w]e cannot place too much weight on these cases, decided upon under different legislation and in a different constitutional context."[84]

The businesses in these different cases argued that they should not be compelled by law to support an activity that according to their faith is immoral. Yet in all of these cases, the owners had decided to offer a service to the public for compensation. Since the law requires that market services be made available in a nondiscriminatory way, no one would see the organization or business as choosing to support these groups and their activities. But more importantly, anti-discrimination laws do not restrict the religious practice of the individual or group and do not require them to participate in a practice they regard as immoral.[85]

---

81   *Ibid* at para 165.

82   [2013] UKSC 73.

83   *Ibid* at para 52.

84   *Ibid* at para 50.

85   In *Yaniv v Various Waxing Salons (No 2)*, 2019 BCHRT 222, the BC Human Rights Tribunal dismissed a series of complaints brought by a transgender woman (who had male genitals) against small, mostly home-based, waxing businesses that had refused to provide their services to the complainant. The tribunal decided that these complaints were made in bad faith and so did not address the s 2(a) issue raised by a few of the businesses.

CHAPTER 5

THE AUTONOMY OF RELIGIOUS ORGANIZATIONS

A. INTRODUCTION

Sometimes an accommodation claim is made not by an individual who is seeking exemption from a law that interferes with their ability to engage in a particular religious practice, but instead by a religious organization or institution that is seeking to govern its internal affairs according to its own rules and practices, even when these are inconsistent with public norms.[1] In these institutional autonomy cases, the key question for the courts is whether the organization's actions will affect outsiders to the spiritual community. The right of the Catholic church, for example, to exclude women from the priesthood (to discriminate against women) is not decided by balancing the religious claim against the claim to gender equality. As a private religious organization, the Catholic church is ordinarily free to govern its internal affairs according to its own rules or norms and is exempted from public anti-discrimination requirements. Similarly, a religious school may dismiss a teacher who enters a same-sex relationship contrary to church doctrine, not because the religious interests of the group or school outweigh the public value of

---

1   As Ayelet Shachar observes, most individual accommodation claims are about inclusion within society—a claim for exemption that enables the individual to participate more fully in the general community—while institutional "autonomy" claims are about "opting out of, or seceding from the effects of the polity's public laws or norms." Ayelet Shachar, "Privatizing Diversity: A Cautionary Tale from Religious Arbitration in Family Law" (2008) 9 *Theor Inq L* 573 at 581.

sexual-orientation equality but simply because the school is understood to be a private religious organization.[2] However, when the group's application of "inside law" affects outsiders to the group, its actions may be subject to public norms.[3]

The starting assumption by the courts in these institutional autonomy cases is that those who choose to become, or to remain, members of a religious group do not require protection from intragroup rules, even rules that are harsh and discriminatory. If the members of a group have voluntarily submitted to the group's rules or decision-making processes, then the state ought not to intervene. The individual's membership in the group may be seen as voluntary as long as they are free to leave the group if they disagree with its actions.

Yet exit from a religious group is seldom costless. There may be a variety of barriers or impediments to an individual's withdrawal from such a group. The protection of religious freedom, then, may sometimes require action by the state to remove or lower these barriers so that individual members, if they choose, are able to leave the group. Whether a barrier to exit should be removed or overridden was an issue in several cases concerning the exit or expulsion of Hutterite colony members. Property in these colonies is collectively owned, and so if a member decides to leave the colony or is expelled, they leave with nothing, in theory not even personal property. The courts have recognized that this rule can be a deterrent to individuals who might want to leave the community. Yet at the same time, they have acknowledged that collective ownership is not just a barrier to exit but is a central tenet of the group's belief system. If a court were to override this practice, it would undermine the group's belief system and organizational structure.[4]

---

2   See *Caldwell et al v Stuart et al*, [1984] 2 SCR 603, in which a teacher was dismissed from her position at a Catholic school after she married a divorced man in a civil ceremony, contrary to Catholic doctrine.

3   A term used by Alvin J Esau, "Living by Different Law: Legal Pluralism, Freedom of Religion, and Illiberal Groups" in Richard Moon, ed, *Law and Religious Pluralism in Canada* (Vancouver: UBC Press, 2008) 110 at 110. A number of church groups challenged government restrictions on worship gathering that were intended to prevent the spread of COVID-19. These challenges were dismissed by the courts, which held that the restrictions on religious practice were justified under s 1. See, for example, *Ontario v Trinity Bible Chapel*, 2022 ONSC 134; *Gateway Bible Baptist Church et al v Manitoba et al*, 2023 MBCA 56; *Beaudoin v British Columbia (Attorney General)*, 2022 BCCA 427.

4   A point also made in Dwight G Newman, "Exit, Voice, and 'Exile': Rights to Exit and Rights to Eject" (2007) 57 *UTLJ* 43 at 65. Newman also notes that there may be ways in which individuals who wish to exit the colony could be "bought out" without the colony collapsing.

In *Hofer et al v Hofer et al* (a pre-*Charter*[5] case), the Supreme Court of Canada had to decide whether members of a Hutterite colony had been lawfully expelled.[6] In addressing this issue, the Court considered whether the members had voluntarily agreed (in contract) to the collective ownership rule and so were bound by this rule when they were expelled from the colony. A majority of the Court found that the expelled members had agreed to the colony's articles of association and were therefore subject to its terms. However, Pigeon J in his dissenting judgment questioned whether the appellants' assent to the colony's rules should be described as voluntary:

> [F]reedom of religion includes the right for each individual to change his religion at will. While Churches are otherwise free like other voluntary associations to establish whatever rules they may see fit, freedom of religion means that they cannot make rules having the effect of depriving their members of this fundamental freedom. In my view, this is precisely what these Hutterians have been attempting to do … The evidence shows that the rules and practices of this religious group make it as nearly impossible as can be for those who are born in it to do otherwise than embrace its teachings and remain forever within it … They have no right at any time in their life to leave the colony where they are living unless they abandon literally everything. Even the clothes they are wearing belong to the colony and, according to the judgments below, they are to be returned to it as its property by anyone who ceases to be a member of the Church.[7]

The difficulty with treating colony membership as voluntary—as a matter of agreement—is that most members were born into the colony. The majority judgment of Ritchie J, though, glossed over this problem: "if any individual either through birth within the community or by choice wishes to subscribe to such a rigid form of life and to subject himself to the harsh disciplines of the Hutterian Church, he is free to do so."[8] However, insofar as they could be said to have agreed to the terms of the "association," they did so as members who were already embedded in a form of life defined by these rules.

---

5   *Canadian Charter of Rights and Freedoms*, Part 1 of the *Constitution Act, 1982*, being Schedule B to the *Canada Act 1982* (UK), 1982, c 11 [*Charter*].

6   [1970] SCR 958 [*Hofer*]. The appellants in the case sought an order winding up the colony and dividing its assets.

7   *Ibid* at 984 & 985: "Such a construction of the contractual relationship between the members of the Colony means that they really cannot exercise their right of freedom of religion." Justice Pigeon also noted that "it is unusual for Hutterian children to be allowed to go beyond Grade 8 education" (*ibid* at 985).

8   *Ibid* at 975.

An individual's identity may be tied to the group so that exit is difficult even when there are few material barriers.[9] A religious community
may be so insular that even if its members are "free" to exit, they may
be unable to imagine living outside the group. Group members may feel
bound to the community by ties of kinship and friendship. These deep
communal connections are an important part of the value of religious life,
which is a source of meaning and structure for group members. At the
same time, these connections may also be the source of what the courts
regard as harm—the lack of meaningful choice or opportunity open to
the members of such communities or the vulnerability of some group
members to oppressive rules.

The protection of the group's autonomy under section 2(a) requires
that we see the group as a voluntary association but also as a source of
identity for its members. If the members feel only a weak connection to
the group, then it is difficult to justify the insulation of group practices
from public norms. But if, on the other hand, the identity of members is
so deeply tied to the group that it is difficult for them to imagine a life
outside the group, then it may be important for the state to protect them
from oppressive internal group rules.

The individual's social and psychological ties to their community
are sometimes described as barriers to their exit, similar to the economic costs that may deter them from leaving the community. The term
"barrier," though, suggests that these ties interfere with the individual's
judgment, preventing them from making the choices they would otherwise make and, like material restrictions, ought to be removed. However,
the claim often made in cases involving the internal affairs of religious
communities is not that the courts, or the state, should remove these
"barriers to exit," as if that were possible or desirable. Instead the claim
is that the courts or the state should intervene to protect the individual from unjust or oppressive internal group rules because they should
not have to choose between leaving the community to which they are
deeply connected and remaining within the community but governed by
unfair rules.[10] The state then may sometimes intervene in the affairs of a

---

9   See the discussion of *Bruker v Marcovitz*, 2007 SCC 54 [*Bruker*], later in this chapter.

10   For a discussion of the importance of respecting group differences while pro-
    tecting vulnerable group members, see Ayelet Shachar, *Multicultural Jurisdictions:
    Cultural Differences and Women's Rights* (New York: Cambridge University Press,
    2001); and Howard Kislowicz, "Judging the Rules of Belonging" (2011) 44 *UBC
    L Rev* 287. The *Divorce Act*, RSC 1985, c 3 (2d Supp), s 21.1, empowers a judge
    in a civil divorce case to exert pressure on a spouse who refuses to give consent to
    a religious divorce by dismissing any application by that spouse and striking out
    any other pleadings and affidavits filed by the spouse. These rules are discussed
    later in the chapter.

religious community that is insular and hierarchical when the community seeks to enforce practices that are thought to be harmful to some of its members, even though the members have, in at least a formal sense, chosen to be or to remain part of the community.[11]

Recognition of the deep connection between the individual and their spiritual community underpins the state's obligation to accommodate the individual's religious beliefs and practices. The autonomy of religious organizations similarly rests on the collective character of religious practice and life. Just as religious groups are made up of individual members, the identity of those members is tied to their association with the group. The Canadian courts have been vague about when a religious organization can make a claim under section 2(a) — and whether an organization simply has standing to bring a claim on behalf of its members or whether it can make a claim on its own behalf — that is, whether it has rights under section 2(a) for which it can seek vindication in the courts.[12] Of course, if religious practice has a collective dimension that is protected under section 2(a), it may not matter whether the organization has rights itself or is simply the vehicle for individual members to claim a right to associate with others and to operate as a spiritual community.

B. THE INTERNAL OPERATIONS OF RELIGIOUS ORGANIZATIONS

Anti-discrimination laws do not ordinarily apply to the operations of a religious organization if the organization is performing a religious function, either serving the members of a spiritual community or carrying out a religious mission within the larger community. If, however, the organization is providing nonreligious services to the general community, it may be viewed as a public or market actor that is subject to public norms.

Each of the human rights codes in Canada includes an exemption from its ban on employment discrimination for a "bona fide occupational qualification" (BFOQ), an exemption that has been applied to

---

11   The Supreme Court, though, has said that religious organizations are not subject to judicial review because they are not public bodies. However, the courts may sometimes intervene in the internal affairs of a religious organization to protect private law rights in contract or property. See *Highwood Congregation of Jehovah's Witnesses (Judicial Committee) v Wall*, 2018 SCC 26, which is discussed later in this chapter.

12   For a discussion see Kathryn Chan "Religious Institutionalism: A Feminist Response" (2021) 71 *UTLJ* 443.

religion-based requirements for employment at religious organizations.[13] Some codes also include more specific exemptions for organizations that serve "the interests of persons identified by their ... creed."[14] A church community, for example, will not be found to have breached the ban on religious discrimination in employment when it selects a minister or pastor based on their commitment to a particular religious belief system.

It is not always clear, though, when it is necessary that an employee of a religious organization adhere to the organization's religious doctrine. Some organizations require all or most of their employees, regardless of the specific tasks the employees perform, to adhere to certain religious practices.[15] For example, in *Caldwell et al v Stuart et al*, the Supreme Court held that a Roman Catholic high school could dismiss a teacher who, although a member of the church, had married a divorced man in a civil ceremony contrary to church doctrine.[16] The Court found that the school's requirement that all teachers adhere to church doctrine was a BFOQ. According to the Court, because teachers are role models for their students, it was reasonable for a religious school to expect them to conform to the doctrines of the church, regardless of the courses they teach. The Court observed that "[i]t will be only in rare circumstances that such a factor as religious conformance can pass the test of *bona fide* qualification. In the case at bar, the special nature of the school and the unique role played by the teachers in the attaining of the school's legitimate objects are essential to the finding that religious conformance is a *bona fide* qualification."[17]

In *Ontario (Human Rights Commission) v Christian Horizons*, the Divisional Court of Ontario had to determine whether the dismissal of an employee, who was a lesbian, by an evangelical Christian group that operated group homes for individuals with developmental disabilities amounted to employment discrimination under the Ontario *Human*

---

13   In the absence of such a provision, an exemption claim could be made directly under the *Charter*.

14   For example, see the Ontario *Human Rights Code*, RSO 1990, c H.19, s 24(1)(a) [*Ontario Code*]. Section 18 provides a similar exception to the ban on discrimination in the provision of services.

15   A number of these cases are discussed in Alvin J Esau, "Islands of Exclusivity: Religious Organizations and Employment Discrimination" (2000) 33 *UBC L Rev* 719. See, for example, *Schroen v Steinbach Bible College*, [1999] MHRBAD No 2 and *Garrod v Rhema Christian School* (1991), 15 CHRR D/477.

16   Above note 2. There may be some unease in insulating religious schools from human rights laws. They may be seen as religious in character or as advancing a religious purpose, but because they educate children, they may also be seen as performing a public role in educating democratic citizens.

17   *Ibid* at 625.

Rights Code.[18] The *Ontario Code* prohibits employment discrimination on the grounds of sexual orientation but recognizes an exception to the ban:

> 24(1) The right under section 5 to equal treatment with respect to employment is not infringed where,
>
> (a) a religious, philanthropic, educational, fraternal or social institution or organization that is primarily engaged in serving the interests of persons identified by their race, ancestry, place of origin, colour, ethnic origin, creed, sex, age, marital status or disability employs only, or gives preference in employment to, persons similarly identified if the qualification is a reasonable and *bona fide* qualification because of the nature of the employment.[19]

The court held that even though Christian Horizons was a religious organization "serving the interests of persons identified by their … creed," the group's religiously based prohibition on same-sex relationships was not a BFOQ for the job performed by the particular employee. The organization's decision to dismiss the employee because she failed to conform to the ban on same-sex relationships amounted to employment discrimination on the grounds of sexual orientation, contrary to the *Ontario Code.*

In the court's view, Christian Horizons was a religious organization operating group homes "for religious reasons—in order to carry out a Christian mission."[20] The organization would not be "assisting people with disabilities in a Christian home environment but for the religious calling of those involved."[21] According to the court, the organization's charitable work was "undertaken as a religious activity through which those involved could live out their Christian faith and carry out their Christian ministry to serve people with developmental disabilities."[22] The court concluded that the organization was "primarily engaged in serving the interest of persons identified by their creed" with beneficial consequences for the individuals residing in the group homes.[23]

Yet would the members of the organization say that their purpose was to serve themselves—to satisfy their desire to perform Christian service? While their motivation may be to do God's will, their purpose is to help others. The court, however, was concerned that if the organization, or any "religious group" doing charitable work in the community, were

---

18   2010 ONSC 2105.
19   Above note 14.
20   Above note 18 at para 75.
21   *Ibid.*
22   *Ibid* at para 77.
23   *Ibid.*

found not to be "primarily" engaged in serving the interests of persons identified by their creed, the organization would not be covered by section 24(1) and so "could not require even its senior officers, who constitute the organization's directing mind, to be adherents to its religious beliefs."[24] But ought this to be a concern if the organization provides general services, pays its employees, and is funded by the state?

The court, however, went on to find that the requirement that employees refrain from same-sex relationships was not a BFOQ for the particular job performed by the employee, Ms Heintz, since she was not involved in religious teaching or conversion.[25] In determining that the organization had a religious mission, the court focused on the shared spiritual commitment of the staff; however, when deciding that conformity with religious doctrine was not a BFOQ for nonmanagement positions, the court's focus shifted to the actual services provided by Ms Heintz and other employees. The court's conclusion is an awkward one: the organization is serving a religious group (its workers), but its workers need not conform to all of the organization's religious tenets.

The court appeared to accept that the organization's practice of hiring only evangelical Christians did not breach the *Ontario Code*. "There was no question," said the court, "that religious commitment is seen by the organization as fundamental to both its approach to service delivery and to the carrying out of the job responsibilities."[26] The court emphasized that Ms Heintz continued to identify herself as an evangelical Christian and "viewed her work with Christian Horizons as the fulfillment of her calling to do Christian ministry" even if she did not accept or conform to the organization's particular beliefs about same-sex relationships.[27] She was, said the court, "a follower of Christian Horizon's ethos in every other way, and is committed and quite capable of performing the job functions of a support worker with the love and care that has typically

---

24   *Ibid* at para 65.

25   The court insisted (*ibid* at para 90) that:

> [t]he qualification, to be valid, must not just flow automatically from the religious ethos of Christian Horizons. It has to be tied directly and clearly to the execution and performance of the task or job in question. A focus that is only on the religious organization and its mission, without regard to how it is manifested in the particular job in issue, would deprive the final element of s. 24(1)(a) . . . of any meaning.

The court found (quoting from the decision of the Ontario Human Rights Tribunal) that the "primary role of a support worker is not to help all residents to adopt a Christian way of life, or to carry out a mission of salvation, or to convert residents to the faith beliefs of the organization" (*ibid* at para 92).

26   *Ibid* at para 99.

27   *Ibid* at para 82.

characterized Christian Horizon's service to people with developmental disabilities and with respect for the Christian activities in the homes."[28] And so the court found that even though a commitment to Christianity might be a legitimate job requirement, it was not necessary for Ms Heintz to accept, and live in accordance with, the organization's religious views about same-sex relationships. A general commitment to the religious ethos of the organization was sufficient to enable her to perform her job properly. The court took it upon itself to decide not just what was essential to Ms Heintz's job, but what was essential to Christian belief—that the rejection of same-sex relationships was not an essential part of the organization's Christian commitment.

There is, however, a larger issue lurking in the background of this case. Christian Horizons employs only Christians and, according to the court, advances a Christian mission. Even if the court is right that the organization does not engage explicitly in religious proselytization, its activities in the group homes are infused with religious content.[29] Yet Christian Horizons is the principal operator in the province of group homes for those with developmental disabilities and is almost entirely funded by the province. If the organization is viewed as "religious," then the province's support for it as the main provider of these services may run afoul of the section 2(a) neutrality requirement.

C. *TRINITY WESTERN UNIVERSITY v BRITISH COLUMBIA COLLEGE OF TEACHERS*

The question of whether the actions of a religious association are simply an internal matter or whether they directly affect outsiders to the community arose in two cases involving Trinity Western University (TWU), a private evangelical Christian university in British Columbia. In both cases, TWU challenged a decision by a regulatory body not to accredit a professional training program proposed by the university.

---

28   *Ibid* at para 104.
29   See *ibid* at para 101:

> The evidence shows that the "Christian environment" that was provided in the homes by the support workers mainly manifested itself through prayer, hymn singing and Bible reading. There is no evidence that Ms. Heintz refused to participate in these activities. In doing so, the support workers are not engaged in converting the residents to Evangelical beliefs or lifestyle.

Since the residents had mental disabilities, it is not clear what the court means when it says the workers were not engaging in converting the residents.

In *Trinity Western University v British Columbia College of Teachers*, the issue was whether the British Columbia College of Teachers (BCCT) breached the freedom of religion of TWU and its community of teachers and students when it was decided not to accredit the university's teacher training program.[30] The consequence of the decision by the BCCT was that graduates of the TWU program would not be able to teach in the province's public school system, although they could teach in private (religious) schools.

The BCCT decided that the TWU program would not adequately prepare students to teach in the public school system because it affirmed the view that same-sex relationships are sinful. In making this decision, the BCCT referred specifically to the contract of responsibilities signed by TWU teachers and students that prohibits "homosexual behaviour" and other activities. According to the BCCT, an institution that wishes to train teachers for the public school system must "provide an institutional setting that appropriately prepares future teachers for the public school environment, and in particular for the diversity of public school students," which, because of the "contract," this program did not do.[31]

The majority of the Supreme Court, in a judgment written by Iacobucci and Bastarache JJ, accepted that the denial of accreditation "places a burden on members of a particular religious group ... preventing them from expressing freely their religious beliefs and associating to put them into practice."[32] In the majority's view, the BCCT decision meant that TWU would have to abandon its religiously based "community standards" if it was to run a program that trains teachers for the public school system. Graduates of TWU "are likewise affected because the affirmation of their religious beliefs and attendance at TWU will not lead to certification as public school teachers."[33] "The issue at the heart of this appeal," said the majority, "is how to reconcile the religious freedoms of individuals wishing to attend TWU with the equality concerns of students in B.C.'s public school system."[34]

The majority, however, found no reason to deny accreditation to the TWU program. They accepted that if a teacher engages in discriminatory conduct, the teacher can be disciplined; but they maintained that the

---

30   [2001] 1 SCR 772 [*TWU*]. Students in the teacher training program previously operated by TWU had completed their school placements under the supervision of faculty from Simon Fraser University. Under the new program proposed by TWU, all elements of the program, including teacher placements, would be supervised by TWU staff.

31   *Ibid* at para 11.

32   *Ibid* at para 32.

33   *Ibid*.

34   *Ibid* at para 28.

right of sexual minorities to be free from discrimination is not violated simply because a teacher holds discriminatory views.[35] In the majority's view, "the proper place to draw the line in cases like the one at bar is generally between belief and conduct."[36] A teacher may believe that same-sex relationships are sinful or wrongful, but as long as they do not act on those views, denying benefits to or imposing burdens on particular individuals because of their sexual orientation, they will not be found to have breached the right to equality. The majority found no evidence that any TWU graduate had acted in a discriminatory way in the classroom. In the absence of "concrete evidence that training teachers at TWU fosters discrimination in the public schools of B.C.," the BCCT had no grounds to deny accreditation to TWU and interfere with the freedom of TWU instructors and students to hold certain religious beliefs.[37]

The majority judgment seemed to say that had there been evidence of direct acts of discrimination by TWU-trained teachers, the BCCT would have been justified in refusing to accredit the TWU teacher training program. Yet it is not clear why this should be so. Once the Court distinguished between anti-gay belief and action and accepted that a teacher may hold such beliefs provided they do not act on them, why was it relevant whether any TWU graduates had engaged in acts of discrimination? If belief and action are separable in this way (public action as wrongful and personal belief as not), then TWU, even though it supported anti-gay and anti-lesbian views, should not be held responsible for any discriminatory actions taken by its graduates. Similarly, the improper actions of some graduates should not affect the accreditation of other graduates who may believe that same-sex relationships are immoral but refrain from engaging in acts of discrimination. The confusion in the majority's reasoning points to a deeper problem with the distinction between belief and action in the school context.

While the distinction between belief and action is central in human rights codes (which prohibit acts of discrimination in the market but do not otherwise regulate an individual's beliefs or the decisions they make concerning private matters), it may not be applicable to the role of a teacher in a public school. An important part of a teacher's role is to teach their students basic values, including tolerance for different religious belief systems and respect for the equal worth of all people. As the majority in *TWU* observed, "[s]chools are meant to develop civic virtue and responsible citizenship, to educate in an environment free

---

35   *Ibid* at para 37.
36   *Ibid.*
37   *Ibid* at para 36.

of bias, prejudice and intolerance."[38] Teachers, though, do not simply instruct students in these values. They are role models and counsellors. If sexual-orientation equality is to be affirmed in the public schools, teachers must do more than simply refrain from direct acts of discrimination against gay and lesbian students. A teacher, when confronted with bigoted words from students about gays or lesbians, should contradict those words, or when approached by a student who is struggling with their sexual orientation should provide support and reassurance or direct them to an individual or group that can offer support. Because the public values of the school curriculum (broadly understood) are taught by example and because they must be affirmed in different ways, it may be that a teacher who is not personally committed to these values cannot perform their role effectively.

This is not to say that individual teachers should be closely examined on their views about sexual-orientation equality (or racial or gender equality). A serious probe into the individual's thoughts or attitudes about sexual orientation might involve too great an invasion into their personal sphere. Nor should we preclude an individual from teaching in the public schools because they belong to a particular church or attended a particular religious school. But this is not the same as saying that it is all right to employ an anti-gay or anti-lesbian teacher provided they refrain from explicit acts of discrimination in the classroom. A teacher should be excluded from the public schools if they have indicated in their public statements or actions that they regard same-sex relationships as sinful or objectionable, even though there is no evidence that they have directly discriminated against gay and lesbian students in the classroom. They should be excluded because discrimination is sometimes subtle and difficult to prove but also because a teacher should do more than simply tolerate gay and lesbian students.

In *Ross v New Brunswick School District No 15*, the Supreme Court held that an individual who holds racist views, as evidenced by their words or actions outside the classroom, may be disqualified from serving as a classroom teacher in the public schools.[39] Justice La Forest, for the Court in *Ross*, upheld the decision of an adjudicator, appointed under the New Brunswick *Human Rights Act*,[40] that ordered the school board to remove from the classroom a teacher who had expressed in a public setting racist views, which he claimed were religiously based. In *Ross*, there was no evidence that the teacher had treated any minority students in his class unfairly or differently from other students or had deviated

---

38   *Ibid* at para 13.
39   [1996] 1 SCR 825 [*Ross*].
40   RSNB 2011, c 171.

from the curriculum and taught racist views. However, because Mr Ross had expressed racist opinions at public meetings and in the local media, students in his school (and the general community) had come to know of his views. The Court found that Mr Ross's public statements had "poisoned" the learning environment in the school.[41]

The Court in *Ross* recognized that a teacher is a role model, an authority figure, and a conduit for public values. Public knowledge of Mr Ross's racist views mattered because his support for such views might have legitimized them in the minds of some students and undermined the school's affirmation of racial equality. If all that is expected of a teacher is that they refrain from teaching racist views, then it might be possible to separate what they say and do in the classroom from what they say and do outside, on their own time. Certainly, there are views that a teacher is not permitted to express inside the classroom but is free to express outside. For example, a teacher should not expressly support the Liberal Party or the Communist Party inside the classroom but is permitted to do so outside. We expect the teacher in the classroom to remain neutral on issues of partisan politics. But in the case of racial equality, we expect more than formal neutrality in the classroom. We expect the teacher to positively support the value of equality. A teacher who publicly affirms racist views cannot perform this role. It would seem even more obvious that a teacher training program that affirms such views does not adequately prepare its graduates to teach in the public school system.

This takes me to the more fundamental error in the Court's decision. The issue in the *TWU* case was not whether a particular graduate and prospective teacher might be anti-gay or homophobic because they attended an educational institute that affirmed anti-gay views. It was, instead, whether a teacher training program that affirms values that are incompatible with the civic curriculum should be denied accreditation because it will not adequately prepare its students to teach in the public school system—a system in which gay and lesbian students should be treated with equal respect and not simply tolerated. Had the BCCT denied accreditation to a teacher training program that had a racist element in its curriculum, it seems unlikely that the BCCT's decision would have been overturned by the Court, even though not every graduate of the program would carry the lesson of racism with them. A program that taught or affirmed values so fundamentally at odds with the civic values of the public school system would not be accredited. Yet TWU sought accreditation for a program that supported values the BCCT thought were

---

41   *Ross,* above note 39 at paras 40–41.

incompatible with the civic curriculum of the public schools—based
on the public commitment to sexual-orientation equality expressed in
provincial and federal human rights codes.

It is worth noting that the existence of TWU, and more specifically
its teacher training program, rests on a belief that the values of those
who teach are important in the education process. TWU recognizes that
its students will become better Christians, or Christian school teachers,
if they are taught in an environment that is fully Christian in its values
and practices. This is why TWU requires that all instructors adhere to
its code of conduct. Even if anti-gay views are not an explicit part of the
teacher training program, they form part of the ethos of TWU.

D. *LAW SOCIETY OF BRITISH COLUMBIA v TRINITY WESTERN UNIVERSITY*

In 2010, TWU applied to the various provincial law societies for accreditation of a law program that it had been planning for several years. Graduates of an accredited law program are eligible to take provincial law
society exams and, if they pass these exams, to be called to the bar in
the particular province following a brief articling period. The graduates
of an unaccredited law program may still be called to the provincial
bar but must satisfy some additional requirements. While many of the
provincial law societies were prepared to accredit the TWU program, the
law societies of British Columbia (LSBC) and Ontario (LSO) declined to
do so.[42] TWU had for some time required its students to sign a covenant
that prohibited them from engaging in certain behaviours, including
sexual intimacy outside heterosexual marriage. The LSBC and LSO were
concerned that this covenant would have the effect of excluding gay and
lesbian students from the program and would therefore limit their access
to the legal profession.

In separate judicial review applications, TWU argued that in refusing
to accredit its proposed law program, the LSO and LSBC had acted outside their powers. TWU claimed that the law societies' statutory mandate
to regulate the legal profession in the public interest did not empower
them to assess the school's admissions practices. TWU also argued that
the decision of the law societies not to accredit the program breached

---

42   Nova Scotia Barrister's Society (NSBS) also declined to accredit the TWU program.
     However, the province's Court of Appeal held that in refusing accreditation, the
     NSBS had acted beyond its powers: *The NS Barristers' Society v TWU*, 2016 NSCA
     59. The NSBS did not appeal the decision.

the TWU community's rights under section 2(a) of the *Charter*. The Supreme Court heard the two cases together and released its decision in each at the same time.[43] The administrative law issues in the two cases were not the same, since the decision-making process followed by each law society was different.[44] However, the freedom of religion issue was the same in both cases. A majority of the Supreme Court held that the decision not to accredit the TWU program was reasonable and that any interference with the TWU community's religious freedom was justified to prevent discrimination against gay and lesbian students in entry to law school and the legal profession. The majority's reasons, written by Abella J, were most fully developed in the BC case. Separate concurring judgments were written by McLachlin CJ and Rowe J. A dissenting judgment was written jointly by Brown and Côté JJ. In the earlier case of *TWU v BCCT*, the Court had focused on the graduates — the output — of the TWU teacher training program and whether they might, as teachers, be more likely to engage in discrimination against 2SLGBTQ+ students. However, in *LSBC v TWU* the focus instead was on the applicants to the program — the input — and whether the covenant would have the effect of excluding gay and lesbian applicants not simply from the program but also from the legal profession.[45]

In determining whether the LSBC's refusal to accredit the TWU program breached the *Charter*, the majority first considered whether the refusal amounted to a restriction on the religious freedom of the TWU community contrary to section 2(a), and second, after finding a breach of section 2(a), whether it was reasonable for the LSBC to conclude that the reasons for restriction outweighed (or were proportionate to) the school's religious freedom interests. Yet despite this framing of the issue by the majority, the Court's task in this and other similar cases is not to balance competing civic and religious interests, but is instead to mark the boundary between the spheres of civic and spiritual life. More particularly, in this case, the issue was whether TWU (in applying to operate an accredited law program) should be viewed as a private religious institution that is free govern itself according to its own norms, or whether because its actions may directly impact outsiders to the religious group it should be viewed as performing a public role and therefore as subject to

---

43 *Law Society of British Columbia v Trinity Western University*, 2018 SCC 32 [*LSBC v TWU*]; *Trinity Western University v Law Society of Upper Canada*, 2018 SCC 33.

44 Notably, the LSBC passed a resolution denying accreditation to the TWU program following a referendum of the society's members on the issue.

45 The majority in the earlier *TWU* decision, above note 30 at para 25, rejected in a cursory way the claim that the covenant would have a discriminatory effect on gay and lesbian applicants.

civic norms. The different judgments begin with different assumptions about the public/private character of TWU (or at least its proposed law program) and so never really address the key issue.

Justice Abella, writing for the majority, held that the LSBC, when deciding whether to accredit a law program, "was entitled to be concerned that inequitable barriers on entry to law schools would effectively impose inequitable barriers on entry to the profession and risk decreasing diversity within the bar."[46] She noted that the law society's overarching statutory objective was "to uphold and protect the public interest in the administration of justice" and that this was stated "in the broadest possible terms."[47] She rejected TWU's claim that the law society, in refusing to accredit its program, was intervening in the internal affairs of a private religious association, because she viewed the covenant as a barrier to entry into law school and into the legal profession.

Justice Abella accepted that the LSBC's decision not to accredit the TWU program breached the religious freedom of the members of the TWU community and of the Evangelical students who might wish to attend TWU to study law. She noted that the members of the TWU community believe that it is important to study with others who share their Christian beliefs "or are prepared to honour those beliefs in their conduct."[48] Justice Abella acknowledged that the mandatory covenant "makes it easier" for Evangelical Christians "to adhere to their faith" because it creates "an environment where their moral discipline is not constantly tested."[49] It followed, then, that the LSBC decision not to accredit the TWU program interfered with "the right of TWU's community members to enhance their spiritual development through studying law in an environment defined by their religious beliefs."[50]

---

46   *LSBC v TWU*, above note 43 at para 39. And at para 31: "In our view, the LPA [*Legal Profession Act*] requires Benchers to consider the overarching objective of protecting the public interest in determining the requirements for admission to the profession, including whether to approve a particular law school." And at para 41: "Limiting access to membership in the legal profession on the basis of personal characteristics, unrelated to merit, is inherently inimical to the integrity of the legal profession."

47   *Ibid* at para 30.

48   *Ibid* at para 65. And further at para 70: "It is clear from the record that evangelical members of TWU's community sincerely believe that studying in a community defined by religious beliefs in which members follow particular religious rules of conduct contributes to their spiritual development. In our view, this is the religious belief or practice implicated by the LSBC's decision."

49   *Ibid* at para 72.

50   *Ibid* at para 75.

However, Abella J went on to find that the decision by the LSBC to deny accreditation to the TWU law program was reasonable and that it reflected "a proportionate balancing of Charter protection with the statutory mandate."[51] She found that the LSBC's decision did not significantly limit religious freedom, first because it only denied approval to the TWU program as long as it included the mandatory covenant, and second because (she understood) that for the TWU community the covenant is desirable but not essential to their spiritual life—"preferred (rather than necessary)."[52] She thought the law society's refusal to accredit a program with such a covenant did not prevent Evangelical Christians from practising their religion "as and where they choose."[53]

On the other side of the balance, Abella J found that the LSBC decision to deny accreditation to the TWU program "significantly advanced ... the public interest in the administration of justice ... by maintaining equal access to and diversity in the legal profession."[54] She recognized that gay and lesbian students would be deterred from applying to the program because of the covenant's ban on same-sex intimacy. The consequence of this is "that the 60 law school seats created by TWU's proposed law school will be effectively closed to the vast majority of LGBTQ students" with the further consequence that qualified 2SLGBTQ+ candidates may be prevented from entering the legal profession.[55] Even though the TWU program would create more law school spaces, the covenant meant that "LGBTQ individuals would have fewer opportunities relative to others ... [thereby] undermin[ing] true equality of access to legal education, and by extension, the legal profession."[56]

Justice Abella's account of the communal dimension of the freedom seemed to involve no more than a recognition that an individual's beliefs and practices are often shared with others and that an individual may sometimes attach value to worshipping with others or joining with others to pursue common spiritual purposes.[57] The individual remains the locus

---

51   *Ibid* at para 79.

52   *Ibid* at para 88. She also noted at para 87 that "the limitation in this case is of minor significance because a mandatory covenant is, on the record before us, not absolutely required for the religious practice at issue: namely, to study law in a Christian learning environment in which people follow certain religious rules of conduct."

53   *Ibid* at para 102.

54   *Ibid* at paras 92–93.

55   *Ibid* at para 93.

56   *Ibid* at para 95.

57   *Ibid* at para 64. The majority accepted that "[t]he protection of individual religious rights under s. 2(a) must ... account for the socially embedded nature of religious belief, as well as the 'deep linkages between this belief and its manifestation through communal institutions and traditions'"; "Religious adherents must

of belief and the focus of protection in her section 2(a) analysis. This allowed Abella J to discount the collective practice as simply a preference of the individual believer to teach or study in an environment in which others share the same beliefs. Justice Abella saw this as a kind of second-order belief.[58] Yet, as noted earlier, it is difficult to account for the value of religious belief/practice from an external or secular perspective (and the obligation of the state to accommodate religious practices or norms) without recognizing the deep connection between the individual adherent and the religious community or tradition with which they associate.[59]

The dissenting judges, Côté and Brown JJ, disagreed with the majority on the two central issues before the Court. First, they thought that the law society's authority to regulate the profession in the public interest

---

be free to "come together and create cohesive communities of belief and practice." In previous judgments, such as *Loyola High School v Quebec (Attorney General)*, 2015 SCC 12 [*Loyola*], which is discussed later in this chapter, the Court made general observations about the communal dimension of religious freedom and the standing of religious organizations to bring challenges under s 2(a) of the *Charter*. But, as in *LSBC v TWU*, the Court in these cases simply recognized that individuals sometimes perform religious practices in combination with others.

58   For a discussion of the institutional standing of TWU to bring such a claim, see Kathryn Chan, "Identifying the Institutional Religious Freedom Claimant" (2017) 95 *Can Bar Rev* 707.

59   Chief Justice McLachlin, in a concurring judgment, thought that the law society was justified in "refusing to condone discrimination against LGBTQ people, pursuant to [its] statutory obligation to protect the public interest" (*LSBC v TWU*, above note 43 at para 137). Yet her argument seemed to be circular, since the law society's decision to accredit the TWU program could be seen as condoning a discriminatory program only if the law society has the authority or responsibility not to accredit such a program. Justice Rowe, in his concurring judgment, found no breach of s 2(a) and so did not need to assess the competing civic and religious claims or to engage in any form of balancing or proportionality analysis. In his view, freedom of religion is about "personal autonomy or choice" and is based on the idea that no one should be "forced to adhere to or to refrain from a particular set of religious beliefs" (*ibid* at para 251, quoting *Syndicat Northcrest v Amselem*, 2004 SCC 47). He accepted that religion has a communal aspect that is protected under s 2(a); but like the majority, he saw the communal aspect of religion as simply an expression of individual choice—the freedom to choose to worship with others or to pursue certain spiritual objectives together with others. He took the position that s 2(a) protects only practices that the individual sincerely believes are required. It is difficult, though, to reconcile this view with earlier Supreme Court judgments in which the Court seemed to say that s 2(a) protects religious practices even if they are not understood by the individual or group to be mandatory. He also thought that the freedom "does not protect measures by which an individual or a faith community seeks to impose adherence to their religious beliefs or practices on others who do not share their underlying faith" (*ibid* at para 251).

did not allow it to intervene in the internal operations of a law school, including the school's admissions policies. Second, the dissenting judges thought that the law society's decision not to accredit the proposed program breached the section 2(a) rights of the TWU community and that this breach was not justified under section 1 of the *Charter*.

According to the dissenting judges, the law society's role in assessing the proposed law program is simply "to ensure that individual graduates are fit to become members of the legal profession because they meet minimum standards of competence and ethical conduct."[60] The law society's public interest mandate enables it to regulate the legal profession in the province but "does not extend to the governance of law schools" and their admissions policies and does not entitle it "to police human rights standards in law schools."[61] Moreover, said the dissenting judges, tolerance for religious diversity is itself a matter of public interest: "Acceptance by the LSBC of the unequal access effected by the Covenant would signify the accommodation of difference and of the TWU community's right to religious freedom, and not condonation of discrimination against LGBTQ persons."[62] The dissenting judges, though, went on to say that even if the LSBC's public interest mandate was broader and allowed the law society to consider factors "other than fitness," the decision not to accredit TWU's proposed program "unjustifiably limited the TWU community's freedom of religion."[63]

The dissenting judges stressed the importance of the "relational or communal" dimension of religious freedom, which involves "more than simply aggregating individual rights claims under the amorphous

---

60   *Ibid* at para 267.

61   *Ibid* at para 273. They further noted at para 290 that the law society's role as gatekeeper to the legal profession does not extend "all the way back to the law school's threshold." And at para 291: "Any harms to marginalized communities in the context of legal education must be considered by provincial human rights tribunals, by legislatures, and by members of the executive, which grant such institutions the power to confer degrees. The LSBC is not a roving, free-floating agent of the state. It cannot take it upon itself to police such matters when they lie beyond its mandate." Indeed, the dissenting judges assumed at para 268 that the TWU covenant is "a code of conduct protected by provincial human rights legislation." But, of course, the BC *Human Rights Code* (RSBC 1996, c 210 [*BC Code*]) does not give general protection to a religious organization's rules; it simply exempts the organization's rules from the application of the *BC Code*'s anti-discrimination requirements. In other words, it does not protect TWU's norms and practices from other forms of regulation or oversight—and it certainly does not entitle its law program to law society accreditation. The dissenters' assertion, of course, assumes that the covenant is an internal rule of a private religious association.

62   *Ibid* at para 269.

63   *Ibid* at para 268.

umbrella of an institution's 'community.'"[64] They noted that members of the TWU community sincerely believe that "studying, teaching and working in a post-secondary educational environment" where all participants agree to adhere to certain principles and practices is spiritually important.[65] According to the dissenting judges, section 2(a) protects "the freedom of members of the TWU community *to express* their religious beliefs through the Covenant and *to associate* with one another in order to study law in an educational community which reflects their religious beliefs."[66] The dissenters thought that the refusal to accredit the TWU law program was a "profound" interference "with the constitutionally guaranteed freedom of a community of co-religionists to insist upon certain moral commitments from those who wish to join the private space within which it pursues its religiously based practices."[67] In their view, the LSBC's decision not to accredit the TWU program "undermines the core character of a lawful religious institution and disrupts the vitality of the TWU community."[68] The dissenting judges also found that this interference with TWU's section 2(a) rights was not justified under section 1. They accepted that religious practices may be limited when they cause injury to others, but found that in this case, because the covenant was simply an internal matter, there was no "legally cognizable injury."[69]

The conclusions reached in the majority and dissenting judgments rest on very different assumptions about the character of TWU (or its proposed law program) as either public or private. Yet the public/private

---

64   *Ibid* at para 315. Justices Brown and Côté further noted at para 327 that "[t]he unequal access to the law program, which the majority judgment finds so troubling, is the consequence of the state's accommodation of diverse religious practices (such as adherence to the covenant) in a liberal pluralist society." In their view at para 335, the purpose of TWU's admissions policy was not to exclude 2SLGBTQ+ students but instead "to establish a code of conduct which ensures the vitality of its religious community."

65   *Ibid* at para 319. And at para 322: "For the members of the TWU community, religious belief and education are inextricably linked."

66   *Ibid* at para 316.

67   *Ibid* at para 261.

68   *Ibid* at para 324 citing *Loyola*, above note 57 at para 67. In the dissenting judges' view at para 268, the decision not to accredit the proposed program "is a profound interference with religious freedom" and inconsistent with "the state's duty of religious neutrality." They insisted at para 332 that secularism "[p]roperly understood . . . connotes pluralism and respect for diversity, not the suppression of full participation in society by imposing a forced choice between conformity with a single majoritarian norm and withdrawal from the public square." The dissenting judges at para 333 defined the scope of state power narrowly: "Simply put, the secular state is a neutral state, which refrains from espousing 'values' that undermine or go beyond what is necessary for the civic participation of all."

69   *Ibid* at para 332.

character of the institution is the very thing that is at issue in the case. The consequence of this — of assuming rather than determining the character of the institution or the law program — is that the two judgments never actually engage with each other. The majority viewed the proposed TWU program as public in character because they understood admission into an accredited law program to be part of the process for determining who enters the legal profession. The majority thought that, in operating an accredited law school and deciding whom to admit to the school, and ultimately to the legal profession, TWU would no longer be acting as simply a private religious organization and its covenant would no longer be simply an internal rule, applicable only to members of the religious community.[70] The dissenting judges, on the other hand, assumed that TWU is a private religious institution that should be free to regulate its internal affairs according to its spiritual norms.[71] In the dissenting judges' view, any interference with a religious association's internal operations or with its ability (as a religious association) to access the benefits of public life would amount to a breach of its religious freedom. The dissenting judges did not consider whether the impact of the TWU program on entry to the legal profession might mean that it was no longer acting simply as a private religious organization serving or overseeing only those who choose to be members of the spiritual community.

In neither judgment was much said about the substance of the competing claims or interests. Because the majority thought the desire to study in a religious community was simply an individual preference, they were able to uphold the restriction with little explanation. For the dissenting judges, because TWU was a private religious organization, any rule regulating entry was simply an internal matter and so caused no real injury to others. As long as the Court seeks to resolve religious freedom issues within the standard model of *Charter* adjudication that

---

70   *Ibid* at para 101: "Being required by someone else's religious beliefs to behave contrary to one's sexual identity is degrading and disrespectful. Being required to do so offends the public perception that freedom of religion includes freedom from religion." And at para 103: "The refusal to approve TWU's proposed law school prevents *concrete*, not abstract, harms to LGBTQ people and to the public in general. The LSBC's decision ensures that equal access to the legal profession is not undermined and prevents the risk of significant harm to LGBTQ people who feel they have no choice but to attend TWU's proposed law school."

71   For example, Brown and Côté JJ, *ibid* at para 265: "a court of law, particularly when dealing with claims of constitutionally guaranteed rights including freedom of religion, must have regard to the legal principles that guide the relationship between citizen and state, between private and public. And those principles exist to *protect* rights-holders from values which a state actor deems to be 'shared', not to give licence to courts to defer to or impose those values."

focuses on balancing, it will engage in a superficial trading-off of competing interests—giving weight to that which cannot be weighed, or arbitrarily discounting one side or the other of the balance in order to reach the result that seems intuitively correct. The balancing/proportionality process allows the Court to avoid providing any real justification or explanation for its conclusion in a particular case.

The issue in *LSBC v TWU*, then, is whether the school (in operating a law program) should be viewed as a private/voluntary religious institution that is free to govern itself according to its own norms, or whether it should be viewed as public, or at least as performing some form of public role, because its actions directly impact outsiders to the religious group, and therefore should be subject to public anti-discrimination norms. Another, more specific way to frame the issue is to ask whether the covenant should be viewed as an internal rule (a rule that applies to the internal operations of a voluntary religious association) or as a rule that applies to individuals who are not part of the TWU spiritual community.

Religious organizations operate in the larger world, and their actions will almost always have some impact on outsiders. The question is what kind or degree of impact is sufficient to say that the organization is no longer operating as simply a private/voluntary religious association?[72] TWU has special privileges granted to it by the state. It has the power to grant degrees. It is eligible to apply for money under various government infrastructure programs. Its students are eligible for state-supported grants and loans. Yet none of these considerations seem (or have been thought) to make TWU "public" and subject to non-discrimination requirements. But TWU now wants to train lawyers and so is seeking accreditation for a law program. TWU can, of course, run a law program without law society approval, but its graduates will not be eligible to practise law, or at least they will only be eligible if they go through some additional steps.

Admission to law school has often been seen as a significant gateway to the profession in Canada. Admission is competitive, with only a

---

72   According to its mandate and objectives, TWU is a religious institution. As noted in Victor Muñiz-Fraticelli, "The (Im)possibility of Christian Education" (2016) 75 *SCLR* 209, TWU seemed to argue against its own interests when it claimed to be public and accessible. As Rowe J pointed out, "[a]lthough TWU teaches from a Christian perspective, its statutory mandate requires that its admissions policy not be restricted to Christian students . . . TWU admits students from all faiths and permits them to hold diverse opinions on moral, ethical, and religious issues" (*LSBC v TWU*, above note 43 at para 240). He continued: "TWU itself states that it is open to 'all students who qualify for admission, recognizing that not all affirm the theological views that are vital to the University's Christian identity': TWU Covenant, A.R., vol. III, at p. 405." This point was earlier made by Chan, above note 58.

small percentage of applicants gaining entry to law school each year.[73] At least until recently, once someone was admitted to law school they were almost certainly going to be called to the bar, since failure rates at both law school and the bar exams were very low. If accredited law schools play an important role in determining who enters the legal profession in Canada, then the accreditation of the TWU program would mean that its norms (and, in particular, its covenant) would have the effect of excluding 2SLGBTQ+ students from the profession.

But is it still the case that law school admission is a significant gateway to the profession? In the last few years, new law schools have been established and funded by the provinces, and several existing law schools have increased the number of students they accept into their first-year program. Perhaps admission to law school is no longer a (the) significant barrier to entry to the legal profession; on the one side, there are so many accredited law school places in Canada (and it is increasingly possible to study abroad and be admitted to practise in Canada), and on the other side, graduation from law school no longer ensures employment as a lawyer in Canada. And of course, there are other significant barriers to law school entry that receive far less attention from the law societies — most notably the high cost of tuition at many accredited schools, which has had the effect of excluding students from less well-off backgrounds.

If, as the dissenting judges assumed, TWU is a private religious institution, then it would be free to discriminate in its admissions not just against gay and lesbian applicants but also against women and racial minorities. A private religious institution could exclude women (or married women, or women with children) from its program if it believed that a woman's role is to care for her children and to provide support in the home for her husband. A private institution could also expel individuals who engaged in interracial dating if it was opposed for religious reasons to "race-mixing." Perhaps TWU's assertion of autonomy in this case has resonance only because as a community we remain ambivalent about

---

73   Elaine Craig, "TWU Law: A Reply to Proponents of Approval" (2014) 37 *Dal LJ* 621 at 633:

> The argument that gays and lesbians can simply go elsewhere to become lawyers is problematic. As TWU noted in its effort to demonstrate to the BC government that there is a need for more law schools in the province: Canada has the lowest number of law schools per capita of any Commonwealth country ... [Applications] currently vastly outnumber the spaces available. Law school seats are a finite public good. Some LGBTQ students may not have the option to attend another Canadian law school. Moreover, as a matter of equality, meaningful access to a legal education in Canada should not differ depending on a student's sexual orientation.

sexual-orientation equality or we still cannot quite let go of the idea that a ban on same-sex intimacy is a restriction on behaviour (that an individual can refrain from engaging in) rather than an act of discrimination against sexual minorities.

Not long after the Supreme Court's decision, TWU announced that it would no longer require students to sign the covenant.[74] Presumably this was done in response to the message from the law societies and the Court that the covenant was the only thing preventing accreditation of the TWU program.[75] But even with the removal of the covenant, there remain two significant concerns about the program's accessibility. The first is that TWU, as a conservative evangelical Christian institution, will remain a hostile place for gay and lesbian students. Even if students are no longer asked to sign an undertaking that they will refrain from same-sex intimacy, the spiritual community will continue to view same-sex relationships as sinful or unnatural.[76] This is hardly a welcoming environment for 2SLGBTQ+ students, even if they are not formally excluded from the program. Second, if TWU is to be the kind of Christian institution it wants to be (a school for Christian students who will then practise as Christian lawyers), then it may have to favour conservative Christian applicants in its admission process. Perhaps TWU assumes that only Christians will apply to its program. But as long as law school places are limited in number, it is likely that non-Christians or non-evangelicals will also apply to TWU. If that is the case, then TWU

---

74   W Stueck & S Dhillon, "B.C.'s Trinity Western University Drops Mandatory Covenant Forbidding Sex Outside Heterosexual Marriage," *Globe and Mail* (14 August 2018), online: www.theglobeandmail.com/canada/british-columbia/article-bcs-trinity-western-university-drops-mandatory-covenant-forbidding.

75   See, for example, McLachlin CJ in *LSBC v TWU*, above note 43 at para 145: "If the community wishes to operate a law school, it must relinquish the mandatory Covenant it says is core to its religious beliefs, with the attendant ramifications on religious practices."

76   Muñiz-Fraticelli, above note 72 at 219, recognizes that this commitment by TWU does not disappear simply with the removal of the covenant but does not believe that either the covenant or culture should prevent accreditation of its law program:

> Given how fundamental the biblical conception of marriage is to TWU's identity, the alternative to TWU Law School *with* the discriminatory CCA [covenant] is not TWU Law School *without* the CCA. The alternative is no TWU Law School at all, and thus no additional places for straight or LGBTQ, religious or secular students. The university is founded on a religious mission — however objectionable some part of it may be to the mainstream of Canadian society. It is a branch of the church. From TWU's perspective, it would be incoherent to claim a Christian identity but not enforce norms that ensure that TWU remains a Christian space, and not merely as a school substantively identical to all others that is merely administered by Evangelicals.

will either choose the strongest students (academically) and its mission will be defeated, or it will give preference to Christian applicants and in doing so will exclude some students from its program on grounds that might be viewed as discriminatory. Either directly or indirectly, it appears that Christian students will be favoured in admission to TWU's program. If it is objectionable to exclude gay and lesbian students, is it not also objectionable to exclude non-Christian students? The answer to this may not be clear. While gay and lesbian people represent a historically marginalized group, the same cannot be said about the general group that includes everyone who is not an evangelical Christian, even if this group encompasses the members of various religious minorities.

E. *LOYOLA HIGH SCHOOL v QUEBEC (ATTORNEY GENERAL)*

In 2008, the Quebec government added an Ethics and Religious Culture (ERC) course to the mandatory curriculum for schools in the province.[77] The course was to be taught in an objective or neutral way and was intended to introduce students to the different cultures and belief systems in the province and to develop in students a capacity to discuss and evaluate different ethical positions. Under the province's education regulations, a private school could apply to the minister of education for an exemption to a required course (such as the ERC course), and the minister could grant an exemption if the school proposed an alternative course that the minister judged to be "equivalent" to the required course.

A private English-language Roman Catholic school, Loyola, applied to the minister for an exemption to the ERC course. The minister, however, decided that the alternative course proposed by the school was not equivalent to the ERC course because all elements of the course would be taught from a Catholic perspective. Loyola challenged the minister's decision, arguing that the minister had acted outside her powers when she refused to grant the exemption. Loyola was successful in its application to the Superior Court; however, the Quebec Court of Appeal reversed the lower court judgment and held that the minister's decision to refuse an exemption to Loyola was reasonable. The school then appealed to the Supreme Court. Prior to its appeal, Loyola made changes to its proposed course. In the revised version of Loyola's alternative course, the doctrines and practices of religions other than Catholicism

---

77   The course was also the subject of *SL v Commission scolaire des Chênes*, 2012 SCC 7 [*SL*], which is discussed in Chapter 3.

would be taught from a neutral or objective perspective; however, Loyola would still teach Catholic doctrine and ethics, as well as the ethical positions of other religions, from a Catholic perspective. The minister maintained her position that the entire course had to be taught from a neutral perspective.

A majority of the Supreme Court, in a judgment written by Abella J, held that the minister's decision (that all aspects of the course offered by Loyola had to be taught from a neutral perspective) interfered with the Loyola community's religious freedom.[78] In Abella J's view, the minister's decision did not reflect a "proportionate balance" between the statutory objective of promoting tolerance and respect for difference and the religious freedom of the members of the Loyola community.[79] Justice Abella accepted that the state has an interest in ensuring that students learn to be tolerant of other cultural and religious traditions and perspectives and develop a capacity to engage with others in a thoughtful and respectful way, but did not think that this justified the state's interference with the religious community's right to hold and manifest different religious beliefs—and in this case the right to manifest and transmit Catholic beliefs to their students. In her view, the requirement that Loyola teach Catholicism ("the very faith that animates its character") from a neutral perspective ("to speak about Catholicism in terms defined by the state rather than by its own understanding of Catholicism") was a serious interference with its religious freedom that would do little to advance the objectives of the ERC course.[80] However, she decided that it was not unreasonable to require Loyola to teach the doctrine and ethics of other religions from a neutral perspective. She thought that any other approach might lead students to regard other religions "not as differently legitimate belief systems, but as worthy of respect only to the extent that they aligned with the tenets of Catholicism."[81] The state does not breach religious freedom, she said, when it requires a school to teach students about other religions in a neutral and respectful way. Justice Abella thought that teaching about other religions and their ethical positions from a neutral perspective may be "a delicate exercise" but is nevertheless an important task.[82]

In her partly concurring judgment, McLachlin CJ went further than the majority and decided that Loyola should be permitted to teach both Catholicism and general ethics from a Catholic perspective—or should

---

78   *Loyola*, above note 57.

79   *Ibid* at para 79.

80   *Ibid* at paras 61 and 63.

81   *Ibid* at para 75.

82   *Ibid* at para 73.

at least be able to emphasize the Catholic perspective when examining ethical questions. She noted that freedom of religion is not limited to the holding and manifesting of religious belief and extends to "the propagation" of religion. In her view, "requiring Loyola to teach its entire ethics and religion program from a neutral, secular perspective" interfered with the school community's right to transmit its faith and so breached section 2(a) of the *Charter*.[83] While a program of "purely denominational instruction" that is "designed primarily to indoctrinate students . . . would not achieve the objectives of the ERC program," "a balanced curriculum" that "presented and respected" all viewpoints, even if "taught from a religious perspective," could be viewed as an equivalent to the ERC course.[84] Loyola, she said, could be required by the province to describe the doctrines of other religions in an objective and respectful way, but should not be prevented from teaching Catholic doctrine and ethical beliefs from a Catholic perspective.

Both judgments included some consideration of the collective dimension of religious practice and the standing of a religious association such as Loyola to make a freedom of religion claim under section 2(a). Justice Abella emphasized that religious freedom protects both the individual and collective aspects of religious belief and practice and noted that in this case "the collective manifestation and transmission of Catholic beliefs through a private denominational school are a crucial part of Loyola's claim."[85] She did not, however, think it was necessary to decide whether Loyola, as an institution, could, in its own right, claim the protection of section 2(a). In this case, she said, Loyola could be seen as representing a community of believers (parents, teachers, and students) and was in the best position to bring the freedom of religion claim on their behalf. Chief Justice McLachlin, in her partly concurring judgment, thought it necessary to say more about the rights of religious institutions under section 2(a) and set out criteria for determining when an institution could make a religious freedom claim. She held that "an organization meets the requirements for s. 2(*a*) protection if (1) it is constituted primarily for religious purposes, and (2) its operation accords with these religious purposes."[86]

Even though the two judgments in the case, by McLachlin CJ and Abella J, reached slightly different conclusions about what could reasonably be asked of a private Catholic high school when teaching about religion, both thought that the school (and its teachers) should not be expected to teach all elements of the course from a neutral or objective

---

83   *Ibid* at para 143.
84   *Ibid* at para 148.
85   *Ibid* at para 61.
86   *Ibid* at para 100.

perspective. Both judgments assumed that the minister's decision meant that Loyola would not be able to teach Catholic doctrine from a committed perspective. Justice Abella, for example, wondered what the point would be of allowing religious schools to teach students if they could not teach from such a perspective.[87] Yet the minister's decision did not preclude Loyola, in its regular religious education classes, from teaching Catholic doctrine as the one true faith.[88] Presumably this was what the other (mostly French-language) Roman Catholic private schools in the province were doing.[89] They had been consulted about the content and approach of the ERC course and had not sought to be exempted from it.

The Court's erroneous assumption that the minister's decision prevented Loyola from being able to teach Catholic doctrine from a committed perspective meant that the Court did not have to defend the problematic claim that it is unfair or unrealistic to ask Catholic teachers/schools in any class to teach Catholic doctrine and ethics from an objective perspective. If it is unrealistic or unfair to expect a Catholic teacher to teach Catholicism from such a perspective, it must also be unreasonable to expect them to teach other religions from such a perspective. Catholicism claims to be the one true faith. If Catholicism is true, then other religions must be false. Or put another way, if Catholic doctrine and ethical issues are taught from a Catholic perspective, can the positions of other religious or secular groups be presented objectively?

If the Court is right that it is unrealistic for a Catholic teacher to teach elements of the course from an objective position, it must also be true that anyone who holds a religious view, or a view about religion, will be unable to teach the program in a neutral way. Yet teachers in the public system who have religious commitments, including to Catholicism, manage to teach the course as designed. There is no reason, then, to think that teachers in private religious schools are incapable of also doing so. In the earlier case of *SL*, which is discussed in Chapter 3, the Court assumed it was possible to teach about religions in a way that was

---

87   *Ibid* at para 70.

88   Note that the principal of Loyola claimed only that "the idea of saying that you cannot be a Catholic for what-ever period of time during the day [when teaching the ERC course] that's where the problem was." Quoted in Azina Zaver, "Teachers and Third Space Realities: The Case of *Loyola High School v Quebec*" (2016) 43 *Religion & Educ* 344 at 346. He did not claim that the course precluded the school from teaching Catholic doctrine elsewhere in the curriculum.

89   *Ibid* at 347: "it appears that confessional schools were ... teaching ERC as a separate course from the Catholic education classes already taught."

descriptive or objective and that this did not involve advancing a form of moral or religious relativism, as Loyola claimed.[90]

Finally, the Court ignored the practical problem raised by Loyola's revised course. The different elements of the course are integrated, and so it will be difficult for a school or teacher to distinguish the parts of the course that are to be taught from a neutral perspective and those that can be taught from a committed Catholic perspective. The Court wrongly assumed that the different elements of the course can be separated practically and normatively.

Chief Justice McLachlin suggested that a Catholic school such as Loyola could teach Catholicism and ethical issues from a Catholic perspective, offering the Catholic view on these matters, without engaging in indoctrination. Yet she says very little about this distinction between religious indoctrination and teaching about a religious belief system—a faith-based system—from a committed position. It is not obvious that the alternative course offered by Loyola, in which Catholicism is taught as the one true faith, will involve an open and reasoned discussion and critique of Catholic doctrine.[91] There is a certain hubris on the part of the Court in imagining that they are able to make these determinations about pedagogy, particularly given the extensive planning and consultation that went into the creation of the course. As Benjamin Berger observes, "the *Loyola* decision might be most telling in its reflection of the difficulties of managing the process of teaching and education from the elevation of constitutional adjudication. The unpredictability and dynamism of the classroom is, in some ways, antithetical to the aesthetic coherence sought through adjudication."[92]

F. PROTECTING VULNERABLE GROUP MEMBERS: THE POLYGAMY BAN

The state may sometimes be justified in intervening in the affairs of a religious community that is insular and hierarchical when the community's

---

90   The majority decided that the Loyola application should be reconsidered by the minister, taking into account the factors and concerns set out in their judgment.

91   Benjamin L Berger, "Religious Diversity, Education, and the 'Crisis' in State Neutrality" (2014) 29 *CJLS* 103 at 118: "a key feature of indoctrination . . . is that its goal is to contain and limit options and alternatives contemplated by the subject." It is "a horizon limiting project."

92   Benjamin L Berger, "The Supreme Court of Canada on Religious Freedom and Education: *Loyola High School v Quebec (Attorney-General)*" (23 March 2015) online (blog): I-CONnect.

practices are thought to be harmful to some of its members, even though the members have, in a formal sense, chosen to participate in those practices.

In *Reference re: Criminal Code of Canada (BC)*,[93] the BC government asked the Supreme Court of British Columbia for its opinion concerning the constitutionality of the *Criminal Code*[94] ban on polygamy. Section 293(1) of the *Code* provides as follows:

> (1) Every one who
>
> (a) practises or enters into or in any manner agrees or consents to practise or enter into
>
>   (i)   any form of polygamy, or
>
>   (ii) any kind of conjugal union with more than one person at the same time, whether or not it is by law recognized as a binding form of marriage, or
>
> (b) celebrates, assists or is a party to a rite, ceremony, contract or consent that purports to sanction a relationship mentioned in subparagraph (a)(i) or (ii),
>
> is guilty of an indictable offence and liable to imprisonment for a term not exceeding five years.[95]

After hearing expert evidence concerning the practice of polygamy, the judge held that the ban breached section 2(a) but was justified under section 1. The ban was justified, said the judge, because Parliament had "a very strong basis for a reasoned apprehension of harm to many in our society inherent in the practice of polygamy."[96]

The judge accepted that the impetus for the ban was the arrival in Canada in the late 1800s of members of the Mormon community (the Church of Jesus Christ of Latter-Day Saints). However, he thought that the criminal ban on polygamy was not the "product of religious animus."[97] The purpose, he said, was not to suppress a religious practice or community but rather to prohibit a harmful activity, which was at the

---

93 2011 BCSC 1588.

94 RSC 1985, c C.46 [*Code*].

95 Section 293(2) of the *Code*, *ibid*, provides as follows:

> Where an accused is charged with an offence under this section, no averment or proof of the method by which the alleged relationship was entered into, agreed to or consented to is necessary in the indictment or on the trial of the accused, nor is it necessary on the trial to prove that the persons who are alleged to have entered into the relationship had or intended to have sexual intercourse.

96 Above note 93 at para 6.

97 *Ibid* at para 896.

time associated with the Mormon Church. The harms "arising out of the practice of polygamy" included "harm to women, to children, to society and to the institution of monogamous marriage."[98]

The judge recognized that women in polygamous relationships face a greater risk of physical and psychological harm. Relationships between co-wives may be difficult because they must compete for emotional and material support from their shared husband. The judge noted that women in polygamous relationships often have more children and tend to live shorter lives than women in monogamous relationships. They also do less well economically and "have less autonomy ... and lower levels of self-esteem."[99] Children in these relationships "tend to suffer more emotional, behavioural and physical problems, as well as lower education achievement than children in monogamous families."[100] This may be due to conflict among co-wives as well as "[t]he inability of fathers to give sufficient affection and disciplinary attention to all of their children."[101] The judge also thought that children in polygamous families are exposed to "harmful gender stereotypes."[102] He noted that girls in polygamous communities often marry at a young age and to much older men. At the same time, young men unable to find wives because of the "sex ratio imbalance inherent in polygamy ... are forced out of polygamous communities."[103] The judge found that polygamy is also harmful to society in general. The harms to society include the creation of a class of unmarried, poorly educated men who are "statistically predisposed" to violent and other anti-social behaviour.[104] Because "patriarchal hierarchy" and "authoritarian control" are standard in polygamous communities, the members "tend to have fewer civil liberties than their counterparts in societies which prohibit the practice."[105]

The judge rejected the argument that these harms could be addressed effectively through more targeted legal measures, such as the existing restrictions on child abuse or sexual coercion. In the judge's view, many of these harms are "inherent" in the practice and are not simply "the product of individual misconduct."[106] Yet at least some of the harms identified by the judge seem to be related to, or at least aggravated by, the insularity of polygamous communities, which as the judge observed

---

98 *Ibid* at para 5.
99 *Ibid* at para 8.
100 *Ibid* at para 9.
101 *Ibid*.
102 *Ibid* at para 12.
103 *Ibid* at para 11.
104 *Ibid* at para 13.
105 *Ibid*.
106 *Ibid* at para 1045.

is wholly or partly due to the criminalization of polygamy.[107] The "lost boys" problem, for example, would be less severe if the young men who were unable to find wives in their religious community did not find themselves effectively exiled into an unfamiliar world. Concern about sexual coercion or denial of education might be more easily addressed if the group was not isolated from the larger community.

Even if some of the harms to women and children could be addressed by regulating or monitoring polygamous relationships, the judge thought there were other significant harms that could not be addressed without banning the practice. In the judge's view, "the positive objective" of the polygamy ban is "the protection and preservation of monogamous marriage."[108] "For that," said the judge, "there can be no alternative to the outright prohibition of that which is fundamentally anathema to the institution."[109] He regarded the institution of monogamous marriage as valuable, a "public good," because "[t]he mutuality inherent in the dyadic structure habituated children to notions of equality and other important norms of citizenship."[110] In the judge's view, "exclusive and enduring monogamous marriage best ensured that men and women were treated with equal dignity and respect, and that husbands and wives, and parents and children provided each other with mutual support, protection and edification throughout their lifetimes."[111] He considered polygamy to be inferior to monogamy because it is structured as an unequal relationship. Even if inequality is part of many monogamous marriages, it is not a structural feature of such relationships.

A preliminary issue for the judge in determining the constitutionality of the polygamy law concerned the scope of the prohibition. The ban, as written, seemed to apply to any form of conjugal relationship (that is "committed, interdependent and of some permanence") involving more than two persons.[112] As a practical matter, such a broadly defined prohibition would be difficult to enforce and might extend to formal and informal polyamorous relationships. The judge, however, determined that the ban applied only when the marriage union is formally recognized by the couple's community. In his view, there must be a "voluntary joining together of two individuals with the requisite intent to

---

107 *Ibid* at para 310: "Wary of legal prohibitions against polygamy, Mormon fundamentalists tend to live covertly in isolated communities."
108 *Ibid* at para 1343.
109 *Ibid*. He continued, "there is no such thing as so-called 'good polygamy.'"
110 *Ibid* at para 174.
111 *Ibid* at para 209.
112 *Ibid* at para 916.

'marry' and the recognition and sanction by the couple's community."[113]
The requirement that there be some kind of formal "sanctioning event"
limits the scope of the ban to polygamous relationships that are supported or mandated by a religious or cultural community. The judge
acknowledged that many of the harms associated with polygamy (and
in particular the harm to the institution of monogamous marriage) may
occur in (or result from) other multi-party intimate relationships; nevertheless, he thought that the harms would be more severe in the case of a
relationship that is religiously or culturally sanctioned and is embedded
in a religious and cultural community, particularly one that is relatively
insular. The inequality in the relationship may be reinforced within a
larger cultural or religious community that regards such relationships
as morally appropriate or even required. Women in such a community
may be pressured into polygamous relationships or may be unable to
imagine any alternatives.

The principal argument against the polygamy ban is that it interferes with the religious freedom of the members of the Fundamentalist
Church of Jesus Christ of Latter-Day Saints and other religious groups
that either permit or require polygamy. Yet, at the same time, the judge
defined the ban so that its focus is on multi-party relationships within
religious or cultural communities. Many of the harms identified by the
judge are connected to the religious or cultural character of the practice.
This highlights a recurring tension in the religious freedom jurisprudence. The deep communal connections that are part of the value of
religious life and commitment may also be the source of what the courts
regard as harm—the perceived lack of choice or opportunity open to the
members of such communities.

G. THE ENFORCEMENT OF PRIVATE LAW ARRANGEMENTS

The courts will not ordinarily intervene in disputes within a religious
community about doctrine and practice. To do so would breach the
requirement that the state, including the courts, remain neutral in religious matters. However, the situation is different when the community's
rules or practices are incorporated into contractual and other private law
arrangements. The courts have been cautiously willing to enforce contracts made between religious group members even when these agreements give legal form to the norms or practices of the group.

---

113 *Ibid* at para 1020.

However, there are a number of reasons why the courts may hesitate to enforce agreements that are based on religious norms or that address religious matters. When enforcing a contract that is based on religious norms, the court may be drawn into disputes about the proper meaning of the norm with no secular or "objective" standard upon which to base its interpretation. The court may find itself in the uncomfortable position of determining religious doctrine and enforcing contested rules on dissenting members of the group.[114] When interpreting commercial and other contractual arrangements, the courts must sometimes consider the customs and norms of different subgroups within the larger community. There are important differences, though, between the enforcement of commercial norms and religious norms. Religious norms, particularly when they are in dispute, cannot be viewed as simply social conventions that a court can discover by examining group practice. They are, for the adherent, part of a higher law and must be respected because they are true or because they are God given. Any dispute between the contracting parties about the proper understanding of these norms is a dispute about spiritual truth. The resolution of such a dispute involves a judgment not about the best interpretation of a social practice but about the proper reading of divine law—about what God has truly commanded. The democratic and secular state, though, is expected to remove itself from such issues and avoid making determinations about spiritual truth.

The courts may also be reluctant to enforce "religious" agreements for the same reasons they have sometimes declined to enforce "family bargains"—because these agreements are embedded in larger relationships and are inseparable from deeper obligations. A contract between religious group members may be based on norms that are faith based, deeply held, and "religiously" binding on the members of a spiritual community. When entering an agreement or "contract," the parties may not understand themselves as creating legal obligations. They may consider themselves bound not by secular law but by the spiritual norms of their community—by higher law—and by their commitment to each other as members of the spiritual community. Even when religious parties make explicit use of private law forms, and may reasonably be understood as creating legal rights and obligations, they may believe that it would be wrong, a breach of their faith and their commitment to their community, to resort to the courts when disputes arise about

---

114 In *Amselem*, above note 59 at para 50, Iacobucci J declared that "the state is in no position to be, nor should it become, the arbiter of religious dogma. Accordingly, courts should avoid judicially interpreting and thus determining, either explicitly or implicitly, the content of a subjective understanding of religious requirement."

the meaning or implementation of the agreement.[115] The reluctance to enforce religious bargains may also rest on a recognition that legal intervention can damage relationships within the religious community. As well, the particular norm or practice that is the subject of the contract may be embedded within—and only understandable in relation to—a larger system of religious norms and practices. For example, the husband's promise in a Muslim marriage contract to pay his wife (deferred) *mahr* if they divorce is tied to his power to divorce his wife unilaterally.[116]

Finally, the courts may be reluctant to enforce religious contracts because they are concerned that one or both of the parties have not made a free and independent decision to enter into a legally binding agreement. The parties to a religious contract may be connected by a common history and a shared commitment to a set of faith-based norms and practices. They may be materially and emotionally tied to their spiritual community. In this context, an individual may be vulnerable to pressure from family and friends to agree to certain terms.[117] The individual may feel "compelled" to agree to contractual terms that are presented as morally binding or as central to community membership or identity. However, it is important not to confuse the inner pressure that an individual may feel to live up to certain values or obligations with the different forms of external pressure that may be brought to bear on them to get them to agree to certain practices or norms. We should not assume that religious commitments negate agency. Each of us is affected by an array of deeply held values, commitments, and associations.

In *Bruker v Marcovitz*[118] and earlier cases involving disputes within Hutterite colonies, the courts have adopted a pragmatic response to the enforceability of "religious" contracts. The courts have been willing to

---

115 For a discussion of the Hutterite prohibition on resorting to secular courts, see Alvin J Esau, *The Courts and the Colonies: The Litigation of Hutterite Church Disputes* (Vancouver: UBC Press, 2004).

116 For a discussion of this, see Pascale Fournier, "In the (Canadian) Shadow of Islamic Law: Translating *Mahr* as a Bargaining Endowment" in Moon, above note 3 at 140. In *Bakhshi v Hosseeinzadeh*, 2017 ONCA 838, the court said that "[t]he outcome of each case [involving an agreement to pay *Mahr*] depends, just as in any other case of contractual interpretation, on the objective intentions of the parties as ascertained through the particular wording of the Maher when read as a whole and considered in light of its factual matrix."

117 Some of those who proposed the establishment of a system of sharia arbitration under the private arbitration law in Ontario (which is discussed later in this chapter) expressed the view that an individual could not be regarded as a good Muslim if they submitted their disputes to the secular courts rather than arbitration under sharia rules. For a discussion of this, see Lorraine E Weinrib, "Ontario's Sharia Law Debate: Law and Politics under the *Charter*" in Moon, above note 3 at 239.

118 Above note 9.

enforce these arrangements if they have a legal form and can be interpreted without the courts being drawn (deeply) into debates about the proper understanding of religious doctrine. More particularly, the courts have been prepared to interpret and enforce such contracts when it appears the parties have relied on the agreement or when the agreement has civic consequences such as the control and ownership of church property. In such cases, judicial abstinence may not be a practical option.

H. JUDICIAL REVIEW OF THE INTERNAL DECISION MAKING OF RELIGIOUS GROUPS: *LAKESIDE COLONY, HIGHWOOD CONGREGATION,* AND *ETHIOPIAN ORTHODOX CHURCH*

In *Lakeside Colony of Hutterian Brethren v Hofer*, the Supreme Court reviewed the decision of a Hutterite colony to expel some of its members from the religious community and from the community's collectively owned property.[119] Justice Gonthier, writing for the Court, found that the colony was a voluntary association and that its members had agreed to its "articles of association." He further found that the colony had the power under these articles to expel members who deviated from the religious beliefs and practices of the community. Justice Gonthier said that while the Court would not review the merits of the colony's decision to expel members, it would consider whether the association had followed its own rules when making such a decision. It is not entirely clear in Gonthier J's decision what the legal basis was for the Court's intervention—whether the Court was reviewing the colony's decision because the colony was a public body or whether the Court was enforcing contractual obligations between colony members.[120] Whatever the basis for the Court's intervention, Gonthier J thought that the decision-making authorities in the colony had failed to adhere to the requirements of procedural fairness, and so the expulsion decision was invalid. Justice Gonthier was conscious of the "entanglement" issue—of the Court

---

119 [1992] 3 SCR 165 [*Lakeside Colony*]. See also the pre-*Charter* case of *Hofer*, above note 6. These and other cases involving the Hutterite colonies in Canada are considered in Esau, above note 115.

120 Justice Gonthier in Lakeside Colony, *ibid*: "If the defendants have a right to stay the question is not so much whether this is a property right or a contractual right, but whether it is of sufficient importance to deserve the intervention of the court and whether the remedy sought is susceptible to enforcement by the court."

being drawn into a dispute about religious doctrine—but thought this was not a significant concern in the case before the Court. He noted that the courts will not generally intervene in doctrinal or spiritual matters but may do so when civil or property rights are involved. According to Gonthier J, once a court assumes jurisdiction over a dispute with religious components, "there is no alternative but to come to the best understanding possible of the applicable tradition and custom."[121]

In *Highwood Congregation of Jehovah's Witnesses (Judicial Committee) v Wall*, Mr Wall, a member of a congregation of Jehovah's Witnesses in Calgary, was "disfellowshipped" by the judicial committee of elders after the committee found that he had engaged in sinful behaviour and was not sufficiently repentant.[122] The consequence of this decision was that members of the congregation were forbidden to speak to Mr Wall and his family about spiritual matters. Mr Wall applied for judicial review of the committee's decision, arguing that the decision should be quashed on the grounds that it was procedurally unfair. In his application to the court, Mr Wall also claimed that his real estate business had been dramatically affected by the loss of customers from the congregation.

The Supreme Court held that Mr Wall's application for judicial review could not succeed. Judicial review, said the Court, "is only available where there is an exercise of state authority and where that exercise is of a sufficiently public character."[123] Even if a body such as the judicial committee has the authority to make decisions that "impact a broad segment of the public," it is not a public decision maker and so its decisions are not subject to judicial review.[124] A decision will be viewed as public and subject to judicial review only when "it involves questions about the rule of law and the limits of an administrative decision maker's exercise of power."[125] The procedural rules of a religious group will often be based on religious doctrine, and the courts "have neither legitimacy nor institutional capacity" to deal with contentious matters of religious doctrine.[126] However, the Court said that it may have jurisdiction when a party has, or claims to have, a legal right based in private law. The Court can address procedural fairness concerns "related to the decisions

---

121   *Ibid* at paras 64 & 65. Justice Gonthier continued: "tradition or custom which is sufficiently well established may be considered to have the status of rules of the association, on the basis that they are unexpressed terms of the Articles of Association. In many cases, expert evidence will be of assistance to the Court in understanding the relevant tradition and custom."
122   2018 SCC 26 [*Highwood Congregation*].
123   *Ibid* at para 14.
124   *Ibid* at para 20.
125   *Ibid*.
126   *Ibid* at para 36.

of religious groups" when "legal rights are at stake" based on contract or tort.[127] The Court, though, found no evidence in this case that the members of the congregation "intended to create legal relations."[128] It noted that the Jehovah's Witness congregation in this case is a voluntary association that is not incorporated and has no articles of association or bylaws and owns no property. So the Court found no grounds in private law to intervene in the operations of the association.

More recently, in *Ethiopian Orthodox Tewahedo Church of Canada St Mary Cathedral v Aga*, several members of a church congregation sought a declaration from the courts that their expulsion from the congregation violated the principles of natural justice and was "null and void."[129] They argued that the church had failed to follow its own internal procedures and regulations when making the decision to expel them. The Supreme Court repeated what it had said in *Highwood Congregation*: that the courts will only review the decision of a voluntary association when that decision affects a legal right such as "property, contract, tort or unjust enrichment and statutory causes of action."[130] The question, said the Court, "is not whether the voluntary association exercises legal rights in general, but whether the particular relief sought by the plaintiff is the vindication of a legal right."[131] If it is not, then "there is no cause of action ... and no basis for relief."[132]

In contrast to the religious association in *Highwood Congregation*, the church in *Ethiopian Orthodox* was incorporated under provincial law and was the owner of the church building and the land on which it was located. The Court noted, however, that the congregation itself was not incorporated and the congregation members who had been expelled were not members of the church corporation. The Court stressed that membership in a voluntary association, such as a church congregation, is not necessarily contractual. To make a claim in contract, said the Court, the plaintiffs must show that the conditions of contract formation had been met, including the intention to create legal relations.[133] The Court found, in this case, no evidence of an intention by the members of the church to enter into legal relations, and so the Court had no grounds to intervene in the affairs of the church community. The Court thought that such an intention is more likely to exist where property or employment

---

127 *Ibid* at para 12.
128 *Ibid* at para 28.
129 2021 SCC 22 [*Ethiopian Orthodox*].
130 *Ibid* at para 29.
131 *Ibid* at para 31.
132 *Ibid.*
133 *Ibid* at para 33.

is at stake but is less likely to be present in religious contexts, as in this case, "where individuals may intend for their mutual obligations to be spiritually but not legally binding."[134]

I. *BRUKER v MARCOVITZ*

At the time of their civil divorce, Mr Marcovitz and Ms Bruker entered into an agreement concerning custody, access, division of property, and support. Their agreement also included an undertaking by each to appear before the Beth Din (rabbinical court) for the purpose of obtaining a *get*, or divorce, under Jewish law.[135] For their marriage to be dissolved under Jewish law, it was necessary for Mr Marcovitz to provide and Ms. Bruker to accept a "bill of divorce," or *get*. Without a *get*, neither party could remarry in the faith, and any subsequent intimate relationship entered into by either of them would be considered adulterous, and any children born of that relationship would be viewed as illegitimate. Mr Marcovitz did not appear before the Beth Din immediately following the civil divorce, despite his promise. Indeed, his consent to a religious divorce came fifteen years later and then only after Ms Bruker had commenced an action for breach of contract. Once Mr Marcovitz gave his consent, and the couple were divorced under Jewish law, Ms Bruker amended her action to seek compensation for the loss she had suffered because of his failure to give his consent at the time of the civil divorce.

In *Bruker v Marcovitz*, a majority of the Supreme Court, in a judgment written by Abella J, held that Mr Marcovitz's promise to consent to a religious divorce was legally enforceable and that Ms Bruker was entitled to damages for the loss she had suffered as a consequence of

---

134 *Ibid* at para 49. Howard Kislowicz & Benjamin L Berger, "Religion, Public Law, and the Refuge of Formalism" (2022) 73 *UNB Law Journal* 67, criticize the presumption that an agreement between members of a religious community that is based on religious doctrine is not ordinarily intended by the parties to create a legal obligation.

135 *Bruker*, above note 9. Clause 12 of their agreement provided as follows: "The parties [agree to] appear before the Rabbinical authorities in the City and District of Montreal for the purpose of obtaining the traditional religious *Get*, immediately upon a Decree Nisi of Divorce being granted" (*Bruker, ibid* at para 107). Strictly speaking, the *get* is not the divorce itself but rather the "bill of divorce," which the husband presents to his wife in the presence of a rabbi and witnesses. When she accepts the bill, the marriage is terminated. Because there is no additional requirement involving the consent of a religious authority, the term *get* is often used to refer to the divorce itself.

her ex-husband's failure to do as he had promised.[136] In Abella J's view, the religious character of Mr Marcovitz's undertaking did not "immunize it from judicial scrutiny."[137] A contract could have a religious object, provided that object was not "prohibited by law" or "contrary to public order."[138] Mr Marcovitz's promise "to remove the religious barriers to remarriage by providing a *get* was negotiated between two consenting adults, each represented by counsel, as part of a voluntary exchange of commitments intended to have legally enforceable consequences."[139] A court, said Abella J, may take jurisdiction when the dispute concerns the legal rights of the parties. She observed that in this case "[w]e are not dealing with judicial review of doctrinal religious principles, such as whether a particular *get* is valid. Nor are we required to speculate on what the rabbinical court would do."[140]

Justice Abella seemed to assume that the contract in this case could be enforced without the Court needing to delve into religious doctrine. She noted that Mr Marcovitz had offered no religious reasons for his failure to perform his undertaking and that, in any event, Judaism recognized no reasons to refuse consent. According to Abella J, the enforcement of the undertaking did not breach Mr Marcovitz's religious freedom, because "[h]is religion does not require him to refuse to give Ms. Bruker a *get*."[141] She noted that under Jewish law he could refuse to give a *get*, which is not the same as him "being prevented by a tenet of his religious beliefs from complying with a legal obligation he voluntarily entered into and of which he took the negotiated benefits."[142] She concluded that

---

136 *Ibid*. For a discussion of the *Bruker* case, see Rosalie Jukier & Shauna Van Praagh, "Civil Law and Religion in the Supreme Court of Canada: What Should We Get Out of *Bruker v Marcovitz*?" (2008) 43 *Sup Ct L Rev* (2d) 381; John C Kleefeld & Amanda Kennedy, "'A Delicate Necessity': *Bruker v Marcovitz* and the Problem of Jewish Divorce" (2008) 24 *Can J Fam L* 205; Richard Moon, "Divorce and the Marriage of Law and Religion: Comment on *Bruker v Marcovitz*" (2008) 42 *Sup Ct L Rev* (2d) 37; and MH Ogilvie, "*Bruker v Marcovitz*: (Get)ting Over Freedoms (Like Contract and Religion) in Canada" (2009) 24 *NJCL* 173.

137 *Bruker*, above note 9 at para 47.

138 *Ibid* at para 59.

139 *Ibid* at para 47.

140 *Ibid*. Earlier, Abella J observed "[t]he fact that a dispute has a religious aspect does not by itself make it non-justiciable" (*ibid* at para 41).

141 *Ibid* at para 69.

142 *Ibid*. A fuller quotation follows (*ibid* at paras 68–69):

> It is not clear to me what aspect of his religious beliefs prevented him from providing a *get*. He never, in fact, offered a religious reason for refusing to provide a *get*. Rather, he said that his refusal was based on the fact that, in his words: "Mrs. Bruker harassed me, she alienated my kids from me, she stole some money from me, she stole some silverware from my mother, she

the enforcement of his promise to consent to a divorce did not compel or pressure him to act in a way that is inconsistent with his religious beliefs. But, of course, Abella J could make this determination only after considering the rules and practices of the religious community.

Justice Abella's judgment involved more (and perhaps less) than a determination that religious contracts are legally enforceable. Underlying her judgment was a desire to mitigate the harshness of the Jewish community's divorce rules. She accepted that religious community members may sometimes require legal protection from the rules and practices of their community. In her view, Mr Marcovitz's promise to consent was enforceable not simply because it was a voluntary obligation but because public policy supported the removal of barriers to religious divorce and remarriage and the protection of gender equality.[143] Not far in the background of Abella J's judgment is the issue of the constitutionality of section 21.1 of the *Divorce Act*,[144] which empowers a judge in a civil divorce case to exert pressure on a spouse who refuses to give their consent to a religious divorce by "dismissing any application by that spouse" and "strik[ing] out any other pleadings and affidavits filed by the spouse."[145] Justice Abella drew from this legislative provision a

---

prevented my proper visitation with the kids. Those are the reasons ..." This concession confirms, in my view, that his refusal to provide the *get* was based less on religious conviction than on the fact that he was angry at Ms. Bruker. His religion does not require him to refuse to give Ms. Bruker a *get*. The contrary is true. There is no doubt that at Jewish law he *could* refuse to give one, but that is very different from Mr. Marcovitz being prevented by a tenet of his religious beliefs from complying with a legal obligation he voluntarily entered into and of which he took the negotiated benefits.

143 While Abella J was prepared to enforce Mr Marcovitz's promise to consent, there is more than a suggestion in her judgment that a husband may not use his consent power as a bargaining lever to obtain or extort concessions from his spouse, in particular concessions relating to custody, support, and the division of property.

144 RSC 1985, c 3 (2nd Supp).

145 *Bruker* above note 9. Section 21.1 of the *Divorce Act* provides as follows:

21.1 (2) In any proceedings under this Act, a spouse (... "deponent") may serve on the other spouse and file with the court an affidavit indicating ...

(c)   the nature of any barriers to the remarriage of the deponent within the deponent's religion the removal of which is within the other spouse's control; ...

(e)   that the deponent has, in writing, requested the other spouse to remove all of the barriers to the remarriage of the deponent within the deponent's religion the removal of which is within the other spouse's control; ...

(g)   that the other spouse, despite the request described in paragraph (e), has failed to remove all of the barriers referred to in that paragraph.

(3) Where a spouse who has been served with an affidavit under subsection (2) does not

public policy supporting the removal of barriers to remarriage. While she insisted that nothing in her reasons "purports in any way to decide the constitutionality of s. 21.1," her judgment would seem to support the constitutionality of the provision.[146]

Justice Abella was prepared to enforce Mr Marcovitz's undertaking because it had been voluntarily given and because, she believed, its interpretation did not require the Court to consider contested religious doctrine. While conscious of the inaccessibility of religious reasons or doctrines to secular institutions, she accepted that religious agreements (or agreements dealing with religious matters) could not lie entirely outside law's purview. She thought that instead of refusing to enforce all religious contracts, the courts should address concerns about undue influence or contractual intention on a case-by-case basis. The courts should decline to enforce a particular contract when there is genuine dispute about the relevant religious values or practices or when there is real concern that the consent of the parties was not given voluntarily. This approach seems both reasonable and necessary. A general decision by the courts not to enforce religious contracts might unfairly deny religious individuals the power to make binding legal arrangements based on their values, practices, and interests. More practically, a general exclusion would require the courts to distinguish religious from nonreligious

---

> (a) within fifteen days after that affidavit is filed with the court or within such longer period as the court allows, serve on the deponent and file with the court an affidavit indicating that all of the barriers referred to in paragraph (2)(e) have been removed, and
>
> (b) satisfy the court ... that all of the barriers referred to in paragraph (2)(e) have been removed,
>
> the court may, subject to any terms that the court considers appropriate,
>
> (c) dismiss any application filed by that spouse under this Act, and
>
> (d) strike out any other pleadings and affidavits filed by that spouse under this Act.
>
> (4) ... [T]he court may refuse to exercise its powers under paragraphs (3)(c) and (d) where a spouse who has been served with an affidavit under subsection (2)
>
> (a) ... serves on the deponent and files with the court an affidavit indicating genuine grounds of a religious or conscientious nature for refusing to remove the barriers referred to in paragraph (2)(e); and
>
> (b) satisfies the court ... that the spouse has genuine grounds of a religious or conscientious nature for refusing to remove the barriers referred to in paragraph (2)(e) ...
>
> (6) This section does not apply where the power to remove the barrier to religious remarriage lies with a religious body or official.

146 *Bruker*, above note 9 at para 35.

agreements. Given the subtle and significant ways in which religious belief shapes individual action, the line between these might be difficult to draw. The problem remains, though, that every time a religious contract is contested, the courts may be drawn, to some extent, into the interpretation (and enforcement) of religious doctrine.

In her dissenting judgment, Deschamps J held that Mr Marcovitz's promise was not legally binding because it lacked a justiciable "object," one of the essential elements of an enforceable agreement at civil law. She was clear that a contract is not legally enforceable under the Quebec *Civil Code*[147] if its object is exclusively religious (or is an object that could only be understood in religious terms). In contrast to the *Lakeside Colony* case (and other church property cases), the contractual obligation at issue in the *Bruker* case had no civic consequences. The contract related simply to Ms Bruker's position or status within the religious community and not to her legal status or property rights.

The religious nature of the contractual right in *Bruker* raises questions about both the appropriateness and the effectiveness of state intervention. In a case such as this, in which the court is not removing a material barrier to exit but is instead seeking to mitigate the unfairness of an internal practice or norm, the court cannot be sure of the effectiveness of its intervention. The religious divorce rules at issue in the *Bruker* case affect the status of Ms Bruker within the Jewish community as married or divorced (and the status of any subsequent relationship). But the state does not have the power to determine her status or standing in the religious community and so is limited in its ability to prevent her marginalization by co-religionists. If the religious community (and in particular the religious authorities) took the view that state pressure on the husband to give a *get* negated its effect, it would be difficult to see what the courts/state could do to protect the interests of Ms Bruker. State intervention appears to be effective in this case because many in the Jewish community—and not just the affected women—are willing to say that indirect state pressure on a husband to give a *get* is acceptable and does not make his "consent" involuntary.

J. SHARIA ARBITRATION IN ONTARIO

In late 2003, a heated debate began in Ontario concerning the arbitration of family disputes on the basis of sharia law under the province's arbitration legislation. The Ontario *Arbitration Act, 1991* provides for

---

147 CQLR c CCQ-1991.

the resolution of disputes in commercial, family, and other areas by an arbitrator chosen by the disputing parties.[148] At the time the sharia arbitration issue arose, the Act provided that the arbitrator was to resolve the dispute on the basis of the relevant provincial law unless the parties agreed to the application of another set of norms or laws, which might include religious laws. The Act further provided that the parties must voluntarily consent to the arbitration process and that the arbitration hearing must conform to basic standards of procedural fairness.[149]

Before the public controversy about sharia arbitration, several religious groups, including Orthodox Jews and Ismaili Muslims, had made use of the legislative framework to resolve family disputes in their communities based on religious laws. However, when a member of the Sunni Muslim community publicly announced the establishment of an Islamic arbitration institute that would resolve family disputes through the application of sharia law, a strong public reaction followed. Contributing to this reaction was the assertion by the institute's founder that all "good Muslims" would be expected to submit their disputes to the "Sharia courts."[150]

A variety of concerns were raised in the public debate about religious arbitration. The principal concern, though, was that Muslim women might feel pressured to submit their family disputes to this process, surrendering their rights under Canadian law. Because arbitration decisions made in accordance with the Act are legally enforceable, there was also concern that the state would be implicated in the enforcement of decisions that were inconsistent with public values such as gender equality.

The province appointed former provincial attorney general Marion Boyd to examine and make recommendations concerning the use of arbitration based on religious norms in family and inheritance matters. The *Boyd Report*, which was released in December 2004, recommended that the *Arbitration Act, 1991* continue to permit the arbitration of family and inheritance disputes based on religious norms.[151] The report found no "evidence to suggest that women are being systematically discriminated against as a result of arbitration of family law issues."[152] The report

---

148 SO 1991, c 17.

149 Most importantly, the parties must each be given a fair opportunity to present their arguments and to hear and respond to the arguments of the other side (*ibid*, s 19).

150 Marion Boyd, *Dispute Resolution in Family Law: Protecting Choice, Promoting Inclusion* (Toronto: Ontario Ministry of the Attorney General, 2004) at 55ff [*Boyd Report*].

151 *Ibid.*

152 *Ibid* at 133.

also identified certain benefits to maintaining a legal framework for the resolution of private disputes between the members of a religious group:

> [I]ncorporating cultural minority groups into mainstream political processes remains crucial for multicultural, liberal democratic societies. By availing itself of provincial legislation that has been in place for over a decade, and that has been used by others, the Muslim community is drawing on the dominant legal culture to express itself. By using mainstream legal instruments minority communities openly engage in institutional dialogue. And by engaging in such dialogue, a community is also inviting the state into its affairs, particularly since the *Arbitration Act*, even in its present form, specifically sets out grounds for state intervention in the form of judicial oversight. Use of the *Arbitration Act* by minority communities can therefore be understood as a desire to engage with the broader community.[153]

Oversight mechanisms in the Act would help to mitigate the unfairness that might sometimes occur in an otherwise private process. More generally, the interaction between state and religious law may contribute to the integration of minority religious groups into mainstream society.

The *Boyd Report* recommended that the Act be amended to include several additional safeguards to protect the interests of vulnerable members of religious groups. The report suggested giving the courts authority to set aside an arbitral award in several circumstances: if the award is unconscionable, if it is not in the best interests of any children affected by it, if either of the parties did not receive independent legal advice or did not waive their right to such advice before the arbitration, or if either of the parties did not receive "a statement of principles of faith-based arbitration" before agreeing to arbitration.[154] The report also recommended that mediators or arbitrators be required "to screen the parties separately about issues of power imbalance and domestic violence prior to entering into an arbitration agreement."[155] The Government of Ontario, though, rejected the report's central recommendations and instead amended the legislation to exclude "faith-based" arbitration. The premier declared that "[t]here will be no Sharia law in Ontario. There will be no religious arbitration in Ontario. There will be one law for all Ontarians."[156]

---

153 *Ibid* at 93.

154 *Ibid* at 134.

155 *Ibid* at 136.

156 Quoted in Jennifer A Selby & Anna C Korteweg, "Introduction: Situating the Sharia Debate in Ontario" in Anna C Korteweg & Jennifer A Selby, eds, *Debating Sharia: Islam, Gender Politics, and Family Law Arbitration* (Toronto: University of Toronto Press, 2012) 12 at 23.

Religious "arbitration," though, is still taking place in Ontario, even if the decisions made by religious authorities are not enforceable in the Ontario courts.[157] More significantly, individuals are still able to enter legally binding prenuptial or separation agreements, dealing with the division of property and the provision of support in the event of marriage breakdown. These agreements may be based on religious principles that differ significantly from the values that underlie family law rules. They will be legally binding as long as they have been entered into voluntarily.[158] The government, understandably, wanted to avoid being implicated in the enforcement of rules or practices that were inconsistent with public values. The question, though, is whether the withdrawal of legal recognition reduces the reliance of religious community members on religious norms and processes in the resolution of family disputes and encourages the integration of religious minorities into the larger community — or whether, as we have seen in other contexts, the "principled" exclusion of religious value systems (or practices) from the public sphere impedes the process of community integration. Religious arbitration (like other religious practices) does not come to an end when it is denied legal recognition, but instead is pushed into the private sphere, where it operates free of legal oversight and contact with public norms.

---

157 For an examination of this debate and the complex issues it raised about the relationship between law and religion, most of which were either ignored or distorted in the public debate, see Korteweg & Selby, eds, *ibid.*

158 As Audrey Macklin points out:

> [T]he question was never whether Muslim men and women could lawfully rely on religious authorities to negotiate domestic contracts, to mediate disputes or to arbitrate the consequences of marital dissolution. They have done so in the past, they do so now, and they will continue to do so in the future. They may participate more or less voluntarily, and abide by more or less fair outcomes. The state possesses neither will nor resources to police whether and how people resolve disputes outside the formal judicial system. In fact, unless one of the parties deliberately engages the formal legal system, the agreement will be insulated de facto from judicial scrutiny.

> Audrey Macklin, "Multiculturalism Meets Privatisation: The Case of Faith-Based Arbitration" (2013) 9 *Int'l JL in Context* 343 at 361. Macklin also makes the point that "the deficiencies attributed to faith-based arbitration are actually instantiations of larger tensions between private ordering and public justice in the specific context of family law dispute resolution" (*ibid* at 345).

K. CHURCH PROPERTY DISPUTES

Generally speaking, the property of a religious organization is held in trust for the purposes of the organization. The trust, which may be either express or implied, is established at the time the property is acquired.[159] When a dispute arises concerning the control or ownership of church property, resulting from divisions within the church, the role of the courts in resolving the dispute is to determine the terms of the trust.[160] In a series of cases beginning with the decision of the UK House of Lords in *General Assembly of the Free Church of Scotland v Overtoun*,[161] British and Canadian courts decided that the property at issue was held in trust for the "church," identified by its adherence to a particular set of religious doctrines. The beneficiary of the property trust in such cases, then, was the group that remained committed to the established (and fundamental) doctrines of the church. In some cases, this meant that the beneficiary of the trust was the group that was splitting from the main body of the organization because it did not agree with significant revisions to established doctrine.

More recently, however, the courts have been less inclined to see the trust as based on adherence to traditional doctrine and have decided that in some cases the property is held in trust for the benefit of the general organization, which has the authority to interpret and revise doctrine. This approach was applied in *Bentley v Anglican Synod of the Diocese of New Westminster*,[162] in which the BC Court of Appeal had to determine who was entitled to hold and use church property following a doctrinally based schism in a diocese of the Anglican Church of Canada. The appellants, who were members and clergy of several Anglican parishes in the Diocese of New Westminster, disagreed with the synod's decision to bless same-sex marriages and so sought to withdraw from the diocese while

---

159 MH Ogilvie, *Religious Institutions and the Law in Canada*, 4th ed (Toronto: Irwin Law, 2017) at 292.

160 See MH Ogilvie, "Church Property Disputes: Some Organizing Principles" (1992) 42 *UTLJ* 377; Alvin J Esau, "The Judicial Resolution of Church Property Disputes: Canadian and American Models" (2003) 40 *Alta L Rev* 767; and *Religious Institutions, ibid* at 291–95. In her book *Religious Institutions*, Ogilvie also discusses the courts' role in overseeing the discipline and dismissal of clergy, which is confined to ensuring that the church follows its internal rules and the standards of procedural fairness (*ibid* at 302). See, for example, *McGaw v United Church of Canada* (1991), 82 DLR (4th) 289 (Ont CA). But see also *Hart v Roman Catholic Episcopal Corp of the Diocese of Kingston*, 2011 ONCA 728.

161 [1904] AC 515 (HL) [*Free Church*].

162 [2010] BCCA 506 [*Bentley*]. See also *Delicata v Incorporated Synod of the Diocese of Huron*, 2013 ONCA 540.

retaining the right to use church property in their parish. Relying on the *Free Church* decision, they argued that parish property was held for purposes consistent with historic, orthodox Anglican doctrine and that because they adhered to traditional church doctrine, they most closely conformed to the conditions of the trust under which parish property was held. The court, however, was unwilling to follow the *Free Church* decision, which did "not allow for the institution in question to adopt changes in doctrine, or at least fundamental doctrine."[163] The court found that the property was held in trust for purpose of "further[ing] Anglican ministry in accordance with Anglican doctrine, and that in Canada, the General Synod has the final word on doctrinal matters."[164] The court recognized that the Anglican church is a hierarchical body and that Anglicanism cannot be separated from the church organization's episcopal authority.[165] The rules of the Anglican Church of Canada provided that doctrinal matters fell within the jurisdiction of the bishop and the synod and that these doctrinal determinations governed all parishes. The court therefore dismissed the appellants' claim to the property.

Courts in different jurisdictions have responded to church property disputes in different ways, trying to resolve these disputes without becoming entangled in matters of doctrine. The commitment in the United States to the separation of church and state has led to two responses to this dilemma: (1) deference to the determination of the highest decision-making body in a hierarchical church, without asking whether this body (the mother or central church) has deviated from traditional doctrine, and even without asking whether this body has adhered to its own rules, including process rules; or (2) the application of "neutral principles," with the court or other civil authority determining the property issue on the basis of the express terms of title deeds, contracts, and perhaps even the church's charter and bylaws, provided these documents can be read in exclusively secular terms without requiring any judgment about religious doctrine.[166]

---

163   *Bentley, ibid* at para 66.

164   *Ibid* at para 76.

165   *Ibid* at para 74.

166   See, for example, *Watson v Jones*, 80 US (13 Wall) 679 (1871); and *Jones v Wolf*, 443 US 595 (1979). In *Pankerichan v Djokic*, 2014 ONCA 709, the Ontario Court of Appeal held that the American "neutral principles" approach has not been adopted by the Canadian courts and that the court's task in church property dispute cases is to construe the terms of the trust under which the property is held.

CHAPTER 6

PARENTS, CHILDREN, AND SCHOOLS

A. INTRODUCTION

Some of the most contentious freedom of religion cases involve the parent–child relationship. In these cases, the claim of parents to make religiously based decisions concerning the welfare of their children, or to transmit their faith to their children, is often pitted against their children's interest in developing as independent agents, capable of making their own judgments, including spiritual judgments, or the interest of the larger community in ensuring the development of children as citizens who are tolerant and able to contribute to society.[1] In this way, the debate about religious freedom in the family context exposes most starkly the central tension in the courts' understanding of religion, as both a personal commitment and a cultural identity, and of religious freedom as both the right of the individual to make spiritual choices and the right of religious believers or communities to live according to their own norms and practices.

---

1   Benjamin L Berger, "Religious Diversity, Education, and the 'Crisis' in State Neutrality" (2014) 29 *CJLS* 103 at 109: "For religious groups and the state alike education is the means by which culture, tradition, value and community are affirmed and sustained."

B. PARENTS' RIGHTS

The right of parents to oversee the spiritual life of their children may simply be part of a more general right of parents to make decisions concerning their children's welfare. It is sometimes argued that parents have this right because they are in the best position to make judgments about what is good for their children. Children require guidance and oversight. Because parents have intimate knowledge of their children and because they ordinarily have the best interests of their children in mind, they are able to provide this guidance. The right (and "right" may not be the proper term) or authority of parents to make decisions concerning the welfare of their children may also, and more substantially, rest on the positive value of the family relationship to the child's emotional and intellectual development and on a recognition that interference with this relationship may be harmful to the child and hinder their development.[2] The right of parents to oversee the spiritual life of their children, or to transmit religious values and customs, then may be based on the importance of the family relationship to the development of children. While it may sometimes be necessary to interfere with the family relationship to protect children from harm, this is never an ideal option and the costs to the children will be significant.[3]

---

2   See K Anthony Appiah, *The Ethics of Identity* (Princeton: Princeton University Press, 2005) at 201–2: "The intimacy of family life; the love of children for parents (and other relatives) and of parents (and other relatives) for children; the sense of a family identity, family traditions: all these would be lost. More than this, the state would be invested with a quite enormous power in the shaping of the citizenry; a power whose potential for abuse is obvious enough."

3   According to the courts, s 7 of the *Canadian Charter of Rights and Freedoms*, Part 1 of the *Constitution Act, 1982*, being Schedule B to the *Canada Act 1982* (UK), 1982, c 11 [*Charter*], ("the right to life, liberty and security of the person") also protects the right of parents to make decisions concerning the welfare of their children. See, for example, *RB v Children's Aid Society of Metropolitan Toronto*, [1995] 1 SCR 315 [*RB*].

   The justification for the restriction of the parents' right is most often based on the interests (or right) of the state or the larger community in the development of citizens who are capable of making independent decisions and tolerating the views of others. But to view this as simply a state interest is to confuse the actor with the reasons for action. The state or the larger community does have an interest in ensuring that children mature into responsible citizens and contribute to the welfare of the larger community, but there is a more basic interest or good at stake here than the effective operation of the democratic process or the economic system, and that is the development of a child's capacity for reasoned judgment and emotional attachment.

C. HARM TO CHILDREN AND INTERNAL LIMITS TO SECTION 2(A)

The Canadian courts have said that section 2(a) of the *Charter* is breached anytime the state interferes (in a nontrivial way) with an individual's religious practice. If the court finds a breach of section 2(a), it then considers whether the restriction on the religious practice is justified under section 1 of the *Charter*. However, some members of the Supreme Court of Canada have said that a religious practice that is "harmful" to others will not fall within the protection of section 2(a), so the state will not be required to justify the restriction of such a practice under section 1. The claim that harmful religious practices should be excluded from the scope of section 2(a) arises principally in cases involving parental oversight of children and seems to reflect our ambivalence about parental "rights." However, in the recent judgment of *Saskatchewan (Human Rights Commission) v Whatcott*, the Supreme Court indicated that even if there is an exclusion of harmful religious practices from the scope of section 2(a), it should be narrowly defined: "Just as the protection afforded by freedom of expression is extended to all expression other than violence and threats of violence, in my view, the protection provided under s. 2(*a*) should extend broadly."[4]

In *RB v Children's Aid Society of Metropolitan Toronto*, Iacobucci and Major JJ in a concurring judgment held that the parents' refusal on religious grounds to consent to a potentially life-saving medical treatment for their infant child was not protected by section 2(a), so that the state's override of that decision did not breach the section:

> The parents['] ... constitutional freedom includes the right to educate and rear their child in the tenets of their faith. In effect, until the child reaches an age where she can make an independent decision regarding her own religious beliefs, her parents may decide on her religion for her and raise her in accordance with that religion. However, the freedom of religion is not absolute ... [W]e are of the view that the right itself must have a definition, and even if a broad and flexible definition is appropriate, there must be an outer boundary. Conduct which lies outside that boundary is not protected by the Charter.[5]

More specifically, Iacobucci and Major JJ found that "the appellants do not benefit from the protection of s. 2(a) of the Charter since a parent's freedom of religion does not include the imposition upon the child of

---

4   2013 SCC 11 at para 154.

5   Above note 3 at paras 223 & 224.

religious practices which threaten the safety, health or life of the child."[6] However, this was not the approach adopted by the majority of the Court in that case. Justice La Forest, for the majority, observed that "[t]his Court has consistently refrained from formulating internal limits to the scope of freedom of religion in cases where the constitutionality of a legislative scheme was raised; it rather opted to balance the competing rights under s. 1 of the *Charter*."[7]

The particular issue before the Court in the *RB* case was the constitutionality of a temporary Crown wardship order granted to the Children's Aid Society under provincial child welfare legislation. The parents, who were Jehovah's Witnesses, had refused for religious reasons to consent to a blood transfusion for their critically ill infant. The wardship order enabled the Children's Aid Society to consent to the transfusion. The parents argued that the order breached section 2(a) and section 7 of the *Charter*. Justice La Forest, for the majority, agreed that the parents had a right under section 2(a) to raise their children in accordance with their religious beliefs and that this included the right to make decisions about the medical treatment of their children; however, he went on to find that the state's interference with this right, in order to protect a child at risk, was justified under section 1. While the Court agreed that parents should be free to care for their children as they think proper and to pass their beliefs on to their children, it recognized that an infant who is denied necessary medical treatment because of their parents' religious beliefs would never reach an age at which they would be able to make their own judgments.

The issue is different when the child is old enough to express a view and indicates their opposition to treatment. Adults have a general right to refuse medical treatment, including life-saving treatment, and are not required to justify their refusal on religious or other grounds.[8] The law

---

6   *Ibid* at para 225. Similarly, in *Young v Young*, [1993] 4 SCR 3 at para 218 [*Young*] (which is discussed later), McLachlin J said that "conduct which poses a risk of harm to the child would not be protected."

7   *RB*, above note 3 at para 109.

8   In *Malette v Shulman*, 1990 CanLII 6868, 67 DLR (4th) 321 (Ont CA), a woman who was injured in accident was unconscious at the time of her admission but had with her a card indicating she was a member of the Jehovah's Witness faith group and refused consent to a blood transfusion. The doctor, although aware of this, nevertheless gave her a transfusion. After her recovery she successfully sued the doctor for battery.

in most provinces extends to "mature minors" the same right to refuse treatment.[9]

The Supreme Court considered the constitutionality of a version of the mature minor exemption in *AC v Manitoba (Director of Child and Family Services)*.[10] The appellant in that case was almost fifteen years old when she was admitted into hospital with severe intestinal bleeding. She was a member of the Jehovah's Witness faith and refused to consent to a blood transfusion even though she had been told by her doctor that a transfusion was medically necessary. The director of Child and Family Services for the province applied for a treatment order from the court. Under the province's child welfare law, a court may authorize treatment it judges to be in the child's "best interests." The legislation created a presumption that the best interests of a child who is sixteen or older will be "most effectively promoted" by allowing their views about treatment to prevail. This presumption will be rebutted only if it is demonstrated that the child does not appreciate the consequences of their decision to refuse treatment. The legislation, though, said that no such presumption is to be made when the child is under the age of sixteen. The trial judge in *AC* held that because the appellant was under sixteen, the "best interests" test applied, so he ordered that the transfusion be given. The child challenged the constitutionality of the legislative scheme, arguing that it breached her section 2(a) rights. A majority of the Supreme Court, in a judgment written by Abella J, held that the "best interests" of the child test should include some consideration of the child's capacity for mature, independent judgment. The capacity of a child who is under the age of sixteen to make such decisions is a relevant consideration in the determination of her best interests. According to Abella J, "[t]he more a court is satisfied that a child is capable of making a mature, independent decision on his or her own behalf, the greater the weight that will be given to his or her

---

9   The history of the common law mature minor exemption is discussed in *AC v Manitoba (Director of Child and Family Services)*, 2009 SCC 30 at para 59ff [*AC*]. In *BH (Next Friend of) v Alberta (Director of Child Welfare)*, 2003 ABCA 109 [*BH*], the Alberta Court of Appeal upheld a medical treatment order under provincial child welfare law. While the *Child Welfare Act*, RSA 2000, c C-12 defined "child" in s 1(1)(d) as "a person under the age of 18 years," it also provided in s 2(d) that a child who is "capable of forming an opinion, is entitled to an opportunity to express that opinion on matters affecting the child and the child's opinion should be considered by those making decisions that affect the child." The court accepted that H lacked the capacity to refuse medical treatment that was necessary to save her life. The court concluded that the treatment order did not breach the *Charter* "where there is no mature minor or no informed decision by one": *BH* at para 13. For a discussion of this case, see Lori G Beaman, *Defining Harm: Religious Freedom and the Limits of the Law* (Vancouver: UBC Press, 2008).

10   *AC*, above note 9.

views when a court is exercising its discretion under [the legislation]."[11] She concluded that when the "best interests" test is interpreted in this way, as taking into account the child's capacity to make medical judgments, it will not be found to violate section 2(a). Because the medical emergency in the case had long passed, and the child was over sixteen when the case was heard, the only issue before the Court was the constitutionality of the legislation.[12]

D. CUSTODY AND ACCESS

When resolving disputes about child custody and access, the courts do not ordinarily pass judgment on the character or value of the parents' religious beliefs.[13] However, the courts will take into account a parent's religious beliefs when those beliefs create a risk of harm to the child. In such a case, a parent may be denied custody or access, or their access rights may be curtailed.[14]

---

11   *Ibid* at para 87. She continued (*ibid*):

> If, after a careful and sophisticated analysis of the young person's ability to exercise mature, independent judgment, the court is persuaded that the necessary level of maturity exists, it seems to me necessarily to follow that the adolescent's views ought to be respected. Such an approach clarifies that in the context of medical treatment, young people under 16 should be permitted to attempt to demonstrate that their views about a particular medical treatment decision reflect a sufficient degree of independence of thought and maturity.

12   The courts have also held that parental practices that are harmful to children, such as physical discipline, even if grounded in religious belief, will not receive *Charter* protection. In *Prince Edward Island (Director of Child Welfare) v SPL*, 2002 PESCTD 74, the Supreme Court of Prince Edward Island granted permanent guardianship of children in a religious commune to the province's director of child welfare and rejected the religious group's argument that use of the "rod" to discipline children and other forms of abusive behaviour were protected by the *Charter* as religious practices. In *Canadian Foundation for Children, Youth and the Law v Canada (AG)*, 2004 SCC 4, the Supreme Court of Canada upheld a narrowly defined exception to the prohibition on assault for the reasonable use of force by a parent in correcting the behaviour of his child.

13   See GD Chipeur & TM Bailey, "Honey, I Proselytized the Kids: Religion as a Factor in Child Custody and Access Disputes" (1994) 4 *NJCL* 101 at 116. But if religion is not a relevant consideration in the application of the child's best interests test in custody and access cases, it is only because we have decided that religion should be treated like a "trait" comparable to gender or race rather than a contestable belief.

14   See Shauna Van Praagh, "Religion, Custody, and a Child's Identities" (1997) 35 *Osgoode Hall LJ* 309 at 318.

Religion most commonly plays a role in a court's decision about custody or access when the beliefs or practices of the separated parents' conflict in a way that may cause stress to the children. When an access parent seeks to teach their children beliefs or practices that are incompatible with the beliefs of the custodial parent, the courts may be willing to limit the access parent's ability to involve their children in their religious life. The courts, though, will curtail the access parent's right to expose their children to their faith only when the religious conflict (and the resulting stress to the children) is significant. The courts recognize that it is generally in the children's best interests to maintain a relationship with the access parent and to be connected as fully as is reasonably possible with their parent's life.[15]

The issue of religious conflict between divorced or separated parents arose in two Supreme Court cases, *Young v Young*[16] and *P(D) v S(C)*.[17] In both cases, the Court considered whether it was in the best interests of the children to limit the ability of the noncustodial parent, the father, to discuss his religion with them or to involve them in his religious practices and, if it was decided that the children's best interests test required the imposition of such a limit on the noncustodial parent, whether this limit breached his freedom of religion rights under the *Charter*.

In *Young*, the mother had been awarded custody of her three children by a lower court, and the father had been granted access subject to the condition that when he was with his children he was not to discuss his religion (Jehovah's Witness), take them to any religious meetings, or involve them in religious canvassing. The father agreed not to take his children on canvassing excursions or to religious services but questioned the prohibition on discussing religious matters with them. The Court accepted that issues of custody and access were to be determined on the basis of the children's "best interests." However, before deciding whether the lower court judge had properly applied the "best interests" test to the case, the Court considered whether this test breached section 2(a) and, if it did, whether it was justified under section 1. Justice L'Heureux-Dubé thought that "even if the Charter were to apply to custody and access orders, no infringement of religious freedoms would occur where such orders are made in the best interests of the child."[18] She argued that "[w]hile parents are free to engage in religious practices themselves, those

---

15   The custody and access cases in which the parents' religious commitments are no longer in harmony make clear that "parents' rights" is just a term of convenience and that the focus is really on the child's interests.

16   Above note 6.

17   [1993] 4 SCR 141 [*P(D)*].

18   Above note 6 at para 137.

activities may be curtailed where they interfere with the best interests of the child without thereby infringing the parent's religious freedoms."[19] Similarly, McLachlin J said that "the Charter guarantee of freedom of religion does not extend to protect conduct which is not in the best interests of the child."[20] The majority of the Court, however, found that in this case the best interests of the children did not require the father to refrain from any kind of "genuine discussion of religious belief" with his children and so ordered the removal of this particular condition of access.[21] The Court made clear that the maintenance of this relationship—and more particularly the father's ability to teach his children about his faith—is protected because it is in the children's best interests and not because the parent has a right of some kind.

In a companion case from Quebec, *P(D)*, the Court confirmed that the sole consideration in matters of custody and access is the child's best interests and that freedom of religion is "inherently limited by the rights and freedoms of others."[22] In this case, the Court upheld restrictions on the noncustodial parent's access that prohibited him from engaging in religious indoctrination. While insisting that religious differences between parents were not "automatically harmful" and indeed might be beneficial, Cory and Iacobucci JJ, writing for the Court, accepted the trial judge's determination that the father's religious practice (described as religious fanaticism) was the source of significant conflict with the children and contrary to their best interests.[23]

As these cases illustrate, judgments about the value or character of religious belief or practice may sometimes play a role in decisions about custody and access. Justice L'Heureux-Dubé in *Young* insisted that in these cases, "where there is conflict over religion, it is important to emphasize that the court is not engaged in adjudicating a 'war of religion' nor are the religious beliefs of the parties themselves on trial. Rather, as courts have often recognized, it is the manner in which such beliefs are practised together with the impact and effect they have on the child which must be considered."[24] Yet, for the father who is a practising member of the Jehovah's Witness community and shares its commitment to

---

19   *Ibid.* "The Charter has no application to private disputes between parents in the family context, nor does it apply to court orders in the area of custody and access. While a child's exposure to different parental faiths or beliefs may be of value, when such exposure is a source of conflict and is not in the best interests of the child, such exposure may be curtailed": *ibid* at para 157.

20   *Ibid* at para 218.

21   *Ibid* at para 186.

22   Above note 17 at para 107.

23   *Ibid* at para 140.

24   Above note 6 at para 135.

active proselytization, this distinction between the beliefs he holds and the manner in which he practises them will make little sense. Shared custody, or generous access for the noncustodial parent, may work when parents are affiliated with the same religious group or with different "mainstream" religious groups that are reasonably compatible or do not come into direct conflict. In such cases, the differences in religious outlook between the parents will not be particularly disruptive or confusing to the children. However, other belief systems that demand exclusive allegiance and regard competing faiths not just as mistaken but as sinful or blasphemous may generate significant tension between the parents and stress in the children. A court, then, may sometimes decide that it is in the best interests of a child to restrict the access of a parent who seeks to involve the child in religious practices that conflict with the beliefs of the custodial parent.[25]

E. SECTION 93 AND SEPARATE SCHOOLS

The right of parents to make decisions concerning the education of their children is understood to include the right to decide whether their children will be educated in a public school or private school (including a private religious school), or at home.[26] At the same time, the state retains the power to oversee private schools and home schooling, and to establish curriculum requirements and instruction standards.[27] The limits of this power were the subject of *Loyola High School v Quebec (Attorney General)*, which was discussed in Chapter 5.[28]

The courts have held that section 2(a) of the *Charter* prohibits state support for the practices or institutions of a particular religion but does not prevent the state from providing general support for religious practices or institutions. A province, then, may fund religious schools as long as it does so in an even-handed way, supporting different religious schools, as well as public/secular schools.

---

25   In *Vojnity v Hungary*, Application no 29617/07, Eur Ct HR, 12 February 2013 at para 41, the European Court of Human Rights confirmed that "a measure as radical as the total severance of contact [access rights] can be justified only in exceptional circumstances."

26   The parental right to send children to private schools seems to be taken for granted. See, for example, the judgment of Iacobucci J in *Adler v Ontario*, [1996] 3 SCR 609 at para 15, and of Sopinka J in *ibid* at para 171 [*Adler*].

27   See *R v Jones*, [1986] 2 SCR 284 and *SL v Commission scolaire des Chênes*, 2012 SCC 7 [*SL*], both of which are discussed in Chapter 3.

28   2015 SCC 12.

There is, however, a constitutional exception to this requirement of equal treatment. Section 93 of the *Constitution Act, 1867*,[29] as well as the Acts establishing the provinces that later entered the union, protect the rights of "Separate" or "Dissentient" schools (principally Roman Catholic schools) that were legally established in a province at the time of its entry into Confederation.[30] The courts have described section 93 as "part of a solemn pact resulting from the bargaining which made Confederation possible."[31]

---

29   *Constitution Act, 1867* (UK), 30 & 31 Vict, c 3, reprinted in RSC 1985, Appendix II, No 5.

30   See the *Saskatchewan Act*, SC 1905, c 42, s 17, and the *Alberta Act*, SC 1905, c 3, s 17. The constitutional terms under which each of the provinces entered the union included a recognition of the rights of denominational schools; however, the courts found that in many provinces the provision had no application since at the time of their entry into the union they had no legally established denominational schools. While the provinces of Quebec and Newfoundland were originally bound under the Constitution to provide support for denominational schools, these obligations were ended (in the case of Quebec) or substantially removed (in the case of Newfoundland) by constitutional amendment.

The full text of s 93 of the *Constitution Act, 1867* is as follows:

93. In and for each Province the Legislature may exclusively make Laws in relation to Education, subject and according to the following Provisions:

(1)   Nothing in any such Law shall prejudicially affect any Right or Privilege with respect to Denominational Schools which any Class of Persons have by Law in the Province at the Union;

(2)   All the Powers, Privileges, and Duties at the Union by Law conferred and imposed in Upper Canada on the Separate Schools and School Trustees of the Queen's Roman Catholic Subjects shall be and the same are hereby extended to the Dissentient Schools of the Queen's Protestant and Roman Catholic Subjects in Quebec;

(3)   Where in any Province a System of Separate or Dissentient Schools exists by Law at the Union or is thereafter established by the Legislature of the Province, an Appeal shall lie to the Governor General in Council from any Act or Decision of any Provincial Authority affecting any Right or Privilege of the Protestant or Roman Catholic Minority of the Queen's Subjects in relation to Education;

(4)   In case any such Provincial Law as from Time to Time seems to the Governor General in Council requisite for the due Execution of the Provisions of this Section is not made, or in case any Decision of the Governor General in Council on any Appeal under this Section is not duly executed by the proper Provincial Authority in that Behalf, then and in every such Case, and as far only as the Circumstances of each Case require, the Parliament of Canada may make remedial Laws for the due Execution of the Provisions of this Section and of any Decision of the Governor General in Council under this Section.

31   *Reference re Bill 30, An Act to Amend the Education Act (Ontario)*, [1987] 1 SCR 1148 at para 27, Wilson J [*Reference re Bill 30*]. See also *Reference re Education Act*

The opening words of section 93 give the provinces exclusive legislative jurisdiction in relation to education. The section, though, goes on to say that the provinces may not "prejudicially affect any Right or Privilege with respect to Denominational Schools which any Class of Persons have by Law in the Province at the Union."[32] The effect of section 93(2) is that the legal rights of denominational schools at the time of Confederation are constitutionally entrenched and cannot be removed or reduced except through constitutional amendment. Under section 93(3), the rights or privileges of these separate schools may be added to by a province, and these additions are protected from *Charter* challenge.[33] These additions, however, are not constitutionally entrenched and so may be repealed by the province at any time. Section 93(3) provides for an appeal to the federal government from any act or decision of a province that affects the rights and privileges of these schools, including any rights that have been granted by the province after Confederation and are not entrenched.

At the time of Confederation, Ontario had a legally established system of Roman Catholic schools, which received funding on the same basis as the nondenominational common schools.[34] In Quebec, both Roman Catholic and Protestant schools were established before Confederation; however, the rights of religious schools in that province were removed by constitutional amendment in 1997. At the time of Confederation, Nova Scotia and New Brunswick did not have legislatively established separate schools, so the courts found that section 93(1) had no application in these provinces. Similarly, Prince Edward Island and British Columbia at the time they joined Confederation did not have legally established separate schools. The Acts establishing the provinces of Manitoba, Saskatchewan, and Alberta each contained provisions similar to section 93, so the separate school rights that existed in each of these provinces at the time of their entry into the union were constitutionally protected. The courts, though, found that no such rights were established in Manitoba when it joined the union. At the time of its entry into Confederation, Newfoundland was also required to maintain its existing separate schools, but the right of these schools to state support was substantially

---

(*Quebec*), [1993] 2 SCR 511 at para 24, Gonthier J: "Section 93 is unanimously recognized as the expression of a desire for political compromise. It served to moderate religious conflicts which threatened the birth of the Union."

32   Section 93(2), which ensured that Protestant (and Roman Catholic) schools would have the same rights as those granted to Roman Catholic schools in Ontario, is no longer operative.

33   *Reference re Bill 30*, above note 31.

34   At the time of Confederation, there were several dissentient Protestant schools in Ontario protected under s 93. These schools were later folded into the public school system.

removed in 1998.[35] Currently, then, separate school rights continue to be constitutionally protected in the provinces of Alberta, Ontario, and Saskatchewan. The constitutional protection granted to separate schools in a particular province depends on what the legal status of these schools was at the time of the province's entry into the union, and so there is some variation among the provinces in the rights established.[36]

The Supreme Court of Canada in *Reference re Bill 30, An Act to Amend the Education Act (Ontario)* considered both the scope of separate school rights under section 93 and the relationship between these rights and the *Charter's* protection of religious freedom and religious equality.[37] The issue in this case was whether the decision of the government of Ontario in 1985 to fund high school grades in Roman Catholic schools (separate schools) without providing equivalent funding to other religious schools breached either section 2(a) or section 15 of the *Charter*. Seventy years earlier in 1915, when the province began funding high school grades in the public school system, it declined to fund the same grades in the Catholic system, arguing that section 93 only entitled the separate school system to funding for the grades that existed at the time of Confederation.[38] In *Tiny Roman Catholic Separate School Trustees v The King*, the Judicial Committee of the Privy Council agreed with the province that this differential funding did not breach section 93, because at the time of Confederation the separate schools in Ontario did not have a legal right to state funding for high school grades.[39] When the government of Ontario decided to reverse its earlier decision and fund high school grades in the separate schools, to the same extent that it funded these grades in the public system, it referred to the courts the question of whether this extension of funding (Bill 30) was constitutional.

In *Reference re Bill 30*, the Supreme Court considered whether the decision of the Ontario government to fund the upper grades of the Roman Catholic schools, which according to the *Tiny School Board*

---

35   For a discussion, see John P McEvoy, "Denominational Schools and Minority Rights: *Hogan v Newfoundland (Attorney-General)*" (2001) 12 *NJCL* 449.

36   For a history (up to 1964) of the application of s 93 in each of the provinces, see Douglas A Schmeiser, *Civil Liberties in Canada* (Oxford: Oxford University Press, 1964) ch 4.

37   Above note 31.

38   The province had also prohibited the separate schools from providing these grades of schooling.

39   [1928] AC 363 [*Tiny School Board*]. According to the court, since the province retained the power in 1867 to regulate separate schools, these schools had no established right to determine what grades could be offered. The Judicial Council of the Privy Council (JCPC), a British-based colonial court, was the final court of appeal for Canada for civil cases until 1949.

decision was not required by section 93 of the Constitution, while declining to fund these grades in other religious schools breached the *Charter*. The Supreme Court assumed that in the absence of section 93 the exclusive support of Roman Catholic religious schools would breach section 2(a) of the *Charter*.[40] It followed then that if the funding of high school grades in the separate school system was not mandated by section 93, the province would be improperly favouring the schools of one religion over those of other religions, contrary to sections 2(a) and 15.

A majority of the Court, in a judgment written by Wilson J, held that the *Tiny School Board* decision was wrong and that the province was obligated under section 93 to fund high school grades in the separate schools. Justice Wilson noted that at the time of Confederation, separate school trustees in Ontario held the same powers as common school trustees, including the power to provide advanced education. As well, in 1867 separate schools in Ontario had been entitled to a proportion of the funding granted to the common schools.[41] Justice Wilson concluded that Bill 30 simply "return[ed] rights constitutionally guaranteed to separate schools by s. 93(1)."[42]

However, Wilson J also said that even if *Tiny School Board* was correctly decided, and the province was not constitutionally required to fund these grades, it was entitled to do so under section 93(3), which contemplates the expansion of separate school rights.[43] Justice Wilson then referred to section 29 of the *Charter*, which specifically provides that the section 93 rights and privileges of separate schools are insulated from *Charter* review. The effect of section 29, she said, is that the preferential treatment of Roman Catholic schools, whether constitutionally required or permitted under section 93, does not breach the *Charter*.[44] Moreover, said Wilson J, even without section 29 of the *Charter*, the province's exclusive support for Roman Catholic schools does not breach

---

40   Justice Wilson, quoting the Ontario Court of Appeal, observed that "[t]hese educational rights … make it impossible to treat all Canadians equally. The country was founded upon the recognition of special or unequal educational rights for specific religious groups in Ontario and Quebec" (above note 31 at para 64).

41   In *Reference re Bill 30*, Wilson J thought that the narrow reading of s 93 adopted by the court in the *Tiny School Board* decision made the constitutional protection of separate schools "illusory" and "undermine[d] this historically important compromise" (*ibid* at para 58).

42   *Ibid* at para 60.

43   *Ibid* at para 29, Wilson J: "Bill 30 is a valid exercise of the provincial power to add to the rights and privileges of Roman Catholic separate school supporters under the combined effect of the opening words of s. 93 and s. 93(3)."

44   Section 29 of the *Charter* provides that "[n]othing in this *Charter* abrogates or derogates from any rights or privileges guaranteed by or under the Constitution of Canada in respect of denominational, separate or dissentient schools."

section 2(a). She thought that, as a matter of constitutional interpretation, a specific right or power established in the *Constitution Act, 1867*, such as section 93, is not repealed or nullified by the later but more general provisions of the *Charter*.[45]

The courts have described separate school rights as the outcome of a political bargain or compromise that was necessary to bring about Confederation. In *Adler v Ontario*, Iacobucci J called section 93 "a child born of historical exigency" that does not "represent a guarantee of fundamental freedoms."[46] Justice Beetz, in *Protestant School Board of Greater Montreal v Quebec (AG)*, said that even though section 93 "may be rooted in notions of tolerance and diversity," it is not "a blanket affirmation of freedom of religion or freedom of conscience ... [and] should not be construed as a *Charter* human right."[47] Justice Wilson, in *Reference re Bill 30*, agreed with this description of section 93 as a historical compromise but did not think that this "foreclose[d] a purposive approach" to the interpretation of the section.[48] She thought that while the courts must be careful not to give a wide interpretation to "a provision which reflects a political compromise ..., it must still be open to the Court to breathe life into a compromise that is clearly expressed."[49]

---

45   Above note 31 at para 623, Wilson J: "It was never intended, in my opinion, that the *Charter* could be used to invalidate other provisions of the Constitution, particularly a provision such as s. 93 which represented a fundamental part of the Confederation compromise." Section 29 served only to create greater certainty about this. In *Waldman v Canada*, Communication No 694/1996, UN Doc CCPR/C/67/D/694/1996 (5 November 1999), the UN Human Rights Committee found that the preferential funding of Roman Catholic schools in Ontario amounted to a breach of Canada's obligations under the *International Covenant on Civil and Political Rights*, 19 December 1966, 999 UNTS 171, Can TS 1976 No 47 (entered into force 23 March 1976). The committee said (*ibid* at para 10.6):

> [I]f a State party chooses to provide public funding to religious schools, it should make this funding available without discrimination. This means that providing funding for the schools of one religious group and not for another must be based on reasonable and objective criteria. In the instant case, the Committee concludes that the material before it does not show that the differential treatment between the Roman Catholic faith and the author's religious denomination is based on such criteria.

46   Above note 26 at para 30.

47   [1989] 1 SCR 377 at 401–2 [*Protestant School Board*]: "As a constitutional text, s. 93(1) may deserve a 'purposive' interpretation but, in so doing, the courts must not improperly amplify the provision's purpose."

48   Above note 31 at para 29.

49   *Ibid*. This purposive reading was necessary to her conclusion that the rights of separate schools in Ontario included the funding of high school grades.

The courts have treated the constitutional protection of separate schools as an anachronism that only constitutional amendment can correct. However unfair it may be for the state to fund only one religious school system, section 93 was part of the Confederation bargain, to which the parties are bound until they agree otherwise. But does this view of section 93, as part of the Confederation bargain, preclude a liberal or principled interpretation of the provision as a minority right? Section 93 was included in the Constitution at a time when the dominant public or common school system in Ontario and most other provinces had a clear Protestant ethos.[50] The protection of separate school rights ensured that Roman Catholic parents would not be financially pressured to send their children to the Protestant common schools. To view section 93 as granting Roman Catholic parents in Ontario the right to educate their children in their own belief system — to indoctrinate children into the Catholic faith or to insulate them from exposure to other beliefs, values, or groups — is to confuse the church's justification for separate schools, which applies whether or not the mainstream schools are Protestant or secular, with the constitutional or public justification for the special funding of separate schools, which may simply have been to protect Catholics from being forced into the religious education system of the majority community. Of course, in 1867 this distinction would not have been obvious, since it would have been difficult at the time to envision an entirely nonreligious or "secular" school system. However, the character of the public school system has changed dramatically since 1867, a change that has been hastened by the *Charter*. Public schools are no longer permitted to advance even a nondenominational religious perspective. A principled reading of section 93, then, might support the ending of separate school rights in Ontario, Saskatchewan, and Alberta now that the reason for the special protection of these schools no longer exists. However, for a variety of reasons, it is unlikely that the courts will be prepared to bring about this change through constitutional interpretation (despite their occasional references to the Constitution as a "living tree"), and that change will only occur through constitutional amendment.[51] A recognition that the reason for section 93(1) no longer exists led to the constitutional amendment ending religious school rights in Quebec and Newfoundland.

---

50 Justice Sopinka, in *Adler*, above note 26 at para 154, referred to the Christian character of the nondenominational common schools in Ontario at the time of Confederation.

51 Such an amendment would require only the consent of the federal government and the government of Ontario.

In the alternative, if the purpose of section 93 was to create a right to religious education for the minority Roman Catholic community in Ontario (a positive right to religious education rather than simply a right not to be forced into the majority Protestant school system), then a principled reading of the section would support the extension of this right to other religious groups in the province. In 1867 there was only one significant religious minority in Ontario. If we believe that section 93 protects the right of Roman Catholic parents to educate their children in their faith, there is no reason why this right should not be extended to other religious groups that have grown since 1867. This has been the approach in Alberta, where "independent" schools receive significant support from the province. Ontario voters, though, rejected this option in the 2007 provincial election—apparently uncomfortable with the idea of state funding for evangelical Protestant and Muslim schools.[52]

Previous attempts to amend the Constitution, such as the Meech Lake and Charlottetown Accords, may have led us to think that constitutional amendment is not a realistic option—that it is simply too difficult to do. However, the formal process for amending the Constitution to remove the special status of separate schools is a simple one that requires only the consent of the federal government and the government of the particular province. In Quebec and Newfoundland, the constitutional rights of religious schools were ended by amendment in the late 1990s. The real barrier to change is political, not constitutional. The irony is that a minority right granted to the Roman Catholic community in 1867 continues to be specially protected (and was even expanded in 1985) because of the political power of that group in the province. It appears, then, that the public funding of the separate school system in Alberta, Ontario, and Saskatchewan will continue for the foreseeable future.

F. THE RIGHTS AND DUTIES OF SEPARATE SCHOOLS

A province is precluded from interfering with the rights or privileges of separate schools that were established by law at the time of the province's entry into the union. Yet despite the courts' description of section 93 as

---

52   During the 2007 Ontario provincial election campaign, the Progressive Conservative Party under leader John Tory proposed an extension of provincial funding to faith-based schools. The defeat of the Conservatives in the election was attributed by many to this proposal. Opposition to the proposal appears to have come from both public school and separate school supporters.

a bargain, they have not regarded the rights of separate schools as static. The Ontario Court of Appeal in *Ontario English Catholic Teachers' Assn v Ontario (AG)* insisted that section 93 be interpreted in a purposive way to ensure that it did not become "a historical strait-jacket."[53] In upholding the court of appeal's decision, the Supreme Court affirmed that "the rights guaranteed by s. 93(1) do not replicate the law word-for-word as it stood in 1867" and that "[i]t is the broader purpose of the laws in force which continues to be protected."[54]

In cases such as *Reference re Bill 30*, the rights claimed by separate school supporters relate to the funding and organizational structure of the schools.[55] However, most of the section 93 cases that have come before the courts have been concerned with the right of separate schools to maintain their denominational or religious character. According to Beetz J in *Protestant School Board*, section 93 protects the "denominational aspects" of these schools as well as the "non-denominational aspects" that are necessary to give practical effect to the denominational guarantees.[56] In that case, the Supreme Court held that the province of Quebec could establish a "uniform curriculum" for nondenominational subjects to be taught in all schools in the province and that this would not breach the section 93 rights of separate schools. Significantly, the courts have said that the state may not interfere with the right of separate schools to hire and retain teachers based on their membership in the Roman Catholic church and their adherence to Catholic doctrine.[57] In *Daly v Ontario (AG)*, for example, the Ontario Court of Appeal held that separate schools have the right to exclude non-Catholic teachers from administrative positions

---

53   [1999] OJ No 1358 at para 18. A purposive approach, said the court, should be applied to "both the provincial power to legislate about education ... and the denominational guarantee of separate schools" (*ibid*).

54   2001 SCC 15 at para 32.

55   See also *ibid*, where the Court held that the system for funding could be altered as long as proportionality in funding between the two school systems was maintained. In *Public School Boards' Assn of Alberta v Alberta (AG)*, 2000 SCC 45, the Supreme Court again confirmed that the funding formula for separate schools could be changed as long as the province funded both separate and public schools in the same way and to the same extent.

56   Above note 47 at 415. The s 93 guarantee does not preclude the establishment of a common school curriculum in the province.

57   See *Casagrande v Hinton Roman Catholic Separate School District No 155* (1987), 38 DLR (4th) 382 (Alta QB). See also *Caldwell et al v Stuart et al*, [1984] 2 SCR 603, in which the Supreme Court held that a Roman Catholic school did not breach human rights legislation when it dismissed a teacher because she had married a divorced man contrary to Catholic doctrine. This case is discussed in Chapter 5.

in the schools.[58] However, the most contentious cases in recent times have been concerned with the conflict or tension between Roman Catholic doctrine and publicly recognized equality rights—particularly those of sexual minorities.

Because of their special status, as the only state-funded religious school system, separate schools (in contrast to other religious schools) are considered by the courts to be government actors that are subject to the *Charter*. Yet there is something odd, even paradoxical, about treating religious institutions as government actors that must respect the rights of citizens, including the right to be free from discrimination. Separate schools are government actors that are permitted to teach Catholic doctrine, including the belief that homosexuality is a moral disorder, and to hire only Catholic teachers. At the same time, there is an expectation that non-Catholic students should be able to attend separate schools and to be exempted from the religious elements of the curriculum. The treatment of separate schools as public actors is an unstable and unprincipled alternative to fixing the current system—by either ending the special rights of these schools or extending the same rights to other religious schools. If separate schools are too public or secular, then they will cease to have any reason to exist. But if they are too parochial, they may lose public support.[59] As the cases discussed below show, it is unclear when separate schools are subject to the obligations of state actors under the *Charter* and when they can operate according to Catholic doctrine.

In *Hall (Litigation Guardian of) v Powers*, a separate school board in Ontario refused to allow a graduating student to attend his high school prom with a same-sex date.[60] The board defended its decision on the grounds that same-sex relationships are contrary to Roman Catholic teaching. The issue for the court was whether section 93 protected the school board's action from the application of the *Charter* ban on sexual-orientation discrimination. The judge found that while the Roman Catholic church regarded "homosexuality [as] contrary to natural law" and "homosexual acts [as] intrinsically disordered," there was "a substantial

---

58   (1999), 172 DLR (4th) 241 (Ont CA). See also *Ontario English Catholic Teachers' Assn v Dufferin-Peel Roman Catholic Separate School Board* (1999), 172 DLR (4th) 260 (Ont CA).

59   In Ontario there has been public pressure on separate schools to establish gay–straight alliances (GSAs) and to fly pride flags. See Jenna Benchetrit, "After a Controversial Vote on Pride Flags in Ontario, LGBTQ+ Students Reflect on Their Meaning," *CBC News* (1 June 2023), online: www.cbc.ca/news/canada/pride-flags-schools-1.6861990.

60   [2002] OJ No 1803 (SCJ) [*Hall*]. For a discussion of the case, see Bruce MacDougall, "The Separation of Church and Date: Destabilizing Traditional Religion-Based Legal Norms on Sexuality" (2003) 36 *UBC L Rev* 1.

diversity of opinion within the Catholic community regarding the appropriate pastoral care and the practical application of [the] Church's teachings on homosexuality"—regarding how the church and its members should treat individuals who identify as gay or lesbian.[61] Even though the bishop with "hierarchical responsibility" for the region within which the school was located had taken the view that excluding same-sex couples from the dance was "an authentically Catholic position," the judge found that this was "not the only Catholic position" and perhaps not even "the majority position."[62] This enabled the judge to find that the board's stance was not an aspect of the denominational character of the separate schools in Ontario that was protected under section 93 and insulated from *Charter* challenge. The judge issued an interim injunction enabling Mr Hall to attend the prom with his date. There was no further litigation and no final determination of the issue.

The willingness of the judge in *Hall* to inquire into church doctrine might seem inconsistent with the Supreme Court's admonition in *Syndicat Northcrest v Amselem* that a court should not decide what is accepted doctrine in a religious community but should consider only whether the individual's belief in a particular practice or value is sincere.[63] At issue in the *Hall* case, though, was not whether an individual's beliefs or practices should be accommodated under section 2(a). Instead, the court had to decide whether the school, a religious institution (and also paradoxically a state actor) that has special rights and privileges under section 93, could rely on a particular understanding of religious doctrine (that was not shared by all members of the religious community) to insulate itself from the application of the *Charter*. The bishop had taken the position that bringing a same-sex date to the prom was contrary to church doctrine; and as the judge noted, one of the bishop's "designated religious duties is to interpret the teachings of the church."[64] The judge's interpretation of church doctrine, or at least his finding that the application of this doctrine was contested (his bypassing of the bishop's interpretation), allowed him to avoid the uncomfortable conclusion that publicly funded separate schools (state actors) could engage in sexual-orientation discrimination. The judge interpreted the Roman Catholic prohibition on same-sex relationships narrowly so that it did not apply to general social activity and did not support the exclusion of individuals who identify as gay or lesbian. He thought that while the Roman Catholic school board sincerely believed that same-sex relationships are sinful, it was

---

61   *Hall, ibid* at para 23.
62   *Ibid* at para 30.
63   2004 SCC 47.
64   Above note 60 at para 30.

mistaken in thinking that this belief or commitment was compromised by Mr Hall's attendance at the prom.[65] The courts may eventually have to address more directly the question of whether the separate school system should be permitted to discriminate against gay and lesbian students based on the constitutional right to operate publicly funded religious schools or whether, instead, the scope of section 93 should be defined more narrowly so that it does not insulate separate schools from basic equality requirements, even when these requirements are inconsistent with Roman Catholic doctrine.

In some districts in Ontario and Saskatchewan, separate schools have opened their doors to students who are not Catholic as a way of maintaining their student numbers. Some non-Catholic parents have objected to school requirements that their children participate in religious rituals and receive religious instruction. The response to this objection might be that a parent who has chosen to send their child to a Roman Catholic school has no basis to complain about them being taught Catholic doctrine or exposed to Catholic rituals. At the same, since the separate schools, for their own reasons, have admitted non-Catholic students, it may be reasonable to expect them to make some accommodation for these students. In Ontario, the *Education Act* provides that separate schools cannot require non-Catholic students to attend religious classes or services.[66] In *Erazo v Dufferin-Peel Catholic District School Board*, the court held that this exemption extended to attendance at liturgies and religious retreats.[67] The school board in that case did not challenge the constitutionality of the *Education Act* provision that granted this exemption.

In *Good Spirit School Division No 204 v Christ The Teacher Roman Catholic Separate School*, a public school board argued that the province's funding of separate schools for non-Catholic students who choose to attend these schools breached section 2(a) and section 15 of the *Charter* because this funding was not mandated by the Constitution and similar funding was not provided to other religious schools.[68] The trial judge agreed with the school board that the funding of non-Catholic students breached the *Charter*. However, the Saskatchewan Court of Appeal

---

65   The judge's reasoning might be compared to that of the Supreme Court in the later judgment of *SL*, above note 27 (which is discussed in Chapter 3). The alternative argument was that simply permitting Mr Hall and his same-sex date to attend the prom (even if same-sex relationships were understood to be contrary to Catholic doctrine) would not amount to support for, or condonation of, a practice that was inconsistent with the school board's beliefs. This, though, would have been a more difficult claim to make given the school's oversight of the event.

66   RSO 1990, c E.2, s. 42(13).

67   2014 ONSC 2072.

68   2020 SKCA 34 [*Good Spirit*].

decided that the province was either entitled or required under section 17 of the *Saskatchewan Act*[69] (which mirrors section 93 of the *Constitution Act, 1867*) to provide funding to separate schools for non-Catholic students. The court noted that the provincial *Education Act Regulations* "confer a right on any child resident in any school division to attend any publicly funded school within that division."[70] Parents then can choose to send their children to either of the two publicly funded school systems in the province—the public or separate system. Non-Catholic students may attend separate schools and Catholic students may attend public schools.

The court of appeal in *Good Spirit* described the two publicly funded systems as parallel. But while they may be parallel in some sense, they are not equivalent—that is, they are not mirror images. While it is true that the courts view separate schools as "public" and as state actors, they are state actors who are permitted to adhere to religious doctrine and maintain their denominational character. The current law in Saskatchewan may allow students to attend either school system, however, the separate schools could, under the *Saskatchewan Act*, refuse to accept non-Catholic students to protect their denominational character.[71] They have not done so, because they want to keep their enrollment numbers up to maintain their funding. Public schools, unlike the separate schools, are constitutionally open to all students, including Catholic students, and cannot decide to exclude students based on their beliefs.

The court of appeal noted that, under the *Saskatchewan Act*, separate schools are entitled to receive funding on the same basis as the public schools—so if public schools receive funds for any student who enrols, so too should the separate schools: "there shall be no discrimination" against the separate schools.[72] This, though, begs the question of what counts as a separate school and what is the reason for the protection of separate school funding.[73] The trial judge thought the *Saskatchewan Act*

---

69   1905, 4-5 Edw VII, c 42 (Can).

70   *Ibid* at para 7.

71   *Reference re Educational System in Island of Montreal / Hirsch v Protestant Board of School Commrs*, [1928] UKPC 10. See also *Reference re Education Act (Quebec)*, [1993] 2 SCR 511, in which the Supreme Court noted that the separate schools in Ontario were "reserved" for Catholic students and that admission of non-Catholic students was not a denominational right or privilege.

72   *Good Spirit*, above note 68 at para 149. Section 17(2) of the *Saskatchewan Act* provides: "In the appropriation by the Legislature or distribution by the Government of the province of any moneys for the support of schools organized and carried on in accordance with the said chapter 29, or any Act passed in amendment thereof or in substitution therefor, there shall be no discrimination against schools of any class described in the said chapter 29."

73   The Court of Appeal described the decision of separate schools to admit non-Catholic students as a matter of religious doctrine—with which the courts should

"presupposes that separate schools are serving the purposes for which they were intended—the perpetuation and protection of the minority's faith through separate education."[74] The court of appeal similarly noted that separate schools were legally established and constitutionally entrenched to protect the province's religious minority from being forced to attend public schools, which at the time had a Protestant ethos.[75] If the reason for the constitutional protection of separate school funding was to ensure the maintenance of an alternative to the secular public system (which once had a Protestant character), then the separate schools may not have the same claim to funding for non-Catholic students—and the requirement of "equivalent" or "proportional" funding may apply only to the funding of Catholic students.

Finally, the court of appeal noted that section 93 permits the enlargement of separate school rights, including the right to accept and receive funding for non-Catholic students. As was decided in the *Reference re Bill 30* case, an enlargement of these rights by the province is insulated from *Charter* challenge. But again, the province's power is to enlarge the rights of separate schools—which are schools for Catholic students. Section 17 (or section 93 of the *Constitution Act, 1867*) is concerned with preserving (and perhaps enhancing the rights and privileges) of separate schools for Catholic students and so should not extend to the funding of non-Catholic students.

G. SECULAR AND RELIGIOUS SCHOOLS: *ADLER V ONTARIO*

In *Adler v Ontario*, the Supreme Court considered whether the provincial government's failure to fund religious schools (other than separate schools under section 93) breached either section 2(a) or section 15 of the *Charter*.[76] The Court concluded unanimously that the Ontario government's nonfunding of religious schools did not violate section 2(a). A majority of the Court also held that the government's practice of funding secular public schools but not religious schools did not breach section 15 equality right. However, two judges, McLachlin and L'Heureux-Dubé JJ, disagreed and found that this practice breached

---

not interfere (*ibid* at para 141). But again, the important question is not whether separate schools are willing to accept non-Catholic students, but why the funding of these schools is constitutionally protected.

74   *Ibid*, quoted at para 142.

75   *Ibid* at para 121.

76   Above note 26.

section 15. Justice McLachlin went on to hold that the breach was justified under section 1, while L'Heureux-Dubé J held that the section 15 violation was not justified.

Justice Iacobucci, writing for the majority of the Court, took the position that section 93 was a complete code for the funding of religious schools. He said that while the government could choose to fund other religious schools, it had no obligation to do so. According to Iacobucci J, section 93 established certain rights for religious schools, and section 2(a) could not be used to expand those rights.[77] In response to the appellants' section 15 claim, Iacobucci J observed that section 93 specifically envisioned state support for public schools. In his view, the reasoning of the Court in *Reference re Bill 30* that the rights and privileges granted to separate schools in Ontario under section 93 could not be challenged under the *Charter* applied also to public schools. According to Iacobucci J, the section 15 "claim fails because the funding of Roman Catholic separate schools and public schools is within the contemplation of the terms of s. 93 and is, therefore, immune from *Charter* scrutiny."[78] The provincial government had the power under section 93 to increase support for both public and separate schools, and the exercise of that power could not be viewed as a breach of the *Charter*.[79] In this way, Iacobucci J sought to avoid the central issue in this case, which was whether the funding of public (secular) schools amounts to discrimination against or the unfair treatment of religious schools.

Justice Sopinka, in his concurring judgment, held that the non-funding of religious schools did not breach section 2(a). As Sopinka J saw it, the appellants were asking for state support for their religious practices. In his view, section 2(a) prohibits state restrictions on religious practice but does not guarantee state support for such practices. According to Sopinka J, provincial support for public schools neither compels the parents in this case "to act in any way that infringes their freedom of religion" nor imposes upon them an unconstitutional burden.[80] He regarded the costs incurred by the parents in sending their children to

---

77   Justice Iacobucci argued that "any claim to public support for religious education must be grounded in s. 93(1) which is a 'comprehensive code' of denominational school rights" (*ibid* at para 27). Later he said that to find that s 2(a) required extension of funding for other religious schools "would be to hold one section of the Constitution violative of another" (*ibid* at para 35).

78   *Ibid* at para 27.

79   Justice Iacobucci's extension of the reasoning in *Reference re Bill 30* to public schools was criticized by Sopinka and McLachlin JJ, who pointed out that section 93 does not specifically grant any rights to public schools.

80   *Adler,* above note 26 at para 171.

religious schools as "a natural cost" of their religion and so distinguished this case from *R v Edwards Books & Art Ltd*:[81]

> The legislation [in this case] is not the source of any distinction amongst all the groups whose exercise of their religious freedom involves an economic cost. This situation is distinguishable from Edwards Books, where one religious group was suffering an additional burden not imposed on other religious groups vis-à-vis non-observers.[82]

In *Edwards Books*, the challenged law had the effect (if not the purpose) of favouring one religious group over another. In contrast, the funding of secular schools in this case did not benefit or disadvantage a particular religious group.

In rejecting the parents' section 15 argument, Sopinka J pointed to earlier judgments, such as *Zylberberg v Sudbury Board of Education*,[83] that prohibited religious practices in public schools. He thought the courts, having ordered the removal of religion (and, more specifically, Christian practices) from public schools to ensure their religious neutrality, could hardly now say that the secular public schools were religiously partisan and that state support for such schools (without equivalent support for religious schools) was unconstitutional.[84] But this may not be quite so straightforward. The parents in *Adler* argued that the exclusive funding of secular schools put pressure on their children to adopt the "faith of secularism" or sent a message that religious adherents are not full members of the political community. The only way to avoid this argument was to find (as Sopinka J did) that secular (nonreligious) schools, in contrast to religious schools, are religiously neutral or inclusive.

Justice McLachlin (with L'Heureux-Dubé J concurring on this point) agreed with Sopinka J that the exclusive funding of public schools did not breach section 2(a) of the *Charter*. Like Sopinka J, she thought that freedom of religion prohibits the state from restricting or compelling religious practice but does not require the state to support such practices: "Absence of state funding for private religious practices, as distinct

---

81   *Ibid* at para 176; [1986] 2 SCR 713 [*Edwards Books*].

82   *Adler*, above note 26 at para 174.

83   (1988), 52 DLR (4th) 577 (Ont CA).

84   *Adler*, above note 26 at para 181: "While it is true that the appellants feel compelled to send their children to private school because of a personal characteristic, namely their religion, and therefore are unable to benefit from publicly-funded schooling, I fail to see how this is an effect *arising from the statute*. The reason why the public school system is not acceptable to the appellants lies in its secular nature. This secular nature is itself mandated by s. 2(a) of the Charter as held by several courts in this country" [emphasis added]. See also *Bal v Ontario (AG)* (1984), 21 OR (3rd) 681, upheld by the Ontario Court of Appeal (1997), 34 OR (3rd) 484.

from prohibitions on such practices, has never been seen as religious persecution."[85] This determination, though, does not fit easily with her other finding that the funding of secular schools breached section 15. Justices McLachlin and L'Heureux-Dubé both held that the state's refusal to fund religious schools amounted to religious discrimination contrary to section 15 of the *Charter*.[86] Justice McLachlin found that "while secular schooling is in theory available to all members of the public, the appellants' religious beliefs preclude them from sending their children to public schools."[87] It followed from this, she said, that the exclusive funding of secular public schools amounted to adverse discrimination against the appellants. They were denied a benefit that was available to others because they believed they could not send their children to public secular schools.

According to McLachlin and L'Heureux-Dubé JJ, the exclusive funding of public (and separate) schools discriminates against those parents who believe that their children must be educated in an environment in which their religious views are affirmed.[88] But if public schools are seen as noninclusive simply because they do not affirm the beliefs and practices of a particular faith, there can be no such thing as an inclusive school, nor indeed can there be any sort of neutral or inclusive public program or institution. Equality on this view can only be achieved through separation—equal support by the state for the institutions or practices of different religions. Not surprisingly, in their section 1 analysis, McLachlin and L'Heureux-Dubé JJ were unwilling to follow to its logical conclusion the idea that the secular public schools are partisan

---

85   *Adler, ibid* at para 200.

86   According to the Supreme Court in *Andrews v Law Society of British Columbia*, [1989] 1 SCR 143 and other decisions, the value or interest protected by s 15 is compromised if a law or other government action distinguishes between individuals on religious grounds (or another enumerated or analogous ground) or has a differential impact on the members of a particular religious group and if this differential treatment is discriminatory, that is, involves stereotyping or reinforces the marginalized position of the group.

87   *Adler,* above note 26 at para 209. Justice L'Heureux-Dubé found, *ibid* at para 68, that for the appellants in this case:

> [m]embership in an identifiable group precludes their accessing the other, publicly funded options. Evidence . . . establishes that to remain a member of the particular religious communities in question, and to act in accordance with the tenets of these faiths, the appellants are required to educate their children in a manner consistent with this faith and therefore outside of the public or the separate schools.

88   It is difficult to reconcile this judgment with the courts' reasoning in *SL*, above note 27, which is discussed in Chapter 3, except that the judgment in this case is based in s 15.

or exclusive. At the section 1 stage, both judges recognized and valued the role of public schools in providing an educational environment in which children from different backgrounds can meet and develop a level of mutual understanding and tolerance toward others. Justice McLachlin described the benefits of a public system:

> Children of all races and religions learn together and play together. No religion is touted over any other. The goal is to provide a forum for the development of respect for the beliefs and customs of all cultural groups and for their ethical and moral values. The strength of the public secular school system is its diversity — diversity which its supporters believe will lead to increased understanding and respect for different cultures and beliefs.[89]

For McLachlin J, the value of the open and tolerant learning environment offered by the public schools (an environment in which no one religious belief system is favoured over another) justified the restriction of the parents' section 15 rights.

Justice L'Heureux-Dubé accepted that the state has an interest in supporting a public school system that is "intended to be universally open and free to all, without discrimination" and in fostering "the values of a pluralist, democratic society, including the values of cohesion, religious tolerance and understanding."[90] However, she thought that the viability of the public system would not be compromised by partial state funding of religious schools, and so she concluded that the breach of section 15 was not justified under section 1. In her view, partial state support for religious schools (something less than full funding) would reduce the burden on parents who want to send their children to religious schools without at the same time leading to a mass exodus from the public schools and compromising the state's goal of maintaining a diverse public school system.

Justice L'Heureux-Dubé believed that parents should be able to send their children to (state-funded) religious schools, but she also thought that the secular public schools perform an important public function and should be protected. Her two concerns, though, are difficult to reconcile. In her view, if state funding of religious schools had a significant impact on public school attendance, the state might be justified in funding only secular public schools. But how does this fit with her earlier claim that the parents were disadvantaged (spiritually compromised) because they were forced for financial reasons to send their children to

---

89   *Adler*, above note 26 at para 212.
90   *Ibid* at para 97.

public schools? Why should the parents' right be limited in any way to protect the viability of public schools? Either it is objectionable, a form of discrimination, to (financially) pressure parents to send their children to a public school, because it supports a worldview that is contrary to their faith, or it is not objectionable because public schools are inclusive and nonpartisan and because it is important that children be exposed to other groups and perspectives in the larger community. On the one hand, if the government is right that exposure to other views and cultures is an important part of a child's civic education, we should be concerned about the removal of any child from the public system. The justification for the exclusive funding of public schools (and support for tolerance and respect) should not depend on the number of parents who would remove their children from the system if religious schools received state funding. On the other hand, if it is wrong for religious parents to be financially pressured into sending their children to a public school, is this not so for all religious parents, including those who cannot afford to pay even partial fees for religious schooling?

The contradiction in the judgments of McLachlin and L'Heureux-Dubé JJ, between their view of public schools as partisan and noninclusive at the section 15 stage and as inclusive and neutral at the section 1 stage, reflects a deeper tension in the public conception of religion as both a cultural identity and a personal choice or commitment. At the section 15 stage of their analysis, McLachlin and L'Heureux-Dubé JJ rely on a conception of religious belief as a cultural identity. A law that has a differential impact on a particular belief system may amount to discrimination against the believers—an identity group. Yet at the section 1 stage, the value that both judges attach to the public schools, in supporting tolerance and mutual understanding or in enabling children to make independent judgments, rests on a different conception of religion as a set of values—of truth claims—that may be right or wrong and may be adopted or rejected by an individual. It is noteworthy that section 1 often plays a limited role in section 15 cases—that once a breach of section 15 is found, a court seldom finds that the breach is justified under section 1. Yet in this case section 1 may have a role because the Court is uncertain about whether or when to treat religious adherence as an identity and therefore as a ground of discrimination.

Children require a structure of values and customs—a cultural framework—to develop as moral and rational agents. As well, the survival of a religious or cultural community depends on its ability to pass its values and practices on to the next generation. At the same time, the development of children as agents and citizens (capable of making their own spiritual and other judgments) requires that they be exposed to different ideas, values, and ways of living. The fact that public schools expose children to other views and values and encourage independent thought does not make these schools partisan or exclusive in the way these terms should be understood in a liberal democracy that is committed to religious freedom and tolerance. Even if there is some value in religious or cultural education, particularly in the early grades, the failure of the state to support religious schools should not be seen as an act of discrimination. The education of children is not simply a private or personal religious matter, similar to praying or wearing a religious symbol, which the state ought to accommodate. It concerns the development of children as agents and citizens.

CHAPTER 7

FREEDOM OF CONSCIENCE

A. INTRODUCTION

At an earlier time, when the moral beliefs of most individuals were rooted in a religious system, the term "freedom of conscience" was used interchangeably with "freedom of religion" to refer to the individual's freedom to hold beliefs that were spiritual or moral in character. However, with the growth of nonreligious worldviews or moral systems, the terms have taken on distinct meanings. Freedom of conscience is now viewed as an alternative to, or extension of, religious freedom. While freedom of religion protects fundamental religious beliefs and practices, freedom of conscience extends protection to fundamental beliefs and practices that are not part of a religious system. Together, then, freedom of conscience and freedom of religion protect the individual's most fundamental moral beliefs or commitments, both religious and non-religious.

The problem of distinguishing religious beliefs/practices from non-religious beliefs/practices, which has bedevilled the US courts, was something that Canadian courts and commentators thought section 2(a) of the *Canadian Charter of Rights and Freedoms* had avoided by creating a single "integrated" right to freedom of conscience and religion.[1] If freedom of conscience and religion protects all deeply held commitments

---

1   *Canadian Charter of Rights and Freedoms*, Part 1 of the *Constitution Act, 1982*, being Schedule B to the *Canada Act 1982* (UK), 1982, c 11 [*Charter*]. See *R v Big M Drug Mart*, [1985] 1 SCR 295.

or beliefs about right and truth, then the courts do not need to embark on the difficult task of determining when a belief/practice is religious rather than "secular."

Yet, despite the courts' formal definition of the scope of freedom of conscience and religion as encompassing both religious and nonreligious beliefs and practices, religious beliefs/practices have been at the centre of the section 2(a) *Charter* jurisprudence. While the Supreme Court of Canada in its earliest section 2(a) decisions said that the right might be breached when the state restricts a deeply held nonreligious practice, it is difficult to find cases in which section 2(a) has been successfully used to protect such practices. It is also worth noting that while the Canadian courts have said that the state must not support particular religious practices, such as the Lord's Prayer, they have not suggested that the state is similarly precluded from supporting (or compelling) nonreligious practices. In other words, while freedom of conscience may (in theory) protect the individual's freedom *to* conscience (their freedom from state interference with their fundamental practices), it does not protect their freedom *from* conscience (their freedom from the imposition of the deeply held nonreligious practices of others).[2]

In *Syndicat Northcrest v Amselem*,[3] the case in which the Supreme Court established the basic test for determining a breach of section 2(a), the Court thought it necessary to offer a tentative definition of religion:

> While it is perhaps not possible to define religion precisely, some outer definition is useful since only beliefs, convictions and practices rooted in religion, as opposed to those that are secular, socially based or conscientiously held, are protected by the guarantee of freedom of religion. Defined broadly, religion typically involves a particular and comprehensive system of faith and worship. Religion also tends to involve the belief in a divine, superhuman or controlling power. In essence, religion is about freely and deeply held personal convictions or beliefs connected to an individual's spiritual faith and integrally linked to one's

---

2   The Court has also said that the state should not support or advocate atheism— the denial of the existence of God—or explicitly reject any or all forms of religious faith. Perhaps the ban on state support for religious belief/practice could in some cases be understood as the protection of freedom of conscience. The complainants in many of the contemporary cases in which state support for religion has been challenged have been agnostics or atheists. Their complaint in these cases is not that the state is supporting one religion over another—the religion of the majority over that of the minority—but rather that it is supporting religious belief/practice generally and sending a message of exclusion to citizens who are not religious, or imposing religion on them, or treating them unequally.

3   2004 SCC 47 [*Amselem*].

self-definition and spiritual fulfilment, the practices of which allow individuals to foster a connection with the divine or with the subject or object of that spiritual faith.[4]

The test set out by the Supreme Court in *Amselem* for determining whether a practice falls within the scope of section 2(a) asks whether the individual (sincerely) believes that the practice connects them to the divine — a test that seems to be concerned exclusively with religious practices.[5] In their section 2(a) decisions, the courts seem to regard religious practices as special or as different from other, nonreligious, practices.

The courts' focus on religious practices has arisen in tandem with its adoption of a neutrality requirement. If religious freedom is understood as a liberty that prohibits the state from coercing individuals in religious matters, then it is easily extended to nonreligious practices. The state ought not to interfere with an individual's practices, religious or otherwise, unless this is necessary to protect the rights and interests of others or the general welfare. Freedom of religion as a liberty has a broad scope but little weight. It precludes the state from compelling a religious practice and from restricting such a practice on the grounds that the practice is erroneous — the wrong way to worship God. However, it does not require the state to compromise its policies to accommodate the individual's religious practices. The state must have a public reason to restrict a religious practice, but any public reason may be sufficient.

However, if religious freedom requires not just that the state refrain from compelling or restricting religious practices without public justification (individual liberty in religious matters), but also that the state remain neutral in religious matters or treat different religious belief systems in an even-handed way, then it is less obvious that equivalent protection should be extended to the individual's nonreligious practices. The neutrality requirement precludes the state from supporting or preferring the practices of one religious system over another (or religious

---

4   *Ibid* at para 39. It is worth recalling, though, that while the Court in *Amselem* indicated that this test was applicable in section 2(a) *Charter* cases, the law applied in that case was the Quebec *Charter of Human Rights and Freedoms*, CQLR c C-12, which protected both freedom of religion and freedom of conscience but listed them as separate rights.

5   *Ibid* at para 46, the Supreme Court defined the scope of s 2(a) exclusively in religious terms:

> [F]reedom of religion consists of the freedom to undertake practices and harbour beliefs, having a nexus with religion, in which an individual demonstrates he or she sincerely believes or is sincerely undertaking in order to connect with the divine or as a function of his or her spiritual faith, irrespective of whether a particular practice or belief is required by official religious dogma or is in conformity with the position of religious officials.

belief over atheism or vice versa) and from restricting religious practices unless there is good reason to do so—or put more positively, the state has a duty to make some accommodation for religious practices.

The requirement that the state remain neutral in religious matters—that it neither support nor restrict religious practice—rests on the idea that religious beliefs/practices are similar to traits or characteristics or that they are a matter of cultural identity rather than political judgment and so should be excluded and insulated (separated) from political decision making. (As discussed in chapter 3, how the courts view a particular belief, as cultural practice or political or moral judgment, will depend on whether they see it as otherworldly in its orientation or instead as addressing civic concerns, such as the rights of others or the welfare of the community.)

If the individual's religious beliefs or moral commitments are "deeply held" or "rooted," a matter of identity rather than choice, it is because they are part of (and grew out of) a shared religious tradition or group culture to which the individual's identity (their worldview) is tied.[6] Such commitments are less likely to originate or be sustained outside a religious or cultural community. The practices of a religious group are protected because they are part of the identity of the group's members and because their restriction may contribute to the marginalization of the group. But, if the requirement that the state accommodate religious practices is tied to the role these practices play in the life of a religious or cultural group, then it is not clear when or whether the accommodation requirement will extend to an individual's nonreligious practices.

Charles Taylor and Jocelyn Maclure argue that (religious) accommodation may be necessary to prevent the "moral harm" that occurs when individuals are required to act in a way that is inconsistent with their deepest convictions or commitments, both religious and nonreligious.[7] Yet, in a democracy, the strongly or deeply held views of citizens on civic issues shape public policy, with the consequence that the views of some citizens prevail over those of others. The courts have been willing to exempt an individual from a particular legal requirement only when their belief/practice can be seen as personal (or as internal to the religious group) and does not relate to a public or civic matter (the rights and interests of others in the larger community). Indeed, most of the

---

6   R Moon, "Religious Commitment and Identity: *Syndicat Northcrest v Amselem*" (2005) 29 *Sup Ct L Rev* 201 at 216.

7   Jocelyn Maclure and Charles Taylor, *Secularism and Freedom of Conscience*, translated by Jane Marie Todd (Cambridge, MA: Harvard University Press, 2011). See also Brian Bird, "Rediscovering Freedom of Conscience in Canada" (2021) 84 *Sask LR* 23 at 61: "conscience touches on core moral commitments that sustain our identity and integrity—who I am and what I stand for—in a fundamental sense."

accommodation claims that come before the courts involve religious rituals or practices (forms of collective worship or markers of cultural identity or group membership that may not even be binding on the individual) rather than religious/moral convictions. Moreover, the focus Taylor and Maclure put on the individual and their personal convictions seems inadequate to explain the other dimension of religious freedom — the duty of the state to remain neutral in matters of religion, to refrain from supporting a particular religious practice or the beliefs and practices of one religious community over those of another.

In the public imagination, the conscientious objector is someone who takes a moral or political stand against the prevailing norms and assumptions of the community. They refuse to conform to the norms of the general community and hold to their own judgment about what is right or just. But if their objection to the law is based on a moral view that the majority in the democratic community has considered and rejected, why should they be exempted from the law? It cannot be enough that the conscientious (or religious) objector is committed to views or values that are inconsistent with state policy. Instead, "freedom of conscience" may extend only to conscientious beliefs that appear to stand outside ordinary political debate — beliefs that are fundamental to the individual but are also part of a distinctive worldview or moral framework. A conscientiously held belief may fall within the scope of section 2(a) when it resembles a paradigmatic religious belief or practice (a faith-based commitment) that is fundamental in significance, specific in content, peremptory in force, and perceived by nonbelievers as inaccessible or unconventional.

Freedom of conscience, like freedom of religion, may protect practices that lie outside (or can be bracketed-off from) political contest and treated as part of a personal or communal set of practices — a distinctive worldview that runs contrary to conventional morality or mainstream practice. Even when the individual understands their objection to the law (and their claim to be exempted from the law's application) as a moral position, it may be viewed by others as personal or cultural rather than universal and political because it is not derived from widely accepted moral principles.[8] Freedom of conscience on this account may extend the same protection to a narrow category of nonreligious beliefs

---

8   As described by Jeremy Webber, "freedom of religion is the primary category, conscience the derivative." Jeremy Webber, "The Irreducibly Religious Content of Freedom of Religion" in Avigail Eisenberg, ed, *Diversity and Equality: The Changing Framework of Freedom in Canada* (Vancouver: UBC Press, 2006) 178 at 179. See also *ibid* at 186: "But the remarkable thing about freedom of conscience is just how parasitic it remains on freedom of religion in all of its most difficult contemporary dimensions." For a different view see Maclure and Taylor, above note 7.

and practices that resemble in content and structure paradigmatic religious beliefs and practices.

B. PERSONAL LIFE AND PUBLIC ACTION

The only reported cases in Canada in which freedom of conscience under section 2(a) was found to have been breached involved a refusal by the federal prison authorities to provide an inmate with vegetarian meals. In *Maurice v Canada (AG)*, an inmate had previously received vegetarian meals on religious grounds, as a member of the Hare Krishna community.[9] After he had disassociated himself from that community, he asked that he continue to receive vegetarian meals in the prison for moral rather than religious reasons. The prison authorities took the position that they were only obligated to provide vegetarian meals for religious reasons. A judge of the Federal Court of Canada, however, rejected this argument, noting that section 2(a) protects both religious and nonreligious beliefs and practices. In the judge's view, the prison could accommodate the inmate's vegetarianism without difficulty, particularly since it was already providing vegetarian meals to inmates on religious grounds.

Two factors may have been critical to the success of this claim, setting it apart from other (possible) claims to accommodation for nonreligious practices. The first has to do with the character of the practice. The judgment provided little information about the inmate's commitment to vegetarianism; however, it appeared that the practice was basic for him and not derived from more general principles, which might have been the subject of debate and disagreement. The practice was both specific in content and peremptory in force and so looked much like a religious duty. The inmate's claim was helped by the similarity of his particular practice, vegetarianism, to a recognized religious practice and indeed by the fact that he had previously been provided with vegetarian meals on religious grounds. Second, the Court may have been willing to protect a practice that in ordinary circumstances is simply a private or personal matter. Outside the prison context, vegetarianism is a practice in which the individual is free to engage and that has no obvious impact on the rights or interests of others and requires no action or cooperation from others. The state ordinarily has no direct involvement in an individual's

---

9   [2002] FCT 69. In *R v Chan*, [2005] ABQB 615, a prisoner had a right to receive vegetarian meals for religious reasons. In *Ewart v Canada*, 2003 FC 1054, the Court found that the prison authorities had interfered with an Indigenous prisoner's religious freedom when they searched his "medicine bundle" without adequate justification.

dietary choices. Within the prison, however, all aspects of an inmate's life are controlled by the prison authorities. The inmate can do nothing without the support or cooperation of the state.

C. FACTUAL DISAGREEMENT IS NOT A MATTER OF CONSCIENCE

A number of lower-court decisions in Canada have considered conscience-based claims to exemption from paternalistic laws such as the requirement that car passengers wear seatbelts or that bicycle riders wear helmets.[10] In each of these cases, the claim for exemption was dismissed with few reasons given. In *R v Locke*, however, the provincial court judge, when rejecting the conscience claim, observed that "Mr. Locke's belief that wearing a seatbelt may cause him more harm than good is not of the same order as the comprehensive value system protected by section 2(a)."[11] Locke's opposition to the legislation was based not on a commitment to a different set of values (concerning personal safety or physical integrity) but instead on a different judgment about the safety consequences of (not) wearing a seatbelt. He believed that he would be safer if he did not wear a seatbelt. The legislature, though, had specifically addressed this question and, relying on empirical evidence, had determined that the safety of passengers will be better protected if they wear seatbelts.

In most of the other lower-court seatbelt cases, the individual's objection to the law seemed to be based on a libertarian view that the state has no right to regulate self-regarding behaviour. The opposition to the law in these cases, then, was based on a "deeply held" moral/political view that is in tension with the state's justification for the law. The difficulty with the accommodation claim, though, is that it represents a direct challenge to the legitimacy of paternalistic laws and perhaps state authority more generally. The accommodation claim is based not on the value the claimant attaches to the particular practice (of not wearing a seatbelt) but instead on their views about the importance of liberty and autonomy and the legitimate scope of state power. A commitment to libertarianism is not itself a reason to refuse to perform a particular act such as wearing a seatbelt. Libertarianism is simply the belief that the individual should have the right to decide whether or not to perform the particular act. Such

---

10   See, for example, *R v Dubbin*, 2009 BCPC 164; *R v Locke*, 2004 ABPC 152; and *R v Warman*, 2001 BCSC 1771.

11   *Locke, ibid* at para 25.

a claim may be too political and too sweeping for the court to contemplate under section 2(a).

Similarly, section 2(a) claims for exemption from vaccine mandates, whether framed in religious or nonreligious terms, should be rejected (even before taking account of the harm that refusal to vaccinate can cause to others) if this refusal rests on a belief about either the effectiveness or risks of vaccination.[12] In *Harjee v Ontario*, the court held that a provincial requirement that an individual show they had been vaccinated before entering certain businesses, such as gyms and restaurants, did not breach the *Charter*.[13] The requirement, said the court, was a justified limit on the individual's rights, including their freedom of religion under section 2(a). In the court's view, the "inability to attend a restaurant or other venue governed by the proof of vaccination requirement does not substantially interfere with [the applicants'] religious observance."[14] The court decided that the requirement breached section 2(a) (but that the breach was justified under section 1), even though the applicants' objection to being vaccinated rested on (erroneous) views about the safety and efficacy of the vaccines and not on religious or moral objections to vaccination.

As noted in Chapter 3, while accommodations may sometimes be made for practices that can be treated as personal to the individual or internal to the community, when a practice has a significant impact on others then it should not be accommodated. It may be that when only a few individuals seek to be exempted from a vaccination requirement, the impact on others will be minor, but when the number of people seeking to be exempted is greater, the impact may be significant. The failure in the community to achieve "herd immunity" will have harmful consequences not just for those who are unable to be vaccinated because of their medical condition or age but for the whole of society.

D. CONSCIENTIOUS OBJECTIONS TO COMPULSORY MILITARY SERVICE

In the late 1800s, Mennonites, Doukhobors, and Hutterites were encouraged to settle in Canada with the assurance that they would be exempted

---

12   The obvious contrast is with the refusal of a blood transfusion by a Jehovah's Witness who is a minor, which rests on a fundamental (scripturally based) objection to receiving the blood of another person and which carries no risk to others.

13   2022 ONSC 7033.

14   *Ibid* at para 64.

from military service.[15] The exemption granted to these groups was extended by the government of Canada after Confederation to the members of any religious group that objected to bearing arms. This exemption was maintained during World War I until its cancellation near the end of the war, although in the end no conscientious objectors were called for active service. Compulsory military service was last imposed in Canada during World War II. The members of two categories of conscientious objectors were granted a postponement of military training and service: (1) Mennonites and Doukhobors who had been exempted from military service by orders in council when they came to Canada in the late 1800s, and (2) other conscientious objectors who were prohibited by their religion from bearing arms. Individuals who were excused from military service were generally required to perform some form of alternative service. During World War II the exemption for conscientious objectors was not extended to Jehovah's Witnesses, a group that was subject to a legal ban during much of the war.

More recently, in *Prior v Canada*, a Quaker who was opposed on religious grounds to government expenditures for military purposes sought to withhold a percentage of her income tax that corresponded to the percentage of the general federal budget allocated to military purposes.[16] The Federal Court of Canada (Appeal Division) rejected her claim. The Court found that the connection between the taxes she was required to pay and the money allocated by the government to the military was too remote to support her claim that the compulsory payment of taxes interfered with her religious freedom.

In the United States, a military service draft was introduced during the Vietnam War in the late 1960s. The *Universal Military Training and Service Act* exempted from military service those who by reason of their "religious training and belief" are "conscientiously opposed to

---

15   In Upper Canada, the *Militia Act, 1793* (UK), 33 Geo III, c 1, exempted Quakers, Mennonites, and Brethren in Christ from compulsory military service. The exemption was intended to encourage the members of different pacifist groups to emigrate from the United States following the American Revolution. For some of the history of conscientious objection to military service in Canada, see Janet Epp-Buckingham, *Fighting Over God: A Legal and Political History of Religious Freedom in Canada* (Montreal: McGill-Queen's University Press, 2014).

16   (1989), 44 CRR 110 (FCA), leave to appeal to SCC refused, [1989] SCCA 441. A complaint by Prior against the government of Canada to the UN Human Rights Committee under the *International Covenant on Civil and Political Rights* [GA Res 2200A(XXI), 21 UNGAOR Supp (No 16) at 52, UN Doc A/6316 (1966) (entered into force 23 March 1976)] was dismissed in *Dr JP v Canada*, Communication No 446/1991, UN Doc CCPR/C/43/D/446/1991 (7 November 1991).

participation [in military service] in any form."[17] In the statute, "religious training and belief" is described as "an individual's belief in a relation to a Supreme Being involving duties superior to those arising from any human relation, but [not including] essentially political, sociological, or philosophical views or a merely personal moral code."[18] The statutory exemption from military service, although confined to religious objections, was interpreted by the US Supreme Court as encompassing objections to military service that are more often considered to be non-religious or conscience-based in character. The Court in *United States v Seeger* noted that the section used the expression "Supreme Being" rather than God and decided that "the test of belief 'in a relation to a Supreme Being' is whether a given belief that is sincere and meaningful occupies a place in the life of its possessor parallel to that filled by the orthodox belief in God."[19] It is not necessary, said the Court, that the individual believe that God had forbidden them to participate in war but only that they believe they are bound by a rule or command beyond their will not to participate in war in any circumstance. This reading of the exemption, said the Court, "embraces the ever-broadening understanding of the modern religious community."[20]

The Court in *Seeger* sought to distinguish the religious objections to military service that fall within the scope of the exemption from those objections that are not exempted because they are part of the individual's personal moral code or based on "political, sociological, or economic considerations."[21] It is difficult, though, to make sense of the distinction between, on the one hand, a duty or obligation that fills the same role in the individual's life as a religious duty and, on the other hand, a personal moral commitment, since the latter, as a moral commitment, must be understood by the adherent as external to their will, binding upon them, and even universal in its application. It is unclear what work the modifier "personal" does here—how it affects our understanding of the scope of the exemption.[22]

---

17   50 USC App § 456(j).

18   *Ibid.*

19   380 US 163 (1965) at 165–66. In that case, the Court found that the exemption did apply to Seeger and several other applicants who the Court accepted may have been "bowing to 'external commands' in virtually the same sense as is the objector who defers to the will of a supernatural power" (at 186).

20   *Ibid* at 180.

21   *Ibid* at 173.

22   Even if we could make sense of the idea of a personal moral commitment that is distinct from a morally binding commitment, it is not clear why the personal claim would be subject to legal regulation while the more general—universal—claim would not.

The more substantial limitation identified by the Court is that the objection to military service must not be based on economic, political, or social factors. The obvious consequence of this limit is that an exemption will not be granted to an individual who objects to participation in a *particular* war for social, political, or economic reasons. Political judgments of this kind, said the Court, have historically been reserved for the government. It appears, then, that the exemption from military service, as defined by the US Supreme Court, will only apply when an individual holds a profound belief that they must not go to war in any circumstance.[23] The individual's conscientious objection must be peremptory in the sense that it does not depend on the contextual application of more abstract principles about which there might be reasonable debate among citizens. Either one accepts that war is wrong (or that it is wrong to take a life, even in self-defence) or one does not accept this and believes that "it all depends" or "it is a complicated matter." A circumstantial objection may be rooted in either a secular or a religious morality, such as the Roman Catholic "just war" doctrine.

Because the individual's opposition to military service (in all circumstances) runs contrary to mainstream opinion or conventional morality, their claim to an exemption from conscription may be viewed by the courts as a personal or communal belief rather than a political position about the rights and interests of others that is subject to democratic contest and regulation. (This may be the case, even though the individual, presumably, believes that it is wrong for anyone to go to war.) If the individual's objection to military service can be seen as an expression of religious commitment or personal conscience, rather than a political statement or civic act, then it may be accommodated, even though exemption from compulsory service will place a greater burden of public service on other members of the community—although it will not directly cause harm to them. Even if compulsory military service during wartime is seen as necessary to the security of the nation, it is an extraordinary intervention into the individual's life. In addition to this concern, there may also be a more pragmatic concern that conscription will result in acts of civil disobedience. In time of war, the risk of civil disobedience may outweigh concerns that the burden of military service will be unevenly distributed. For these reasons, governments (and courts) have been prepared to treat objections to military service as a matter of conscience that should be accommodated.[24]

---

23   See also *Gillette v United States*, 401 US 437 (1971).

24   Part of the motivation for the US Supreme Court's broad reading of the conscientious objection exemption in the military service legislation (which by its terms seemed only to protect religious objections) may have been to ensure that a law

Conscientious objection to military service has been an issue in several recent European Court of Human Rights decisions, mostly involving Jehovah's Witnesses in Russia, Turkey, and Armenia. See, for example, *Savda v Turkey*, in which it was held that the state has a duty under article 9 of the *Convention for the Protection of Human Rights and Fundamental Freedoms* to establish a system for determining whether an individual has a conscientious objection to military service.[25] In *Dyagilev v Russia*, the court reiterated "that opposition to military service, where it is motivated by a serious and insurmountable conflict between the obligation to serve in the army and a person's conscience or his deeply and genuinely held religious or other beliefs, constitutes a conviction or belief of sufficient cogency, seriousness, cohesion and importance to attract the guarantees of Article 9 of the Convention."[26] The determination that an individual's objection to military service falls within the scope of section 9 protection "must be assessed in the light of the particular circumstances of the case."[27] The court found that in this case the applicant had not demonstrated "a serious and insurmountable conflict between the obligation to serve in the army and his convictions."[28]

E. FREEDOM OF CONSCIENCE AND AUTONOMY

Freedom of conscience was employed in a very different way by Wilson J in the Supreme Court of Canada's decision in *R v Morgentaler*.[29] In her concurring judgment, she held that the *Criminal Code*[30] ban on abortion

---

that was intended to protect the "free exercise" of religion did not at the same time breach the "establishment clause" of the First Amendment, which precludes the state from favouring religion over nonreligion. The argument sometimes made is that when the state exempts a religious practice from the application of ordinary law without also exempting a similar nonreligious practice, it is preferring religion over nonreligion, contrary to the establishment clause. Yet when the state accommodates a religious practice, it is not preferring religious over nonreligious practices rather it is maintaining the separation of religion and politics—excluding and insulating religion from politics—for the reasons earlier described related to the value and standing of religious associations in the larger society.

25   Application No 42730/05, ECtHR (12 June 2012); *Convention for the Protection of Human Rights and Fundamental Freedoms*, Rome, 4 November 1950.

26   Application No 49972/16, ECtHR (10 March 2020).

27   *Ibid* at para. 59.

28   *Ibid* at para 94.

29   [1988] 1 SCR 30.

30   RSC 1985, c C-46.

breached section 7 of the *Charter* because it deprived a woman of her liberty and security of the person in a way that was not in accordance with principles of fundamental justice. To interfere with the decisions a woman makes concerning her body, and more particularly concerning reproduction, would be to deprive her of her liberty and security of the person. This deprivation, said Wilson J, would interfere with the woman's freedom of conscience, a principle of fundamental justice. According to Wilson J:

> [T]he decision whether or not to terminate a pregnancy is essentially a moral decision, a matter of conscience. I do not think there is or can be any dispute about that. The question is: whose conscience? Is the conscience of the woman to be paramount or the conscience of the state? I believe, for the reasons I gave in discussing the right to liberty, that in a free and democratic society it must be the conscience of the individual.[31]

In Wilson J's decision, conscience refers to a sphere of autonomous judgment. The individual has the right to make decisions about deeply personal matters such as reproduction. This, I think, is different from the standard section 2(a) freedom of religion or freedom of conscience claim. The standard claim is not that the state should refrain from regulating a particular matter (that all persons should be exempted from legal regulation) but rather that those individuals, and only those individuals, who have a deep moral commitment that is inconsistent with the law should be exempted from its application. It may be that an exemption will be granted only if the (religious) practice is sufficiently "private" (that is, limited in its impact on the rights and freedoms of others), but that is not the same as defining a sphere of autonomous judgment that applies to all persons.

F. THE LIMITED SCOPE OF SECTION 2(A)

Despite their formal claims, the courts have done little to accommodate religious practices and, unsurprisingly, even less to accommodate non-religious practices. A nonreligious belief or practice that is fundamental to the individual, does not directly address civic or public concerns, and rests on moral premises that are not widely shared in the community may be insulated from political action. It might then be said (as discussed in Chapter 2) that when "religion" looks like civic morality,

---

31   *Ibid* at 175–76.

it will be subject to the give-and-take of ordinary politics, and when "conscience" (secular morality) looks like religion, it will fall within the protection of section 2(a). Cases in which the courts find a breach of freedom of conscience will, I suspect, continue to be rare and will occur only when the restricted practice is similar in structure and content to familiar religious practices.

CONCLUSION

The Supreme Court of Canada in *R v Big M Drug Mart*[1] determined that section 2(a) of the *Canadian Charter of Rights and Freedoms*,[2] freedom of conscience and religion, protects the individual's autonomy in matters of religion. The Court held that section 2(a) prohibits the state from compelling an individual to engage in a religious practice and from restricting their engagement in such a practice, at least without a good public reason to do so. In other words, the section protects both the freedom from, and the freedom to, religion. Yet in the *Big M Drug Mart* decision, the Court seemed, at times, to advance a very different understanding of religious freedom—as a form of equality right. The Court said, for example, that the Federal *Lord's Day Act*[3] was objectionable because it "creates a climate hostile to, and gives the appearance of discrimination against, non-Christian Canadians ... The theological content of the legislation remains as a subtle and constant reminder to religious minorities within the country of their differences with, and alienation from, the dominant religious culture."[4]

In subsequent judgments, the Court explicitly adopted this equality based conception of religious freedom.[5] Freedom of religion, in this

---

1   [1985] 1 SCR 295 [*Big M Drug Mart*].

2   Part 1 of the *Constitution Act, 1982*, being Schedule B to the *Canada Act 1982* (UK), 1982, c 11 [*Charter*].

3   RSC 1970, c L-13.

4   *Big M Drug Mart*, above note 1 at para 97.

5   *SL v Commission scolaire des Chênes*, 2012 SCC 7.

account, requires that the state remain neutral in matters of religion. The state should take no position on religious issues. It should not support the practices of one religious tradition over those of another, and it should not restrict the practices of a religion without a substantial reason to do so. However, if religious freedom is a form of equality right, it cannot be based simply on the importance of individual autonomy and must rest instead on a recognition that the individual's religious membership or commitment is deeply rooted, a matter of identity rather than simply a choice or judgment. On this view, when the state favours the practices of one religious group over those of another or restricts the practices of a particular religious group, it treats some members of the community as less deserving or worthy based on their religious "identity," or it marginalizes the members of a particular religious group.

While both branches of the religious freedom right (the freedom to and the freedom from religion) rest on a concern about the equality or status of different religious groups, the courts have developed different approaches to determining the breach under each branch. In cases in which the Court has determined that the state has supported a particular religious practice or belief, and therefore breached section 2(a), it has invariably gone on to find that the state's action cannot be justified under section 1. In the Court's view, state action that supports a religious practice such as the Lord's Prayer or the Sunday Sabbath involves a direct denial of the religious freedom right and so necessarily fails the first step of the *Oakes* test.[6]

On the other hand, the Court has said that when the state restricts a religious practice (in a nontrivial way), even though it may be pursuing a legitimate public purpose, it breaches section 2(a) and must justify the restriction under section 1. The courts' significant analysis in restriction cases occurs at the section 1 limitations stage. However, at this stage the Court has set a low standard for justification of the breach and has often been quick to uphold the restriction.[7]

---

6   *R v Oakes*, [1986] 1 SCR 103. Even when the Court attributes a more general purpose to a state practice, such as the recitation of the Lord's Prayer at the opening of the public school day, it inevitably goes on to find that the restriction fails the minimal impairment element of the *Oakes* test. (*Zylberberg v Sudbury Board of Education*, [1988] OJ No 1488 (Ont CA)).

7   With that said, the Court has not always kept the different branches of the right separate. In *Mouvement laïque québécois v Saguenay*, 2015 SCC 16 [*MLQ*], for example, the Court confirmed that when the state enacts a *law* that supports a particular religious practice or belief system, not only will the law breach s 2(a), it will not be justified under s 1. However, the Court also said in *MLQ* that when a state official, through their *actions*, supports a particular religious practice, s 2(a) will be breached only if the official's actions "interfere" with the complainant's

The courts have said that the state must remain neutral in matters of religion (that it must not support the practices of a particular religion), and yet they have not excluded religion entirely from the public sphere. A religious belief should not play a role in political decision making (and will be treated as a matter of cultural identity) if the action it calls for is spiritual in character—that is, if it is concerned with the worshipping or honouring of God. However, when a religious belief addresses a political or civic matter, the courts will treat it as a political or moral judgment that may play a role in political decision making. Religiously grounded beliefs about civic issues may be adopted or rejected by law makers based on a public judgment about the beliefs' contribution to human good or public welfare.

In deciding that the commitment to religious neutrality does not preclude political actors from relying on religious "values" in public life, the courts must rely, at least implicitly, on a distinction between the spiritual and civic elements of a religious belief system. Where the courts draw the line between these different elements will reflect their views about the nature of human welfare and the proper scope of political action. If law makers are permitted to rely on religious beliefs/values when formulating public policy, they should also be free to reject or repudiate such beliefs/values. In other words, (religiously grounded) civic values should be neither excluded nor insulated from political decision making. The state may remain neutral on spiritual matters, such as when or how to pray or what clothes to wear, but it cannot be neutral on civic issues, such as the recognition of same sex-marriage, the prohibition of gender discrimination, or the regulation of abortion.

According to the Canadian courts, the *Charter*'s section 2(a) right to freedom of religion is breached any time the state restricts a religious practice in a nontrivial way. Even when a law advances a legitimate public purpose, the state must justify, under section 1 of the *Charter*, the law's nontrivial interference with a religious practice. However, the courts have been willing to uphold a restriction on religious practice if the restriction has a legitimate objective that would be noticeably

---

freedom of religion. In such a case, the complainant must show that the state actor supported a religious practice, and also that this support interfered with the beliefs of others in the community. In establishing this requirement, the Court seemed to confuse the two branches of religious freedom—the two ways in which s 2(a) may be breached by the state. In the end, however, it appears that this additional requirement has no real role to play. The Court in *MLQ* decided that it was sufficient to satisfy this requirement that an individual who identified as a nonbeliever reported that he felt excluded or hurt by the recitation of the prayer at the opening of the town council meeting. This, of course, could be claimed in every case in which a state actor supports or performs a religious practice.

compromised if an exception were made. In other words, even though the courts have structured their approach to section 2(a) so that it has the form of an equality right, they have adopted in practice a very weak standard of justification under section 1 so that the right protects only a limited form of liberty.

When deciding whether a particular limit on religious practice is justified (or whether accommodation should be made for a particular practice), the courts say they are balancing competing religious and civic interests. Yet, from a secular or public perspective, a religious belief/practice has no necessary value. The secular concern is not with the belief/practice itself but rather with its importance and meaning to the group's members and with the potential impact of its restriction on the position of the group in the larger society. The requirement that the state make some accommodation for religious practices is intended to prevent or limit the marginalization of minority religious groups.

While the courts do not engage in anything that could properly be described as the "balancing" of competing public and religious interests (in which the state's objectives might sometimes be subordinated to the claims of a religious community), they have sometimes sought to create space for religious practices at the margins of law by adjusting the boundary between spheres of religious and civic life. Religious practices (forms of worship) that are "personal" in character, such as the wearing of a turban or kippa, are sometimes indirectly or incidentally limited by state action, such as a police uniform requirement. The issue for the court in these cases is whether the state can pursue its objective as (or almost as) effectively in another way that will not interfere to the same extent with the religious practice.

Sometimes, however, the conflict between law and religious practice is more direct, in the sense that the law is pursuing a policy that is directly at odds with a religious practice. In such a case, the conflict between the law and the religious practice cannot be avoided or reduced by the state simply adjusting the means it has chosen to advance its civic purpose. For example, if some parents, on religious grounds, object to the enforcement of a legal ban on corporal punishment, the court must decide whether these parents should be exempted from an otherwise justified ban on physical discipline because they believe that God has mandated them to discipline their children in a way the law has forbidden. In such a case, then, the court's task is not to decide the proper balance or trade-off between competing interests or values (in accordance with the ordinary justification process under section 1 of the *Charter*), but is instead to decide whether space should be given to a different normative view—a view that the legislature has rejected. In the case of a ban on corporal punishment, however, the conflicting religious belief/practice cannot be viewed as simply a private matter, given the significant impact of this form of action on others—that is, on the children who will be harmed by the practice.

Sometimes an accommodation claim is made not by an individual who is seeking exemption from a law that interferes with their ability to engage in a particular religious practice, but instead by a religious organization or institution that is seeking to govern its internal affairs according to its own rules and practices, even when these are inconsistent with public norms. In these institutional autonomy cases, the key question for the courts is whether the organization's actions will affect outsiders to the spiritual community. The right of the Catholic church, for example, to exclude women from the priesthood (to discriminate against women) is not decided by balancing the religious claim against the claim to gender equality. As a private religious organization, the Catholic church is ordinarily free to govern its internal affairs according to its own rules or norms and is exempted from public anti-discrimination requirements. However, when the group's application of its "internal" rules affects outsiders to the group, its actions may be subject to public norms. In exceptional cases, the state may also intervene in the affairs of a religious group that is insular and hierarchical when the group seeks to enforce practices that are thought to be harmful to some of its members, even though the members have, in at least a formal sense, chosen to be or to remain part of the community.

In most religious accommodation cases, an individual (or group) asks to be exempted from a law that prevents them from engaging in a religious practice—for example, from wearing religious dress or keeping religious holidays. In conscientious objection cases, however, the individual asks to be exempted from a law that requires them to *perform* an act that they regard as immoral (or sinful). In many of these cases, the claimant wishes to be excused from performing an act that is not itself immoral but that supports or facilitates (what they see as) the immoral action of others, and so makes them complicit in this immorality. The issue in conscientious objection cases is not, as the courts sometimes claim, the reasonable balance between the individual's religious interests and the interests of others in the community, but is instead whether the individual's religiously based objection to performing a particular act should be viewed as an expression of personal religious commitment that ought to be accommodated, provided this can be done without noticeable harm to others, or instead as a (religiously grounded) civic position or action that falls outside the scope of religious freedom protection and may be the subject of legal regulation. In determining whether a particular (conscientious) objection should be viewed as a personal/ spiritual matter or instead as a civic/political position, two factors may be relevant. The first is whether the individual is being required to perform the particular act (to which they object) because they hold a special position not held by others, notably some form of public appointment. The other factor is the relative remoteness/proximity of the act that the objector is required to perform from the act they consider to be inherently immoral. When the act the objector is required to perform is far removed from the "immoral" act, we are more likely to see their objection as a political position rather than an expression of personal religious commitment.

At issue in these different religious "accommodation" cases is the line between the political sphere (of government action) and the private sphere (of religious practice). The courts may sometimes draw the line so that a religious practice is exempted from the application of an otherwise justified law. In this way, they may create some "private" space for religious practice without directly challenging the state's authority to govern in the public interest and to establish public norms. A religious practice will be accommodated only if it can be seen as private—as not impacting the rights and interests of others in any significant way. Accommodation, though, cannot be extended to beliefs or practices that explicitly address civic matters (the rights or welfare of others in the community) and are directly at odds with democratically adopted public policies. Because there is no principled way for the courts to determine the appropriate "balance" between democratically selected public values or purposes and the spiritual beliefs or practices of a religious individual or community (an alternative normative system), the insulation of religious belief/practice from public decision making will be at best minor. However, this pragmatic response to the competing claims of state policy and religious practice does not fit well with the courts' commitment to resolving issues in a principled way, a commitment that underpins the legitimacy of judicial review.

Under both branches of the religious freedom right—the freedom from and the freedom to religion—the court must separate—draw a line between—the sphere of personal or communal religious practice and the sphere of secular civic life. An individual's personal spiritual practices are both insulated and excluded from political decision making. However, a person's beliefs concerning civic issues, such as the rights and interests of others or the just arrangement of social relations, even if grounded in a religious system, must be subject to the give-and-take of ordinary politics. Religious belief/practice, then, is sometimes treated by the courts as an aspect of the individual's identity that should be excluded and insulated from politics, and other times (when it addresses civic matters or affects the interests of others) as a judgment about truth and right that may play a role in public decision making. Religious belief is not simply a fixed attribute or characteristic; nor is it simply a personal choice or judgment. The challenge for the courts is to fit this complex conception of religion into a system of constitutional rights that distinguishes between immutable or deeply rooted traits that must be respected by the state as part of a commitment to human equality, and choices or commitments that are protected as a matter of human liberty but subject to laws that advance the public interest. Because religion can be seen through both lenses, as cultural identity and personal commitment, this shifting by the courts between equality- and liberty-based conceptions of section 2(a) may be unavoidable.

TABLE OF CASES

INDEX

ABOUT THE AUTHOR

Richard Moon is Distinguished University Professor and Professor of Law at the University of Windsor. In addition to this book, he is the author of *The Life and Death of Freedom of Expression* (Toronto: UTP, 2024), *Putting Faith in Hate: When Religion is the Source or Target of Hate Speech* (Cambridge: Cambridge University Press, 2018) and *The Constitutional Protection of Freedom of Expression* (Toronto: UTP, 2000); the editor of *Law and Religious Pluralism in Canada* (Vancouver: UBC Press, 2008); the co-editor of *Religion and the Exercise of Public Authority* (Oxford: Hart/Bloomsbury, 2016), *Indigenous Spirituality and Religious Freedom* (Toronto: UTP, 2024) and *The Surprising Constitution* (Vancouver: UBC Press, 2024); and a contributing editor to *Canadian Constitutional Law* (Toronto: Emond-Montgomery, multiple editions).